PRAISE FOR
THE DEATH OF DEMAND

"Every once in a while, a book comes along that makes you rethink your basic notions about the world around you. This is one of those books."

*Seth Godin*
*Author of* Purple Cow

"In plain English, Osenton provides a truly unique perspective of the global economy's half-century journey to undreamed of outputs since World War II. More importantly, he sheds new insight on the inescapable dilemma that all businesses face today: survival and growth in a maturing economy."

*Norma V. Rosenberg*
*Former Director, Global Strategy Group,*
*PricewaterhouseCoopers*

# THE DEATH
# OF DEMAND

**FT** Prentice Hall
FINANCIAL TIMES

In an increasingly competitive world, it is quality
of thinking that gives an edge—an idea that opens new
doors, a technique that solves a problem, or an insight
that simply helps make sense of it all.

We work with leading authors in the various arenas
of business and finance to bring cutting-edge thinking
and best learning practice to a global market.

It is our goal to create world-class print publications
and electronic products that give readers
knowledge and understanding which can then be
applied, whether studying or at work.

To find out more about our business
products, you can visit us at www.ft-ph.com

Pearson
Education

# THE DEATH
# OF DEMAND

## FINDING GROWTH
## IN A SATURATED
## GLOBAL ECONOMY

Tom Osenton

FT Prentice Hall
FINANCIAL TIMES

FINANCIAL TIMES PRENTICE HALL
An Imprint of PEARSON EDUCATION
Upper Saddle River, NJ • New York • London • San Francisco • Toronto • Sydney
Tokyo • Singapore • Hong Kong • Cape Town • Madrid
Paris • Milan • Munich • Amsterdam
**www.ft-ph.com**

Library of Congress Cataloging-in-Publication Data

Osenton, Tom.
    The death of demand : finding growth in a saturated global economy / Tom Osenton.
        p. cm.
    Includes index.
    ISBN 0-13-142331-2
        1. Corporations--United States--Growth. 2. Consumption (Economics)--United States.
    3. Consumer behavior--Unites States. 4. Business cycles--United States. 5. Supply and
    demand. 6. United States--Economic conditions--21st century. I. Title.

    HD2785.O824 2004
    658.4'06--dc22'

                                                            2003069003


Production Editor and Compositor: *Vanessa Moore*
VP, Executive Editor: *Tim Moore*
Editorial Assistant: *Richard Winkler*
Full-Service Production Manager: *Anne R. Garcia*
Marketing Manager: *Alexis R. Heydt-Long*
Manufacturing Buyer: *Maura Zaldivar*
Manfacturing Manager: *John Pierce*
Cover Design Director: *Jerry Votta*
Cover Design: *Mary Jo DeFranco*
Interior Design: *Gail Cocker-Bogusz*

 © 2004 Pearson Education, Inc.
Publishing as Financial Times Prentice Hall
Upper Saddle River, NJ 07458

**Financial Times Prentice Hall offers excellent discounts on this book when
ordered in quantity for bulk purchases or special sales. For more information,
please contact: U.S. Corporate and Government Sales, 1-800-382-3419,
corpsales@pearsontechgroup.com. For sales outside of the U.S., please contact:
International Sales, 1-317-581-3793, international@pearsontechgroup.com.**

Printed in the United States of America
2nd Printing

ISBN 0-13-142331-2

Pearson Education Ltd.
Pearson Education Australia Pty., Limited
Pearson Education Singapore, Pte. Ltd.
Pearson Education North Asia Ltd.
Pearson Education Canada, Ltd.
Pearson Educación de Mexico, S.A. de C.V.
Pearson Education—Japan
Pearson Education Malaysia, Pte. Ltd.

# FINANCIAL TIMES PRENTICE HALL BOOKS

*For more information, please go to www.ft-ph.com*

**Business and Society**

Douglas K. Smith
*On Value and Values: Thinking Differently About We in an Age of Me*

**Business and Technology**

Sarv Devaraj and Rajiv Kohli
*The IT Payoff: Measuring the Business Value of Information Technology Investments*

Nicholas D. Evans
*Business Innovation and Disruptive Technology: Harnessing the Power of Breakthrough Technology…for Competitive Advantage*

Nicholas D. Evans
*Consumer Gadgets: 50 Ways to Have Fun and Simplify Your Life with Today's Technology…and Tomorrow's*

Faisal Hoque
*The Alignment Effect: How to Get Real Business Value Out of Technology*

**Economics**

David Dranove
*What's Your Life Worth? Health Care Rationing…Who Lives? Who Dies? Who Decides?*

John C. Edmunds
*Brave New Wealthy World: Winning the Struggle for World Prosperity*

Jonathan Wight
*Saving Adam Smith: A Tale of Wealth, Transformation, and Virtue*

**Entrepreneurship**

Oren Fuerst and Uri Geiger
*From Concept to Wall Street: A Complete Guide to Entrepreneurship and Venture Capital*

David Gladstone and Laura Gladstone
*Venture Capital Handbook: An Entrepreneur's Guide to Raising Venture Capital, Revised and Updated*

Thomas K. McKnight
*Will It Fly? How to Know if Your New Business Idea Has Wings… Before You Take the Leap*

Erica Orloff and Kathy Levinson, Ph.D.
*The 60-Second Commute: A Guide to Your 24/7 Home Office Life*

Jeff Saperstein and Daniel Rouach
*Creating Regional Wealth in the Innovation Economy: Models, Perspectives, and Best Practices*

Stephen Spinelli, Jr., Robert M. Rosenberg, and Sue Birley
*Franchising: Pathway to Wealth Creation*

**Executive Skills**

Cyndi Maxey and Jill Bremer
*It's Your Move: Dealing Yourself the Best Cards in Life and Work*

**Finance**

Aswath Damodaran
*The Dark Side of Valuation: Valuing Old Tech, New Tech, and New Economy Companies*

Kenneth R. Ferris and Barbara S. Pécherot Petitt
*Valuation: Avoiding the Winner's Curse*

**International Business**

Peter Marber
*Money Changes Everything: How Global Prosperity Is Reshaping Our Needs, Values, and Lifestyles*

Fernando Robles, Françoise Simon, and Jerry Haar
*Winning Strategies for the New Latin Markets*

**Investments**

Zvi Bodie and Michael J. Clowes
*Worry-Free Investing: A Safe Approach to Achieving Your Lifetime Goals*

Aswath Damodaran
*Investment Fables: Exposing the Myths of "Can't Miss" Investment Strategies*

Harry Domash
*Fire Your Stock Analyst! Analyzing Stocks on Your Own*

David Gladstone and Laura Gladstone
*Venture Capital Investing: The Complete Handbook for Investing in Businesses for Outstanding Profits*

D. Quinn Mills
*Buy, Lie, and Sell High: How Investors Lost Out on Enron and the Internet Bubble*

D. Quinn Mills
*Wheel, Deal, and Steal: Deceptive Accounting, Deceitful CEOs, and Ineffective Reforms*

John Nofsinger and Kenneth Kim
*Infectious Greed: Restoring Confidence in America's Companies*

John R. Nofsinger
*Investment Blunders (of the Rich and Famous)…And What You Can Learn from Them*

John R. Nofsinger
*Investment Madness: How Psychology Affects Your Investing…And What to Do About It*

H. David Sherman, S. David Young, and Harris Collingwood
*Profits You Can Trust: Spotting & Surviving Accounting Landmines*

**Leadership**

Jim Despain and Jane Bodman Converse
*And Dignity for All: Unlocking Greatness through Values-Based Leadership*

# CONTENTS

## CHAPTER 4 DESPERATE TIMES, DESPERATE MEASURES 105

*To my parents.*

# ACKNOWLEDGMENTS

First and foremost I want to thank my wife Mary-Ellen for enduring endless hours of droning monologues that I am certain made her mind numb. My sincere thanks for putting up with all that again. To my daughter Curran and son Matt, who also endured during the process. Thanks to you both. I am a very lucky dad.

It was again a great pleasure to work closely with Tim Moore, VP and executive editor at Prentice Hall. Tim is one of the great ones—he gets it. Many thanks also to Russ Hall who helped to make whatever I put down on paper much, much better. To John Nofsinger and Louis Columbus for their invaluable feedback and advice during the entire process, thank you so much. To Vanessa Moore, thank you for making it look great and for putting up with all my changes!

To my agent Dianne Littwin, a very special thanks for everything you do. To Rick Winkler, editorial assistant at Prentice Hall, for always keeping things moving forward.

To Bruce Miller and Marci Cohen, a special thanks for everything that you've done to help me—both professionally and personally. I will always remember. Also, many thanks to the entire crew at Market Data Corporation in Chicago, especially Mary Berry, Jen Kolar, Freida Chiu, Jon Fairman, Kitty Conlin, and of course, Valerie Cooper. Thanks for putting up with all the things stuck to the wall! Thanks to the staff of the Boston office of the Customer Share Group LLC—you guys are the greatest.

I will also always remember Tom Stein and his great support through it all. Most people are too selfish to care about other people—not Tom. To John Rawlings who still inspires me. My only regret is that we worked together for too short a time. To Michael Rosengarden, a great friend. I will never forget. To long-ball hitting Steve Alley of The Alley Company, a world-class adviser, but an even greater human being.

To Donna Dowdle and the infamous Henry. My sincere thanks to both of you for making my day job a whole lot easier.

To the outstanding staff at the University of New Hampshire's Dimond Library in Durham, NH. My sincere thanks to Claudia Morner for graciously allowing me access to her remarkable library and staff. Special thanks to Cliff Poulin and Jean Putnam for lugging all those dusty Moody Industrial Manuals up and down stairs for two years! Thanks also to Deanna Wood, Debbie Watson, and Louise Buckley at the reference desk for helping me find the most obscure facts.

To Bill Perkins who always provides a fresh and helpful business perspective. And I would be remiss if I didn't say a special thank you to Michael McFadden for all that he has done over the years. Michael, what can I say?

Lastly to our family dogs, Dakota and Jolie, who sleep in the cubbyhole under my desk, and keep my feet warm at four o'clock in the morning.

Soli Deo Gloria
*"To God alone be the Glory"*

# INTRODUCTION

*There once was a man from Wales,*
*Whose performance his boss mostly hails,*
*One day he got canned,*
*For lack of demand,*
*His supply far outnumbered his sales.*

When I was growing up in Boston in the 1950s, we had one telephone, one car, one television, and one turntable for playing LPs and 45s. The turntable and TV were actually both built into a large piece of dark mahogany furniture complete with hidden speakers—what must have been the home entertainment center of its day.

A half-century later, my own household has three cars, five telephones (not including three cell phones), three televisions, and eight different types of devices in which we can play our music CDs. We are oversized, over-entertained, over-informed, and definitely over-consumed. We have more than we need, more than we could ever consume, yet the call to arms from economists, business leaders, and government officials alike is "Grow, grow, grow."

We can't buy any more consumer electronic devices, we can't eat any more food, we can't drive more than one car at a time, or talk on more than one phone at a time, or watch more than one movie at a time. We are not broadband consumers. We can't expand our capacity for hamburgers, toothpaste, or shampoo, and there is no economic stimulus that will cause us to change our consumption habits for the long term.

The signs of saturation are all around us, but we prefer to characterize them as *soft spots*, or temporary periods during which corporations work off inventories. But it's more than that. Consider these statistics:

- There are 15 million vacant homes in the United States—enough to house every family in Australia.
- There are 31 million more registered vehicles than licensed drivers in the United States—enough to provide every man, woman, and child in Canada with his or her own car.
- There are more than 310 million personal telephone numbers (residential and cellular) in the United States, not including business numbers—one for every man, woman, and child in both the United States and Australia.

We have more TVs than people to watch them, more telephones than people to talk on them, more homes than families to live in them, and more cars than people to drive them. We can buy a hammer and nails, rent a DVD, or buy a pound of ground beef at four different locations within five miles of our homes. For the first time in history, the law of demand and supply is being put to the test: Have we pushed consumption to the edge of saturation, unable to stimulate new demand at any price?

Why the sudden lack of demand and fear of deflation? Because over the last 100 years we have nearly exhausted the three variables of consumption:

1. **Number of consumers.** Not only has the world's population quadrupled since 1900, the number of people participating in each category of product has greatly expanded over the last 100 years. The emergence of the middle class in developed countries gave rise to hundreds of millions who entered product categories for the first time in the 20th century. Today, there's barely a product category in which the rich and poor don't participate as consumers together.

2. **Number of categories.** The number of categories of products and variations of products has greatly expanded since 1900. Consider, for example, the vast number of options for shampoo or toothpaste at your local supermarket.

3. **Frequency and volume.** The amount of product consumed both in terms of frequency and volume has greatly expanded since 1900. The developed world rationed and sacrificed for the first 50 years of the 20th century. Since 1950, we have been on a consumption binge that borders on gluttonous. Obesity has reached epidemic proportions. Consumer debt continues to grow while the number of personal bankruptcies is at record levels, approaching 2 million additional families or individuals a year.

While pushing the edge of the consumption envelope over the past 100 years, we did all that we could to continually establish new sales records. First, we expanded domestically and used all of the creativity and media buying power of Madison Avenue to reach and influence anyone with a television set. Then we moved the show on the road, expanding distribution to international markets. Then we increased the number of products and line extensions to satisfy every desire and every taste: Italian salad dressing, lite Italian salad dressing, zesty Italian salad dressing, lite zesty Italian salad dressing. Somewhere along the road to progress while we were building a better life for our children and ourselves, we killed the golden goose.

We killed demand by using our drive, ambition, and creativity to convince more consumers in more categories to consume more products more often and in larger quantities than ever before. Our relentless push for more has caused us to reach a destination that few, over the past 300 years, thought possible: saturation.

So now what? What lies ahead for corporations, their employees, and their shareowners? Will we continue to grow? Probably. But will we continue to grow at a rate to which we have become accustomed? Probably not. And therein lies the rub. We have all been operating in a *new economic reality* for quite some time now; we just didn't know it. We must start thinking about the next 12 years, not just the next 12 months, and how we intend to manage maturing corporations in maturing industries that provide little momentum to a maturing economy.

How does a 45-year-old CEO, for example, manage a low-to-no-growth corporation in the 21st century? Is it possible to fuel earnings growth for two decades largely by cutting costs? Campbell's Soup's strategy was to reduce its dividend to fund a retooling of its soup-making process. Will that strategy help them sell more cans of soup? Can any strategy help the airline industry sell more seats? Can any strategy help the auto industry sell more cars and trucks? Can any strategy help McDonald's sell more Big Macs? For the first time ever, the answer to these questions might simply be "no."

This is the *new economic reality*—a reality that requires businesses to consider the possibility of selling a relatively fixed number of units each year for the foreseeable future and without a whole lot of pricing power. In the *new economic reality*, the rate of growth of corporations—any corporation—trends UP for just one period of its life. After that UP trend—which often takes decades—the corporation's rate of growth trends DOWN. UP once and DOWN once—not multiple times as suggested by those whose Holy Grail is the short-term business cycle. The long-term business cycle—one that views results over decades instead of years or quarters—does not follow an "S-shaped" pattern. It follows an inverted or upside-down "V."

Like the townspeople watching the naked emperor at the front of the ceremonial parade, few have had the courage to tell it like it is for fear of appearing stupid or incompetent, as the fairy tale goes. However, that doesn't mean avoiding the issue will make it go away.

In many ways we are the spoiled brats of capitalism, always expecting more. When we don't get more, we throw a temper tantrum. We also tend to not take serious the undeniable signs that suggest big fundamental economic problems are on the horizon. We have not yet realized the seriousness of the problem. On a recent front page of *USA Today*, the lead story trumpeted the approval of $87.5 billion to help rebuild Iraq. Directly under that story was an article announcing that the U.S. Department of the Treasury was redesigning the U.S. nickel. Do we have any clue as to how stupid that looks, and how much it shows that we are not yet serious about a fundamentally troubled economy?

The emperor is naked, and has been for years. It's now time to stop whining about it and accept the fact that what we have is a bearish economy for the foreseeable future. An economy that might require us to rethink our very purpose and, to redefine precisely what it is we mean when we say *we are making progress.*

# I THE DRIVE FOR GROWTH

The battle cry has been the same for generations: Growth, growth, and growth. It is an absolutely necessary ingredient in a capitalist system. For the last 150 years, that ingredient has been consistently delivered by the generations who accepted the challenge and pushed for more and more each year.

In many ways, this is a tribute to the tens of millions whose blood, sweat, and tears helped build the world's economy. Those who came before did their jobs, and did them well—maybe too well.

In the first decade of a new century, there are undeniable signs that suggest that our forebears pushed the consumption envelope as far as it could be pushed.

# 1 THE LIFEBLOOD OF CAPITALISM

Kraft Foods is one company that has enjoyed an incredible market-dominating ride. From its humble beginnings as a wholesale cheese business in Chicago in 1903, to its initial public offering (IPO) as a multibillion-dollar global company in 2001, the company that James L. Kraft started with horse-drawn delivery wagons has blossomed into the largest branded food and beverage company in North America, and the second largest in the world.

What North American home is without at least one of its many famous brands? From Velveeta, Maxwell House, Oscar Mayer, Nabisco, Philadelphia Cream Cheese, to Post cereals, walk through any supermarket in North America and you will see Kraft brands in almost every aisle. In fact, according to A.C. Nielsen, Kraft's brands can be found in more than 99 percent of all households in the United States.

Although market dominance is what every company desires, it does come with a unique set of challenges made possible by the capitalist society that created it. Ironically, Kraft's impressive dominance across a number of categories makes it harder for the Northfield, Illinois–based marketer to grow. In fact, six of Kraft's mega-brands generate more than $1 billion each in sales, commanding overwhelming market share leadership with little opportunity for significant increases in either volume or pricing.

After decades of robust growth, this $30 billion company is having a difficult time growing the top line at all. In fact, since 1995, Kraft Foods has more often delivered negative revenue growth than positive revenue growth on a year-over-year basis. The exception occurred when Philip Morris acquired Nabisco in 2001 and folded most of its assets into Kraft.

Long gone are the golden days of delivering consistent double-digit revenue growth, especially in the United States. Companies such as Kraft Foods might have reached the outer limits of their ability to generate substantive revenue gains from market share gains. For mature industries such as consumer-packaged goods, generating a 1 or 2 percent increase in revenue growth from year to year is becoming more the rule than the exception. When a company markets its vast portfolio of brands in more than 145 countries to billions of customers and dominates almost every category in which it competes, how much more cream cheese, cookies, and cereal can it sell?

## LIFE AND DEATH

When British economist Alfred Marshall first wrote about the concept of demand and supply in his 1890 book *Principles of Economics,* he made a profound observation about the life of a business and that of a human being. Each followed a strikingly similar path starting with birth, moving through growth, to maturity, and finally into decline, and ultimately death. In his words:

> A business firm grows and attains great strength, and afterwards perhaps stagnates and decays; and at the turning point there is a balancing or equilibrium of the forces of life and decay. And as we reach to the higher stages of our work, we shall need ever more and more to think of economic forces as resembling those which make a young man grow in strength until he reaches his prime; after which he gradually becomes stiff and inactive, till at last he sinks to make room for other and more vigorous life.

Lost, however, over the last century of extraordinary growth, is Marshall's observation that nothing lasts forever. Implied in his statement is that demand is also not immortal, regardless of endless price decreases. More than 100 years ago when Marshall first captured the essence of the law of demand and supply, there wasn't a whole lot to demand beyond the basic categories of food, clothing, and shelter. However, as the 20th century dawned, the arrival of the automobile, first in Europe and then in North America, signaled the start of a long and remarkable run for demand. At one time easily controlled by simple price adjustments, demand shows almost no sign of vitality today, and there is no evidence to suggest that it will change anytime soon.

As the 21st century dawned, there were more consumers in more countries consuming more products in more categories than at any other time in history. The events of the early part of the 20th century, including the introduction of mass production, helped make all products affordable not just for the rich, but for the growing number of people who were rapidly populating an entirely new group in the social strata between the rich and the working class: the middle class. The significant and concurrent conditions that allowed for such a unique growth dynamic were:

■ Population growth.
■ The development of thousands of new categories of products and services.
■ The ability to rapidly communicate with an increasing number of consumers everywhere.

By the end of the 20th century, there was hardly a category that was not populated by all three major classes. Even the poor had cell phones, cars, houses, televisions, Play Stations, computers, and e-mail.

## NOT JUST ABOUT CHEESE

The lack of worldwide demand today is neither an indictment of corporations such as Kraft Foods nor the mature consumer packaged goods industry in which it competes. In fact, quite the opposite might be true. The folks at Kraft Foods might have done their jobs too well over the last 50 years, effectively hastening the onset of saturation by influencing as many people on the planet who can afford to do so to consume as much cream cheese, cookies, and cereal as they possibly can. With the universe of bagel noshers largely fixed, even some of the most successful marketers in the world can't convince them to increase their consumption of schmeers. Now, satiated consumers worldwide are increasingly saying, "No mas! Nicht mehr! No, I do not want fries with that!"

Countless corporations in dozens of industries across all sectors are flirting with flat or even shrinking year-over-year revenue growth. Even a decade of aggressive mergers and acquisitions has largely resulted in simply creating bigger corporations with little or no organic growth.

Obscured by the events of September 11, 2001 and the 2003 war in Iraq, is an underlying trend that has gone largely unnoticed over the last quarter-century: demand, and the rate of unit and revenue growth for corporations around the world, has gradually slowed to a trickle.

However, as the rate of revenue growth has dwindled, the global investment community's expectations for consistent earnings growth have intensified. A rigid and unrelenting demand for increased profit growth, in the absence of an accompanying boost in natural revenue, has created a mathematical dilemma that is sending some corporations on acquisition shopping sprees, many on the cost-cutting warpath, and others beyond the boundaries of ethical business behavior. The rash of financial fabrications involving high-profile public corporations certainly raised the specter of impropriety in the early years of this century. It also increased our awareness of the lengths to which corporations will go to deliver the level of earnings that Wall Street expects.

On the surface, this revenue problem seems imminently fixable. A stimulus package here, zero percent financing there, and we are magically back on the growth track. However, there are new fundamental symptoms that suggest otherwise. Although productivity gains have greatly helped in the delivery of earnings growth over the last decade, our ability to continue to increase output per worker is fading. Sometimes forgotten is the fact that revenue is the single most important element in generating earnings. Without revenue, there can be no earnings at all, and without a constant inflow of new revenue, the long-term prospect for delivering earnings growth in perpetuity for some of the most established and historically successful businesses in the world could be at risk.

## WORLD POPULATION GROWTH

Many point to the billions of potential consumers in third-world countries that have yet to be exploited as the answer to every CEO's prayers. However, don't expect it to happen all at once. It's true that geographical expansion will bring growth to many corporations over the next 20 years, but it will happen at a much slower pace than many expect. For major corporations like the Coca-Cola Company, markets such as China are no longer new territory. Now more than 30 years after former U.S. President Richard Nixon's historic visit there in 1971, some corporations have already marketed to several generations of Chinese consumers.

Now layer on top of this the fact that the world's rate of population growth has been decreasing since the 1960s and you have a formula that suggests slow growth over a long period of time, not necessarily what an anxious and demanding Wall Street wants to hear. Figure 1-1 shows that world population growth rates have been in decline since 1963 and are projected to continue to decline until at least 2050. So although the world's population will continue to rise slowly, it will do so at an ever-decreasing rate—a rate that is currently a little more than 1 percent.

Similarly, U.S. population growth rates have also been in decline, but actually for a longer period of time. Driven by the baby boom in the 1950s, the rate of U.S. population growth peaked in the mid-1950s. Growth rates slid through the 1960s, 1970s, and 1980s, before making a minor comeback in the first half of the 1990s (see Figure 1-2).

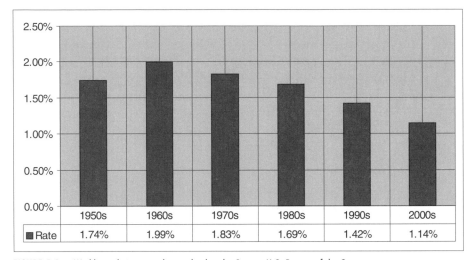

FIGURE 1-1    World population growth rates by decade. Source: U.S. Bureau of the Census.

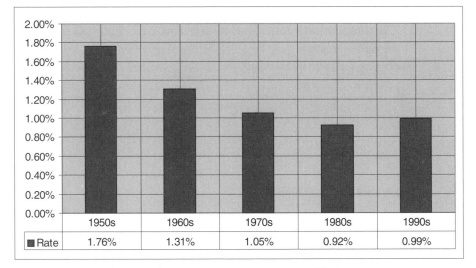

FIGURE 1-2    U.S. population growth, 1950 to 2000. Source: U.S. Bureau of the Census.

The *echo boom* that sociologists had anticipated when baby boomers became parents occurred later and was of a shorter duration than many expected. The reason was that many childbearing boomers delayed the start of their families until after spending a decade or two establishing their own professional careers. The delay resulted in many women over 40 having babies for the first time from 1990 to 1995. However, the population up-tick was short-lived, and since 1996, the population growth rate in the United States has been sliding once again.

Those who point to population growth as the savior to the world's demand woes will be disappointed that more consumers aren't being produced, and the rate of population growth is expected to continue to shrink for the balance of the 21st century. At least one of the major developed economic powers in the world will experience a population decrease over the next quarter of a century. Experts predict that not only will Japan's population shrink over the next 25 years, it will do so as citizens over the age of 65 outnumber those under the age of 15 for the first time ever. The implications of this shift are significant. As the number of people entering the workforce shrinks, a growing universe of retirees will live longer, consume less, and require a disproportionate amount of medical attention.

Although the population in the United States continues to grow, retirees also create a significant problem for the government, especially as the oldest baby boomers turn 65-years old beginning in 2011. This will be the first generation with a significant number of retirees relying primarily on voluntary 401(k) plans instead of full corporate pensions. Those investing in such plans have been greatly hurt by the stock market backslide since mid-2000, while others have simply chosen not to pay in to their 401(k) plans at all. Add to this the fact that for every two retiring boomers, only one new body will enter the workforce in the United States to help fund an already under-funded Social Security system. Cleary, we are headed for a nasty intersection of economic reality over the next 10 years that fundamentally has little to do with the stock market.

## WORLD'S LARGEST GDPS HURTING

The issue at hand is one of global proportions and requires a radical rethinking of the business status quo. Consistent with a decline in the rate of population growth is the declining rate of growth for gross domestic product (GDP) figures around the world. Not unlike the United States, Japan has been a victim of its own success, emerging from the ashes of World War II and transforming itself into one of the world's most significant economies in a remarkably short period of time. But the slow-down in growth in recent years has created serious problems for Japan that is experiencing its worst economic crisis since World War II. According to Japanese officials, the primary cul-prit responsible for the slowdown has been sluggish sales. The government is considering instituting a permanent tax cut to bring some life back into the economy. However, such a move presumes a certain level of demand exists among consumers—an assumption that is no longer a sure bet in any of the world's developed nations.

The sustained and robust economic growth during the 1960s and 1970s created an expectation that growth was a post-World War II given in Japan, the United States, and Ger-many. All three countries continued to expand assets in order to continue to grow market share into the 1980s. Japan and the United States also fell victim to major diversification efforts when times were good, and a burgeoning top line could fund expansion and mask mistakes. However, as economic growth began to slow in the 1980s and 1990s, many of Japan's leading corporations sought to shed businesses in order to refocus on core competencies.

Japan's maturing auto industry, for example, has already started to experience the pain of consolidation—a certain pre-view of what is to come for stagnant U.S. automakers by 2010. Some believe that without earlier investment from U.S. corpo-rations, under-performing Japanese automakers such as Isuzu (General Motors) and Mazda (Ford Motor Company) would have disappeared long ago.

The 12-nation Eurozone economy has been terribly weak in recent years, with growth projections in the 0 to 1 percent range from the European Central Bank for the near term, hardly robust. Germany's economy—the largest in the Euro-zone—continues to struggle due, in part, to massive financial losses from the stock market crash there in 2002, which has greatly dampened investment activity.

From a macroeconomic perspective, the world's economy has been slowing for some time now. In the United States, real GDP has been growing at a steadily decreasing rate since the 1960s. The distractions of the day-to-day buzz that swirls around the business world often obscure the bigger picture, especially when the bigger picture is more often communicated in terms of cumulative dollars, euros, or yen as opposed to rates of growth.

When you step back and take a look at the economy—any economy—from 100,000 feet, the picture is quite different. No longer are we measuring in increments of days, weeks, months, and years, but decades, quarter-centuries, half-centuries, and centuries. Figure 1-3 shows that real GDP growth rates have been declining in the United States since the 1970s. That certainly is not the impression we have been given by the economic powers that be. More often we are served up statements like that of an MSNBC financial reporter who, when asked about the annual surge in sales during the holidays, proclaimed, "Holiday sales will always increase. They can never go down." Unfortunately, this is the prevailing perspective among those whose livelihoods revolve around the stock market.

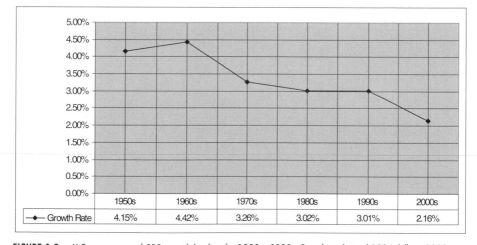

|  | 1950s | 1960s | 1970s | 1980s | 1990s | 2000s |
|---|---|---|---|---|---|---|
| Growth Rate | 4.15% | 4.42% | 3.26% | 3.02% | 3.01% | 2.16% |

FIGURE 1-3    U.S. economy real GDP growth by decade, 1950s–2000s. Based on chained 1996 dollars. 2000s figure based on 2000, 2001, and 2002. Source: Bureau of Economic Analysis.

The United States' Congressional Budget Office issues a series of reports each year on the state of the budget and the economy. The purpose of these reports is to provide "impartial analysis" relating to all aspects of current and future budgets that fund national and local programs and services and are funded by taxpayers' dollars. In August 2003, the office issued a sobering report suggesting that, while the budget will work its way back into the black around 2012 and 2013, the overall deficit may during the same period reach a staggering $7 trillion—doubling the already record deficit levels of 2004. The practice of passing on such levels of debt to the next generation in an economy that is trending at an ever-decreasing rate of growth is extremely dangerous. Economic time bombs such as a growing universe of retirees who are living longer, and a sizable number who creep toward retirement with no pension and no voluntary 401(k) participation make the aggregation of debt today not only ill advised but irresponsible.

Keynesian economics had its time. Borrowing from the future works when the economy is growing at an increasing rate of growth—when aggregate demand is trending up. What would happen to the insurance industry if everyone entering the work force for the first time opted against life insurance? Without an inflow of new premiums it would be extraordinarily difficult to continue to pay claim obligations. The government is experiencing economic impotence due to saturation, unable to jump-start the economy through traditional monetary policies that usually work when demand has life.

## THE BASICS

Over the course of the last 25 years, some have confused stock market performance with the actual operational performance and health of the corporations that are traded on Wall Street. More often than not, when graduates from the Class of 1990 and later are asked, "How's the company doing?" they respond with information about the corporation's stock performance: "It's up 2 percent this quarter." Without operational performance, it's difficult to see an appreciation in stock performance over the long term. Have we already forgotten about the dot-com debacle? Some have become so blinded by the prospect of building personal wealth that they forget that the operational performance of a corporation really comes down to three basic elements:

1. Costs
2. Revenue
3. Earnings

However, we don't always remember that these elements follow a natural progression: investment (costs), income (revenue), and profit (earnings). There are no earnings at all without revenue. When asked if the pace at which earnings are outgrowing revenues troubled her, one high-profile Wall Street analyst simply brushed off the question remarking, "Earnings have always grown faster than revenues." Obviously, she never launched a business.

The most frightening aspect of this statement was that she believed she was right. This dangerous perspective illustrates that we have effectively created two separate, often disconnected worlds: the world of Wall Street and the world of business. The connection between the two worlds has been reduced to a single number every three months—earnings—with little regard for the means taken to deliver those earnings. The lack of demand and, therefore, lack of revenue growth is causing corporations to take actions that they never had to before.

Dow component corporation Eastman Kodak is a good example. Caught in a rapidly changing industry, Kodak is essentially the same size it was a decade ago (about $13 billion in sales), but with about 40,000 fewer employees. It's been a tough decade for Kodak, as well as for the greater Rochester, New York area where the company is headquartered.

## RATE OF GROWTH: TRENDING UP OR DOWN?

Someone once said, "No business ever stands still. It's either moving up or moving down." Because we are so intent at looking at business on a monthly, quarterly, and yearly basis, it is sometimes hard for us to spot trends that might be significant to the future of the business. Even though we can't feel that the earth is rotating, we know that it is in constant motion. Similarly, the rate of revenue growth for a corporation is always in motion, trending in one direction or the other. A corporation's rate of revenue growth is either trending up or trending down, especially if viewed over decades.

Obviously, when a company launches, its rate of revenue growth trends upward. For a period of time it experiences an increasing rate of growth, the period when the rate of revenue growth is in a consistent state of upward movement over a number of years. Corporations can spend decades in this phase, but as a rule of thumb, it usually lasts 20 to 30 years or less.

A decreasing rate of growth occurs when the rate of growth is in a consistent state of decline over a period of years. Although the corporation might still be expanding from year to year, its rate of revenue growth is trending on a downward path. Corporations can spend decades in this phase, fighting off negative growth through innovation and acquisition.

Of course, most corporations do continue to grow, but at a rate much slower than historical levels. In fact, the rate of revenue growth—one of the most important factors in generating long-term earnings growth—has consistently eroded for most established corporations over the last 25 years, reflecting the fact that there are natural limitations to growth for all businesses.

## NEVER LOOKING BACK

Even with the exploitation of more than one billion consumers in China on the horizon, there are only so many people on this planet and, according to recent population growth studies, we might be facing population shrinkage over the next decade. This is not good news for the corporations that rely on population growth for sales growth.

Because we rarely look back on results, especially results over decades, it becomes almost impossible to recognize the impact of a gradual erosion of revenue over a 50-year period. We have been trained to look ahead to next quarter or next year, so we generally explain away recessions as the result of temporary economic downturns and the impact of events such as September 11. However, a new study from Chicago-based Customer Share Group LLC suggests that the rate of revenue growth for many of the world's leading corporations has been sliding since the mid-1970s.

For the last five decades, management has been showing slides—and now Microsoft PowerPoint presentations—of a galloping top line that seems to defy gravity. Was Isaac Newton wrong? Is it possible that everything that goes up keeps going up? Figure 1-4 provides a view of collective revenue growth of the Dow Jones component corporations on a decade-by-decade basis since the 1950s.

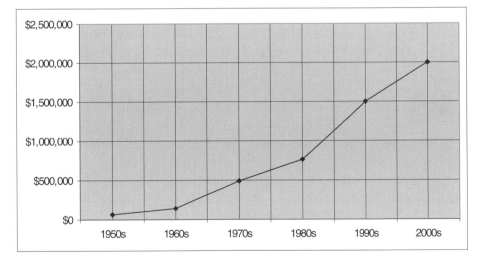

FIGURE 1-4    The Dow 30 total revenue by decade, 1950s–2000s, inflation-adjusted. (Millions U.S. dollars). Source: Moody's (Mergent) Industrial Manuals.

Figure 1-4 shows continuous upward movement in revenue, an ever-increasing stairway of sales that provides the corporate optimist with the good news that a board of directors wants to hear. Although actual revenue appears to be trending positively for the Dow 30, this view of revenue growth distorts the reality of the difficulty that corporations are experiencing in the trenches when trying to push the revenue line upward.

In many ways, this is the "glass half-full" perspective on revenue growth. The emperor appears to be fully clothed in new silky and colorful garments, yet you will see later on that some corporations have simply been unable to perpetuate this illusion.

## THE INVERTED V

Using the very same data from Figure 1-4, Figure 1-5 provides a very different perspective, showing the steady rise in the rate of revenue growth for the 30 Dow component corporations as a group coming out of World War II. However, after approximately 25 years of steadily climbing growth rates through the 1950s, 1960s, and into the 1970s, this group, and most individual corporations, hit a wall in the 1970s when rates of growth peaked and started to decline.

The 1980s followed with truly disappointing revenue growth. After experiencing extraordinary growth during the 1970s, why would senior management expect that level of growth to subside? As the natural double-digit growth of the 1970s faded, the 1980s began to reflect an economy that was not only bigger and thus harder to grow, but also an economy that was made up of rapidly maturing industries. The 13.6 percent average rate of revenue growth from the 1970s gave way to a dramatic drop to an average 4.7 percent for the Dow 30 as a group during the 1980s.

A modest comeback in the 1990s was largely fueled by three temporary events:

- An echo boom population spike from older baby boomers.
- Extraordinarily aggressive mergers and acquisitions activity that added wholesale revenue gains to the top lines of corporations such as General Electric.

■ The wholesale adoption of the Personal Computer both by businesses and by consumers, mostly driven by the advent of e-mail and the World Wide Web.

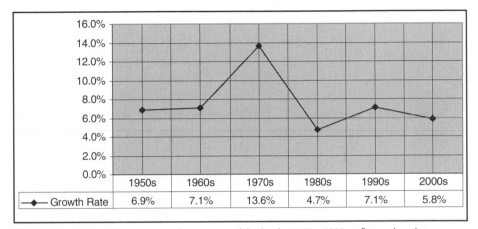

| | 1950s | 1960s | 1970s | 1980s | 1990s | 2000s |
|---|---|---|---|---|---|---|
| Growth Rate | 6.9% | 7.1% | 13.6% | 4.7% | 7.1% | 5.8% |

FIGURE 1-5    The Dow 30 average rate of revenue growth by decade, 1950s–2000s, inflation-adjusted. Source: Moody's (Mergent) Industrial Manuals.

However, the short-lived up-tick has given way to more sobering rates of growth. In many cases, we are witnessing the lowest growth rates in more than 50 years, and in the case of some corporate juggernauts such as young Dow component The Home Depot, negative growth rates for the first time ever.

Certainly, many corporations continue to grow, but at a rate much slower than historical levels. In fact, the rate of revenue growth, an important contributing factor in generating long-term earnings growth, has consistently eroded over the last 25 years. Though most corporations have been able to deliver acceptable earnings levels over this period, it's been aggressive cost-reduction and productivity gains that have made it possible.

## EBBING TIDE

Drilling all the way down to the corporation level, it becomes clear that the building blocks that make up the economy's foundation are simply unable to generate the type of dynamic growth necessary to create upward movement. The chart in Figure1-6 shows that Procter & Gamble's rate of revenue growth actually stopped increasing and started decreasing in the 1970s. The significance is this: Procter & Gamble's extraordinarily expensive efforts to grow market share over the last quarter-century have certainly generated growth, but at an ever-decreasing rate. Most corporations that existed prior to 1950 follow a similar pattern of growth, so this is by no means unique to Procter & Gamble.

This chart provides a particularly jolting view of a trend that started nearly 30 years ago and shows no signs of a turn-around. The reason is simple: Procter & Gamble has effectively maximized its penetration in most of the categories in which it competes, and consumption levels within those categories have stabilized. Procter & Gamble has actually done a very good job of introducing new categories, even in recent years, which helps add entirely new revenue streams to the mix as opposed to simple line extensions that can often cannibalize core brands.

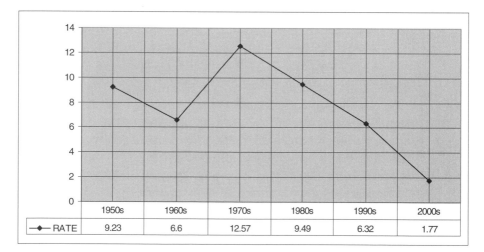

| | 1950s | 1960s | 1970s | 1980s | 1990s | 2000s |
|---|---|---|---|---|---|---|
| ◆ RATE | 9.23 | 6.6 | 12.57 | 9.49 | 6.32 | 1.77 |

FIGURE 1-6    Procter & Gamble's rate of revenue growth by decade, 1950s–2000s, inflation-adjusted. All of its consumer product colleagues look relatively the same. Source: Moody's (Mergent) Industrial Manuals.

As the rate of revenue growth at many such large corporations has dwindled over the last quarter-century, Wall Street's expectations for consistent earnings growth have only intensified making life for the CEO of the maturing corporation in the 21st century much more than just challenging.

## NEGATIVE RATE OF GROWTH

Many corporations are already flirting with flat or even shrinking year-over-year revenue growth. The Dow 30, for example, has experienced a steady decline in their collective rate of revenue growth since the beginning of the 21st century.

The rate of revenue growth for the Dow 30 decreased eight straight quarters to kick off the 21st century. The troubling slide ultimately hit the trough when the group delivered negative revenue growth for three consecutive quarters for the first time since the Great Depression, posting negative numbers in Q3 2001 (–1.6%), Q4 2001 (–2.6%), and Q1 2002 (–1.5%). During this period, 60 percent of the Dow components reported negative year-over-year revenue growth, the worst collective performance for the Dow 30 in 70 years. The group finally rebounded in Q2 2002 with a meager 1 percent growth rate for the quarter.

This first-ever revenue recession for the blue chips underscores the fact that revenue growth is not only a serious issue, but also that some of the elements that drive an economy are simply tired and maxed out, simply unable to generate the steam they once did. Although their performance improved in 2002, Dow component corporations were still unable to beat prior-year revenue results 40 percent of the time. Is this a temporary soft spot, as U.S. Federal Reserve Chairman Alan Greenspan might characterize, or a more permanent issue of satisfied demand?

## McDONALD'S: NOT-SO-HAPPY MEALS

Dow component sibling McDonald's Corporation has also hit a wall. The world's largest restaurant chain, with more than 30,000 restaurants in 120 countries, announced its first-ever quarterly loss since going public in 1966, losing $343.9 million in the fourth quarter of 2002. The fast-food giant has had a tremendous run, but like so many other corporations that grew rapidly through the 1970s, even McDonald's can't keep expanding indefinitely. Its mega-aggressive expansion strategy had been averaging more than 1,700 new store openings a year. That's one every five hours! However, that strategy has been greatly adjusted. In fact, in 2003 more than 700 McDonald's restaurants closed and tore down the golden arches.

Vaunted 20th-century economist John Maynard Keynes believed that economic downturns were short-term phenomena that could be fixed. He believed that these downturns were driven by a short-term lack of demand and were merely temporary setbacks. However, much of Keynesian economic theory relied on future growth and, in many cases, borrowed from the future. Did Keynes ever consider the possibility of sapped demand, of saturation, and little or no future growth? That for every two retiring Boomers expecting to draw from Social Security there will be one new worker entering the workforce paying into Social Security?

The concept of more permanent saturation levels probably never occurred to economists down through the ages. Economic slowdowns have always been fixable: Lower the price and increase demand. However, even the Federal Reserve is finding that demand in the 21st century is difficult to ignite, and that deflation may be a real possibility.

## ALL SECTORS HAVE HIT THE WALL

Look across all the major sectors of the economy and a clear trend has developed since the 1970s. The rate of growth for all major sectors of the economy has been decreasing for a quarter century—with the exception of technology. And today, not even technology is delivering the rate of growth that it once did. That's not to say there is no growth on a sector-by-sector basis. There certainly is, but it's being delivered at an ever-decreasing rate.

Figure 1-7 identifies the economy's major sectors, the industries that make up those sectors and a sampling of some of the leading corporations that make up the industries. It also shows the inflation-adjusted average collective growth rate of the listed corporations for the 1990s and for the first three years of the 2000s. What sectors are growing at increasing rates? What industries are growing at increasing rates? What corporations are growing at increasing rates?

■ Some might say: *The business cycle is very resilient. We always bounce back.*

That's because we look at economic performance in such small increments that it obscures our ability to identify long-term trends. A 25-year declining trend can be slowed, but it cannot be stopped. The theory that a corporation's performance follows the classic "S-curve" is a myth. The pattern of a corporation's rate of growth over the course of its life looks like an *inverted V.*

■ Some might say: *We can be successful at a lower rate of growth.*

Not forever, and not without a steady inflow of top line growth. There are limits to productivity, and to cost cutting. Also, a 25-year trend of declining revenue rates does not necessarily stop at 3 percent because we need it to. An average rate of growth measured over decades that was 5 percent and is now 3 percent is on its way down to 2 percent—not back up to 4 percent.

■ Some might say: *That may be true for mature corporations, but not for us.*

The definition of *mature* is certainly a relative term. If your company is more than 20 years old, then you are probably growing revenue at decreasing rates. Procter & Gamble's rate of revenue growth is decreasing—at 165+ years old, you would expect it to be. So is Microsoft's— and Microsoft's rate of decrease is occurring significantly faster than P & G's did. So are both companies mature?

| SECTORS | INDUSTRIES | CORPORATIONS | AVERAGE RATE OF GROWTH 1990s | AVERAGE RATE OF GROWTH 2000s |
|---|---|---|---|---|
| Consumer staples | Beverages (alcoholic), beverages (nonalcoholic), tobacco, household products, personal care, food, food retailers | Anheuser-Busch, The Coca-Coca Company, Altria Group, Procter & Gamble, Gillette, General Mills, Safeway | 4.98% | 1.95% |
| Consumer cyclicals | Retail (general), retail (specialty), retail (specialty apparel), retail (department stores), retail (drugs), broadcasting, recreation, entertainment, automotive, publishing, restaurants, lodging, footwear | Wal-Mart, The Home Depot, The Gap, Federated, CVS, Disney, General Motors, Tribune, McDonalds, Hilton, Nike, Kodak | 10.44% | 7.73% |
| Technology | Software, hardware, networking, semiconductors, peripherals | Microsoft, Oracle, Cisco, Intel, Texas Instruments, Hewlett-Packard, IBM, Dell, Sun Microsystems, Apple, EMC | 13.59% | 3.67% |
| Communication | Telephone service, telephone equipment, cellular/wireless, long distance | Verizon, Bell South, SBC, Qualcomm, Motorola, Alltel, AT&T Wireless, Nextel, AT&T, Sprint | 12.53% | 1.53% |
| Health care | Pharmaceuticals, biotechnology, medical products, managed health care | Pfizer, Johnson & Johnson, Eli Lilly, Merck, Wyeth, Schering-Plough, Genentech, Genzyme, Medtronic, Health Management | 14.30% | 9.82% |

| | | | | |
|---|---|---|---|---|
| Financial | Money center, regional banks, insurance, diversified, investment banking/brokerage | Citigroup, Bank of America, MBNA, JP Morgan Chase, Wells Fargo, AIG, American Express, Merrill Lynch, Morgan Stanley, Charles Schwab | 22.64% | 5.37% |
| Energy | Oil, oil drilling | Exxon/Mobil, Chevron Texaco, Conoco Phillips, Halliburton, Schlumberger, Baker Hughes, Occidental Petroleum | 2.21% | −0.39% |
| Utilities | Electric, gas, water | Southern, FPL, PG&E, Exelon, Consolidated Edison, Entergy, Dominion Resources, Progress Energy | 7.48% | 6.39% |
| Basic materials | Chemicals, paper and forest, aluminum | Dupont, Dow Chemical, International Paper, Alcoa, Weyerhauser, Praxair, Air Products | 7.53% | 4.69% |
| Transport | Air freight, railroads, airlines | Federal Express, UPS, Union Pacific, CSX, Burlington Northern, AMR, Southwest, Delta, Roadway | 5.08% | 2.44% |
| Capital goods | Electric equipment, aerospace, manufacturing | GE, Honeywell, Emerson, Rockwell, United Technologies, Lockheed Martin, 3M, Boeing | 9.84% | 1.92% |

FIGURE 1-7    Where's the growth? What industries are capable of energizing the economy? Source: SEC Filings, Moody's (Mergent) Industrial Manuals.

■ <u>Some might say</u>: *The sky is not falling.*

No it's not, but we are tracking on a collision course that has a mathematical certainty of failure unless we take action now. All corporations in all industries in all sectors are moving on a continuum toward saturation. Why? Because that is the natural destination for intelligent, ambitious, creative, hungry societies whose goal is to convince consumers to consume at maximum levels.

What is the significance of a slide that has trended down for more than 25 years? From a long-term perspective, growth rates will never trend up again. Certainly, there will be up years and down years, but from a trending standpoint, increasing rates of growth are a thing of the past for most industries. So simply rubbing the bottle and expecting the genie to deliver increased consumption is a naïve notion.

The perception that only those *mature* corporations are having difficulty growing is also a naïve notion. Just ask the folks at McDonald's, Intel, Hewlett-Packard, and The Home Depot. If your company is more than 20 years old, it is probably already past the top. This is the reality of the *business life cycle*: a one-time journey through *Birth* followed by *Growth* followed by *Maturity* followed by *Decline* and ultimately *Death*. And, ironically, the better we are at our jobs, the faster we move through these five phases.

A close look at the major sectors and more than 50 major industries suggests that many components of the current economy resemble Alfred Marshall's 1890 description of *a young man who, after reaching his prime, gradually becomes stiff and inactive, until at last he sinks to make room for other more vigorous life.*

The overwhelming majority of industries identified in Figure 1-7 have already seen their best days relative to top-line growth. Most of the sectors identified here are a century or more old, from consumer staples and telecommunications to capital goods and transport. To be sure, these sectors continue to grow, but at ever-decreasing rates. All of the sectors have

seen the introduction of a number of discontinuous innovations over the last century, such as the introduction of the airplane to the transport sector, television to the consumer
cyclicals sector, and penicillin to the health care sector. Even
so, these sectors are very large and quite mature having
reached a level of saturation decades ago. Now they grind forward with less and less momentum, increasingly the victims of
more and more cost scrutiny.

The health care sector, viewed by some as the next great
economy driver, does appear to have the best potential for
near-term robust growth among all existing sectors. This sector enjoys a very unique dynamic that most other sectors do
not: industries such as pharmaceuticals and biotechnology are
essentially in the business of developing discontinuous innovations; that is, categories of products (drugs and biological rem-
edies) that never existed before. Most other industries focus on
improving a single innovation such as the automobile.

Even though the pharmaceutical industry can be traced
back thousands of years, it continues to grow at very healthy
rates because of constant introduction of new categories of
drugs. Another unique element that also helps the industry
plow forward, often at double-digit rates, is that not all new
drugs replace other existing drugs. This is why the overall universe of medications grows each year, resulting in more
patients consuming more drugs. Even though a medication
might have been discovered decades ago, it could still be the
popular choice of a physician today.

This unique dynamic—one that is funded with the constant development of new categories of drugs—actually makes
for a powerful business model that creates the potential for
explosive and sustained growth.

The sister industry of biotechnology, also with roots thousands of years in the past, appears to be the only industry
today with a rate of revenue growth that is on the rise and has
yet to hit the top. However, the fledgling industry has far to go
if it is expected to greatly impact its sector and ultimately the
economy. Currently, the largest 20 public biotechnology
firms collectively are about the same size as The Coca-Cola

Company—around $20 billion. With U.S. GDP approaching $10 trillion, the top 20 biotechnology firms would have to quintuple in size just to reach 1 percent of the U.S. GDP.

Although pharmaceuticals and biotechnology are strong growth engines within the health care sector, it is extraordinarily difficult for just one or two dynamically growing industries to have an impact on an economy that has grown so large.

## EVEN TECHNOLOGY HAS SEEN ITS BEST DAYS

Even the youngest sector of all—technology—is in decline. It wasn't long ago when there was no technology sector, when technology essentially amounted to room-sized IBM mainframes. Then the computer found its way first onto the desktops of businesses around the world, and then to the desktops of consumers around the world. Technology experienced the fastest rise to innovation saturation of any sector in history. The technology sector's meteoric rise lasted only about 20 years while the rate of revenue increased during the widespread adoption phase. After a glorious run up, technology had joined most other sectors, growing at ever-decreasing rates by the late 1990s.

If you think that the technology sector as we now know it will generate enough juice to drive the economy as it has for much of the last 20 years, think again. Technology has already experienced its golden years of growth, with historically high rates of growth behind it. Hewlett-Packard delivered double-digit growth in 2002 due largely to its acquisition of Compaq, yet for the second consecutive year lost money. Revenues for IBM and Intel have screeched to a halt and have mostly been flat or down since the turn of the century.

Even industry leader Microsoft, although hugely profitable, has seen its rate of revenue growth slide from growth rates beyond 50 percent per year to mere mortal rates in the high single digits in 2003, as shown in Figure 1-8.

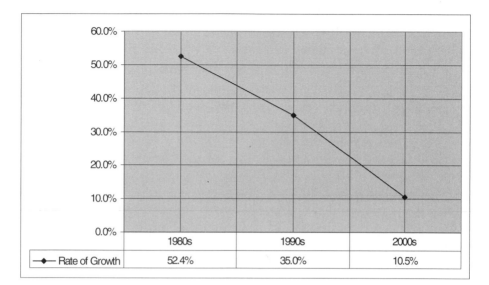

**FIGURE 1-8**   Microsoft Corporation's average rate of revenue growth, 1980s–2000s. Source: Moody's (Mergent) Industrial Manuals, SEC filings.

Herein lies the truly significant problem for the world economy: *There is currently no sector experiencing the growth rates necessary to drive any economy.* Similarly, even though there are several robust industries growing at dynamic rates, the relative size of those industries, such as biotechnology, is simply not yet big enough to impact the world's economy, or even an individual country's economy.

Coming out of World War II, most existing industries experienced burgeoning rates of revenue growth through the 1970s. Then, as the major industries' respective rates of revenue growth began to mature, technology arrived in a big way with the introduction of the personal computer circa 1978. In many ways, technology served as the savior for the U.S. economy over the last 25 years of the 20th century generating new spending from both individuals and corporations that had entirely new categories of products to buy.

Now the question is this: As the robust growth that we've experienced in technology fades, what sector can provide the energy to keep the economy moving onward and upward? While technology was there in the 1980s to add new growth to a maturing economy, it is unclear whether another savior sector is on the horizon and capable of providing new growth.

## THE SHRINKING BIG THREE

Few industries reflect the overall health of an economy more than the auto industry. If car and truck sales in the United States since 1999 are any indication, we might be reaching fundamental limits in the number of cars that are bought each year. The erosion of sales and market share among the Big Three U.S. automakers has always been directly linked to the success of Asian imports since the 1970s. Although losing market share has always been troubling to the Big Three (Ford, Daimler-Chrysler, and General Motors), at least the overall universe of unit car sales in the United States was growing each year. Losing share when the overall pie was getting bigger was bad enough, but losing share when the pie is getting smaller has inflicted a much deeper hurt on the Big Three—one that they all are unlikely to survive.

The rate of growth of total U.S. retail car and truck sales has been trending down since the late 1980s. Although total U.S. retail car and truck sales hit an all-time high of 17.8 million units in 2000, actual unit sales declined three years in a row in 2001, 2002, and 2003.

The Big Three accounted for more than their share of the overall shortfall in sales. The Big Three sold half a million fewer cars in 2002 versus 2001, giving up 1.6 percentage points in market share to the competition. General Motors used liberal financing tactics (e.g., zero-percent financing) to gain back some of the ground it lost during the first 11 months of the year. Even a whopping 36 percent increase in December 2002 sales did not help the top automaker avoid a sales shortfall for full year 2002 versus 2001.

The woes of the Ford Motor Company also continued in 2002 when Ford sold fewer cars and trucks in the United States than it did a full decade earlier. U.S. car and truck sales for Ford slumped to 3.6 million units in 2002, fewer than the 3.7 million units sold in 1993 when the Ford family of cars did not yet include sales from Volvo and Land Rover. With little pricing power due to fierce competition from both domestic cars and imports, there is no making up for the loss in volume with price increases.

Each of the Big Three moved surprisingly fast through new contract negotiations with the United Auto Workers (UAW) union in September 2003. Within days of signing a new four-year contract, all three automakers received union approval to close or sell plants and other operations that would impact close to 12,000 autoworkers, something that the three were unable to do under the terms of the last contract. Though the cost structures of the Big Three have historically trailed Japanese automakers in efficiency, this move also suggests that supply was significantly disconnected from demand, especially after 2000 when inventory levels at many dealerships reached record high levels. Detroit's first three-year losing streak since the inflationary 1970s is a very bad sign for both the industry and the economy.

**A Chicken in Every Pot and a Car for Everyone.** When candidate Herbert Hoover campaigned for the U.S. presidency in 1928, his message to voters was the promise of prosperity for all Americans. His famous campaign slogan, "A chicken in every pot and a car in every garage," said it all to voters who were winding down the Roaring 20s and heading for a depression. Although Hoover's campaign claim certainly did not come true during his presidency, it has subsequently been fulfilled beyond his wildest dreams.

By 1950, Hoover's dream of a car in every garage was just about fulfilled when 50 million motor vehicles were registered in the United States. However, the number of registered motor vehicles in operation in the United States has increased every year since the end of World War II, outpacing population growth in most of those years. According to U.S. Department of Transportation figures, more than 221 million motor vehicles were registered in the United States in 2000, or close to 31 million more registered motor vehicles than licensed drivers.

That's a lot of cars. Picture a four-lane highway, jammed bumper-to-bumper, and wrapped all the way around the earth—and that's just the 31 million cars in surplus. No wonder we can't sell any more cars.

**There are 31 million more registered cars than licensed drivers in the United States. With that surplus alone, the United States could supply every man, woman, and child in Canada with his or her own car.**

Back in 1950 when the automobile was still a novelty for many, the number of licensed drivers far outnumbered the available registered motor vehicles to drive as shown in Figure 1-9. But the ratio of drivers to cars quickly crossed over with cars outnumbered drivers sometime in the early 1970s. That means that the United States has had more cars than drivers for more than 30 years. It is difficult to imagine that there is much more room for growth in the automotive industry when you consider that the United States could supply every resident of Canada with his or her own car, just from the surplus 31 million registered cars to licensed drivers.

| YEAR | NUMBER OF REGISTERED U.S. MOTOR VEHICLES | NUMBER OF LICENSED U.S. DRIVERS | SURPLUS OF CARS TO DRIVERS |
|---|---|---|---|
| 1950 | 49,161,691 | 62,193,495 | –13,031,804 |
| 1960 | 73,857,768 | 87,252,563 | –13,394,795 |
| 1970 | 108,418,197 | 111,542,787 | –3,124,590 |
| 1980 | 155,796,219 | 145,295,036 | 10,501,183 |
| 1990 | 188,797,914 | 167,015,250 | 21,782,664 |
| 2000 | 221,475,173 | 190,625,023 | 30,850,150 |

FIGURE 1-9    Registered motor vehicles and licensed drivers. There were nearly 31 million more registered cars than licensed drivers in 2000. Source: U.S. Department of Transportation.

With the overall U.S. car sales pie getting ever smaller, and the Big Three's share of that shrinking pie diminishing, will Ford, Daimler-Chrysler, and General Motors ever grow domestic car and truck sales in the United States again? Add to this a slowdown in population growth, and we might have to consider that we have reached natural saturation levels for new car sales in the United States.

**Zero-Percent Financing.** Although General Motors might have posted its greatest December on record in 2002, the world's largest automaker might ultimately pay a much higher price for that record in the future. Giving up all interest on financing terms to motivate consumers to buy more cars before the end of the calendar year certainly worked like a charm. But GM's 2002 year-end promotion that pushed 60-month terms might actually hurt the automaker over the long haul.

Zero-percent financing certainly can work wonders for the short term, but it can unwittingly lengthen the buying cycle for consumers taking advantage of the deals. Now, instead of buying a new car in three years when financing terms expire, many consumers won't be in the market for a new car until two years beyond that when their last payment is made at the end of the fifth year.

Consumers are also not stupid. Why buy a new car in July when by October 1 of the same year favorable financing plans will be widely available? General Motors' strategy has been to lure as many new customers as possible with attractive financing and then retain their loyalty over time. Historically, however, the automotive industry has done poorly in the area of customer retention, largely because their marketing efforts are almost exclusively focused on luring new acquisitions. Additionally, discounting tactics usually attract fringe buyers, by far the hardest to retain.

The celebration over such year-end programs is usually short-lived as the new year rolls around quickly and the meter on new car sales for another year is reset. Also, a record-breaking month of December in one year that is driven largely by artificial means sets the bar even higher for the company to clear the following year. Consider this: Even with unusually generous financing ploys, total U.S. auto sales—including the imports—have more often decreased than increased in recent years. This industry is headed for major changes over the next decade, including some shocking consolidations that few thought would ever happen.

## THE AMERICAN DREAM

Homeownership has always been considered a part of living the American dream. That dream has come true for more and more Americans each year since the end of World War II. In 2000, homeownership topped 121 million for the first time ever, more than double the number of homes owned in 1960. Today, there are many more homes than there are families in the United States.

**There are 15 million vacant homes in the United States. With that surplus alone, the United States could house virtually every family in Australia.**

However, new home starts have gradually eroded over the last 30 years, dropping in number each decade since the 1970s. It's not surprising that this figure is slowing because the vacancy rate of homes in the United States has been steadily rising since the 1970s. In 1970, approximately 69 million homes were owned in the United States, and some 6 million of those homes (8.7 percent) were vacant. In 2000, nearly 12 percent of all homes were vacant in the United States; that's nearly 15 million homes, or enough to house the entire country of Australia.

It's difficult to imagine that basic supply and demand pressures will allow us to continue to build new homes when an increasing number of the homes that we already have are vacant.

## RATIONALIZING THE DOLDRUMS

The explanations for the early 21st-century business funk vary greatly, from the terrorist attacks of September 11 to corporate malfeasance at the likes of Enron, Tyco, and WorldCom. Most economists, however, rationalize the sluggish economy as cyclical in nature, and therefore a temporary setback.

The resulting fear, however, has dampened consumer confidence in the equity markets. Coupled with an extraordinarily cautious venture capital community, the lowest levels of merger and acquisition activity since the mid-1990s, and reduced research and development budgets at major public corporations, there is little evidence to suggest that there is any new revenue growth driver on the near-term horizon.

Through it all, though, cheerleaders for an up, up, and away economy abound. Optimism is certainly a good thing, especially in difficult times. However, narrowing rates of growth in all industries raise new questions about new economic fundamentals that could be more permanent in nature. The lingering inelasticity in demand that we are witnessing today suggests the possibility that we are approaching real saturation levels in some sectors. Normally, demand inelasticity is a temporary condition, ordinarily fixed by downward price adjustments. However, saturation could change that and create a more permanent condition of "maintenance sales" that provides no growth.

## CONVENTIONAL REMEDIES

Meanwhile, back in the day-to-day corporate world, senior managers must deal with the realities of slower revenue growth with age-old marketing tactics that are designed to stimulate demand. We have already pushed the limits of expansion, both domestically and internationally. We have already created a seemingly endless number of line extensions that more often result in the cannibalization of our own sales. More often line extensions slice the pie into many more and smaller pieces and add unnecessary costs to an equation that rarely brings us new revenue. How many variations of salad dressing do we need, and does it really help the corporation grow?

Discounting has become commonplace as we adjust the manufacturer's suggested retail price, trading profit for volume. In the process, we have conditioned consumers to always expect a discount, and more often adjust their buying patterns to times of the year that they know will be more advantageous to them.

In many ways, we already have a built-in stimulus package in the form of consumer credit card debt. Each year Americans buy more and more on credit and pay less and less of the outstanding balance. According to The Nilson Report (nilson-report.com), consumer credit card spending nearly tripled from $466 billion in 1990 to $1.3 trillion in 1999. Outstanding balances on that spending have historically hovered around 50 percent, or $243 billion and $614 billion for 1990 and 1999, respectively. To put that into perspective, the outstanding debt of $614 billion in 1999 would have translated into nearly $2,500 for every man, woman, and child in the United States. Is it really possible to stimulate the U.S. economy any more?

## WHEN ALL ELSE FAILS, CHEAT

Cooking the corporate books is another symptom of our inability to generate new revenue growth. Although many point to greed as the reason many corporate executives cheat, greed has been part of the human condition since Adam and Eve. We now know, in fact, that some corporations cheat. We even know how they cheat. But we really haven't fully answered the question of why they have to cheat. The question, then, really should be this: What has changed over the last 25 years to force some corporations to cheat in order to deliver expected earnings growth?

As a corporation runs the natural course of maximizing both revenue strategies (domestic and international distribution, and merger and acquisition activity) and cost-cutting strategies (downsizing, consolidation, and productivity efforts), it ultimately reaches an ethical fork in the road, forcing a choice between delivering reduced earnings or simply faking the numbers. Obviously, some have opted for the latter. Although the Enron, Tyco, and WorldCom debacles represent extreme cases of revenue and expense manipulation, these cases demonstrate what can happen when revenue slows or is greatly reduced.

Pushing the boundaries of Generally Accepted Accounting Practices (GAAP) to paint a rosier financial picture than actually exists has been raised to an art form in recent years. Such practices have largely been the result of corporate revenue reservoirs drying up, and include such common practices as the inflation of revenues through bogus inter-company billings, inventory stuffing, or simply an overstatement of sales.

Xerox's stock price suffered greatly in the wake of an SEC investigation that focused on the firm's alleged artificial inflation of lease revenues. The original intention of such practices can often backfire, depressing revenue, earnings, and ultimately the stock price. Although the matter is now considered settled, Xerox's stock price has taken a beating since the investigation began in June 2000, dropping by nearly 75 percent over a two-year period.

Drug manufacturer Bristol-Myers created a serious problem for itself when pipeline inventories expanded in the fourth quarter of 2001. The inflation of wholesale inventories created a short-term sales windfall of 10 percent in Q4 2001 when wholesalers aggressively stocked up. As a result, this helped cause a sales shortfall for Q1 2002, and the company was forced to restate sales and earnings estimates both for the quarter as well as for the full year 2002. Bristol-Myers' stock price also suffered, losing nearly 60 percent of its value in less than a year.

These cases represent some of the more public examples of alleged numbers manipulation. It would be nearly impossible to identify and penalize every public corporation that has strayed from strict adherence to accounting standards in the name of self-interest over the last decade. Although tougher laws and heightened accountability on the part of senior executives for their numbers are important and necessary steps, it doesn't solve the fundamental underlying problem: the lack of revenue growth.

## HITTING THE MARKET-SHARE WALL

Sometime around 1975, the post-World War II growth explosion fizzled. Revenue growth became more difficult to deliver, as many of the fundamental product categories reached market share highs. The 25-year run-up was over. We had hit the *market-share wall*—the point at which the rate of revenue growth stops increasing and starts decreasing. It also marks the relative peak of the population of two important groups that make up a particular industry or sector:

1. *Consumers in the category.* The universe of consumers that make up the category has largely been determined. New consumers entering the category are primarily the young who replace that segment of the category population that dies. Population gains over time add minimally to the number of consumers in the category.

2. *Competition in the category.* The universe of competitors that are part of the category has also been largely determined. This is not to say that more competitors won't join the category along the way, or that competitors in the category from the outset won't exit the category. It merely means that the chief producers for the category—along with market-share levels—are greatly established.

In fact, many category leaders have historically experienced their most significant market-share levels just prior to hitting the market-share wall. After hitting the wall, market-share levels, especially for category leaders in industries such as automotive, soft drinks, and other consumer products begin to erode from historical highs. The market-share leaders are usually victims of dozens of category options offered not only by competitors, but also by their own line extensions.

## VICTIMS OF OUR OWN SUCCESS

In many ways, we have become victims of our own success, raising the bar year in and year out, requiring us to jump even higher the next year. In the world of business, the more you grow, the more you have to grow if you want to keep fueling the delivery of increased earnings.

Consider General Electric, for example. Here's a company that has a history of acquiring 100 or more companies in recent years. Why? Because it takes an ever-increasing amount of new revenue to push General Electric's top line ever upward. As internal businesses mature, an increasing amount of revenue growth at the $140 billion industrial giant must come from acquired businesses, and a $1 billion acquisition today barely impacts General Electric's top line. However, this wasn't always the case.

Throughout the 1970s, General Electric experienced outstanding revenue growth, averaging more than 10 percent a year. The 1980s, however, were far less kind to General Electric's top line with an average rate of growth of just over 3 percent. General Electric nearly tripled its revenue from 1970 to 1979, yet was only able to muster a 25 percent increase in sales from 1980 to 1989. Even more striking is the fact that a much bigger General Electric more than tripled its revenues in the 1990s, topping $100 billion for the first time in 1998. General Electric's revenue grew by nearly $80 billion in the 1990s, from $33 billion in 1990 to $111 billion in 1999.

After disappointing sales in the 1980s, General Electric became an acquisitions machine, gobbling up more than 500 companies over the course of Jack Welch's final five years as chairman. Once hooked on the revenue juice from acquisitions over a period of years, it becomes a difficult habit to kick, and puts immense pressure on any successor to continue the drill: acquire, consolidate, and increase productivity. For Jeffrey Immelt, General Electric's new chairman, it makes it difficult to run the company in any other fashion.

There is little doubt that corporations are finding it more difficult to generate revenue growth by any means, including acquisitions. Since the turn of the 21st century, revenue growth has greatly slowed. So what's the big deal? The big deal is that there is an undeniable connection between revenue and earnings. If revenue stops growing, ultimately so will earnings. For now, most public corporations have been able to put all of their energy into delivering the type of growth that Wall Street expects, and that makes senior management wealthy beyond their wildest dreams. However, the roadmap to earnings delivery has shifted dramatically since 1980 with cost-cuts gaining in importance as the primary earnings driver.

Nonetheless, earnings growth has taken center stage as the Holy Grail for analysts, the business press, shareowners, and management alike. Grow earnings and everybody wins. That is, until you can no longer grow earnings.

## PUTTING EARNINGS AT RISK

This global sales bump in the road won't be fixed by simply firing the vice president of sales or dismissing the advertising agency. This is a new phenomenon for the world's economy. Since the end of World War II, there has always been at least one industry with a rate of growth that is trending up instead of down, until now. Why is this significant? The consistent lack or absence of revenue growth will ultimately put the delivery of earnings growth at risk. In some cases, it already has.

Too many simply brush aside the lack of revenue growth as a short-term problem caused by a number of factors, from September 11 to diminished consumer confidence. The bottom line is this: Management's ability to deliver sustained earnings growth is in jeopardy because of its troubling inability to deliver sustained revenue growth. This puts a tremendous amount of pressure on management to increasingly rely on cost-cutting to deliver earnings.

Wholesale layoffs, dramatic cuts in marketing spending and research and development budgets, and compromising on the fundamental quality of products to save a buck can certainly all contribute to this quarter's earnings target, but at what long-term cost to the health of the corporation and the livelihoods of future generations of workers worldwide?

Ever since the first general store opened near Boston in the 1620s, we have looked forward to a bigger, better year next year. For the most part, we have lived up to that ideal over the last 380 years. We have always believed that growth is unlimited, almost an inalienable certainty, even if it means growing at a slower rate. We believe that the inability to grow is due to someone's inability to deliver. We now know this not to be true in most cases.

We are beginning to understand that growth might not be an economic certainty. If our ability to deliver increased revenues in perpetuity is limited, and our ability to deliver increased productivity in perpetuity is limited, then our ability to deliver increased earnings in perpetuity is also limited.

## THE CULTURE OF MORE

We have truly been conditioned to expect more and more in this culture and we are bombarded by the hyperbole everyday. The World's Largest Bookstore. Billions and Billions Served. Now even Google, the popular Web search engine, is puffing it up on its home page: "Searching 3,000,000,000 Web Pages!" There is only one direction: Up. There is only one quantity: More. Our perspective on revenue growth is no different. In many ways, our view toward our economy has largely been warped since World War II, and why not? We continue to deliver record revenues. We continue to deliver record earnings. Incredibly, we expect our winning streak to continue ad infinitum.

Just when we think we have seen the greatest golfer of all time, along comes Tiger Woods. Just when we thought we've seen the greatest woman's tennis player of all time, along comes Serena Williams. Just when we thought we've seen the greatest home run output of all time, along comes Mark McGwire, and two years later Barry Bonds. Because of such rare feats, we think that there are no limits; there is nothing that we can't do.

Our optimism abounds, and that's not a bad thing. We look at any slowdown as temporary, any shortfall as an aberration. In fact, we measure the health of our economy not on what we sell but on what we produce, and even that measure has steadily eroded over the last quarter-century. We are a highly educated and rational society, yet we most often look at business and its promise with childlike enthusiasm, emotionally and irrationally.

We are problem solvers. We intently study each problem and come up with solutions, and we have solved a lot of problems, from bad breath to grass stains, to getting from point A to point B, to communicating with someone across the street or around the world.

We have flooded the domestic market as well as international markets with thousands of product categories over the last quarter-century. We sell everything to everyone, everywhere, yet we still believe that we can convince a consumer in Des Moines to drink one more Coke a week. In many ways, we have tapped out the planet. Those who have the means and access essentially have everything that they need, in any quantity in which they need it. Those without the means are currently not prospective buyers of Lucky Charms. Sure, China is a vast untapped commercial market, but even China has its limits.

For the first time in history, we might be facing the stark reality that there are limitations to consumption, and that just kicks demand square in the teeth. There are no longer any new consumers entering the categories of toothpaste, soft drinks, or breakfast cereals. Therefore, gains come from fractional shifts in market share that cost marketers billions in investment spending each year.

We have super-sized and line-extended ourselves into a corner of saturation where volume is flat and price is powerless. There's an excess of industrial capacity in the United States that makes raising prices virtually impossible. This is an economy of slumbering demand, increased inventories, and dangerously declining rates of revenue growth. We must wake up to that reality. This change in our economy is fundamental in nature. It is real, it is here for a while, and if you are part of the business world, you are dealing with it. To make matters worse, you will have to deal with it in what will likely be an unstable geopolitical climate for the foreseeable future.

You can thank the generations that went before you because they accomplished what they set out to do: innovate, build, and push the boundaries of progress. Introducing countless new products, expanding distribution to every corner of the world, acquiring every possible company. Ever since the end of World War II, the world has increasingly sought to drive record sales, post record revenues, and to deliver record earnings. By any measure, the mission was a huge success, but over the course of the struggle, capitalism's best friend died.

This is why there will be no economic turnaround and no getting back on a growth track. Not the way some think, anyway. The ambition of many generations that pushed for more has unwittingly killed demand. The lifeblood of capitalism is dead, the victim of hundreds of years of progress. A century ago expectations were low and sacrifice was high. Now, in the first decade of a new century, expectations are high and few in developed countries have ever experienced real sacrifice. It's never been harder to increase revenue or to reduce costs.

In some ways, the curtain is still coming down on a century of remarkable progress that spins the head. It just may be that because of that progress, the world's economy will simply turn at a slower pace. Like an aging man who has successfully negotiated the hills in the past, our easy climbs are behind us, and our tough climbs are just beginning.

# 2 BUILDING REVENUE AND MARKET SHARE: 1950 TO 1980

So much of life is about timing, and so much about the success or failure of an individual's business career can depend on when he or she enters the business world. The same can be true for the birth of a new business. Launching a business on October 28, 1929, probably would not have been the best time to convince people to take an investment flyer. Consider the difficulty Ray Kroc would have had gathering momentum to build a hamburger empire if he launched McDonald's in 1929 instead of 1955.

Fast-forward from 1929 to 1946, and the world was a very different place. It was the first full year after World War II, and the world was much more focused on building up than tearing down. Ironically, it was the year that John Maynard Keynes died. Keynes was the fabled economist whose theories played a major role in postwar economic policy, especially as it relates to the role of government in the economy. Unfortunately, he would not live to see his theories in practice in a postwar world. It was also the year movie director Frank Capra introduced the world to *It's a Wonderful Life,* a movie that would not only define the spirit of the times, but the hope for a better life for generations to come. For many, it truly was the beginning of a wonderful life—a life so many had been forced to delay.

The first year after the war ended was the year that the world was introduced to Tide—the washing miracle—and its phenomenal success helped Procter & Gamble plow even more money into research and development to develop other block-buster brands such as Crest toothpaste in 1955. The parlay proved enormously successful, especially when the American Dental Association essentially endorsed Crest when it added tooth-decay fighting fluoride to its formula later in the decade.

Events of the immediate postwar years set the tone for the rest of the century, one of growth, building, and rebuilding:

- Over 1 million U.S. GIs enrolled in colleges under the GI Bill of Rights.
- General George Marshall became U.S. Secretary of State and called for a plan to help Europe recover from the war—*The Marshall Plan*.

Conditions were perfect to create an upward growth trend in virtually all sectors of the economy. A world of driven individuals who had sacrificed so much for so long had an opportunity for a fresh start and the sky truly was the limit. Hopes were high, and the conditions and timing to ignite a demand frenzy were perfect.

## THE FABULOUS FIFTIES

At the start of the 1950s, the Dow Jones Industrial Average hovered around 175. The largest of the Dow components—General Motors at $7.5 billion—was also the largest company in the world. The smallest of the Dow components was General Foods at $124 million. Sears & Roebuck, also a Dow component, was becoming a retailing giant with $2.2 billion in net revenue in 1950. The largest corporation in the world in 2003 didn't even exist in 1950. In fact, Wal-Mart was 12 years away from opening its first store in 1962. Some of the fastest growing of the Dow 30 corporations in 1950—Allied Can (18.5%), American Smelting (27.4%), National Steel (26.6 %), and Corn Products (22.7%)—don't even exist today.

The world, although certainly not without geopolitical strife, was beginning to get back on its feet. Market conditions and consumer dynamics created a perfect environment for building and, in the case of Europe and Japan, rebuilding. For the two generations of men and women who crawled through the mud on virtually every continent, sold apples on street corners to earn money for a meal, and rationed food and other materials, it was time to live life, time to pursue the great benefits of freedom and the simple dreams of buying their own homes and driving their own cars.

GIs returned from the war eager to build new lives for themselves, and a new generation of consumers was just beginning to enter the world at record birth rates. The opportunity to fulfill the pent-up demand of at least two generations that had sacrificed so much had never been better:

- The quality of life for most was not extremely high.
- The desire for a higher quality of life was extremely high.
- The energy, motivation, and hard-work ethic necessary to create a better quality of life was extremely high.
- The ability to produce goods and services was extremely high.
- Demand had been suppressed for decades through years of self-sacrifice.
- Creativity abounded in the development of new categories designed to help make life easier.
- A growing percentage of the population was earning more money.
- Money was essentially reinvested into corporations by way of more and more consumption.
- Vast numbers of consumers entered product categories for the first time ever (buying homes, cars, televisions, telephones, washing machines, vacuums, etc.).
- 78 million babies were born between 1946 and 1964. The baby boomer generation was beginning to make an impact: first as children, then as adults and heads of their own households starting in the late 1960s.

■ Television, the most powerful mass communication tool in history, was born.

It was the golden age of market share, an opportunity for consumers to consume and for corporations to lay claim to their share of countless virgin markets that appealed to the masses. As for the masses, their hopes were high to build a better life for themselves, and if not specifically for themselves, at least for their children.

## THE RIPPLE EFFECT

With the population booming, consumption was booming, and new product development was booming. All of this activity created a ripple effect that helped virtually all industries grow. As the population boomed, certainly the basic food and clothing industries benefited immediately. However, so did the housing market, as well as the commercial real estate market that served the ever-expanding corporations that were responding to the increase in demand.

More houses, retail outlets, and corporate offices meant more wood, steel, cooper, water, electricity, and telephones, boosting demand in the basic materials, utilities, and communications sectors. More real estate meant more mortgages, driving growth in the financial sector. More cars meant more gas and oil, boosting the energy sector. More pregnancies meant more baby deliveries, and the rapid increase in the number of people in the world meant more people needed medical care from cradle to grave.

In the 1950s, there was a rapid increase in the number of people living and dying in the world, and the ripple effect of growth that this caused was a remarkable one-time event that corporations quickly learned how to harvest.

## GROWTH STRATEGIES

Although mostly relying on creative thinking and research from their own laboratories in the development of new products, corporations also utilized a mix of growth strategies to build sales and capture market share from 1950 to 1980:

1. *Product development.* Hundreds of new products and new product categories were introduced to meet the demands of a growing populace. Successful new product introductions frequently resulted in the development of line extensions that introduced a new consumer benefit.

2. *Domestic distribution.* As new products and line extensions were introduced and accepted as mainstream additions to daily life, the next logical step for corporations was to expand distribution domestically. If it played in Peoria, it would probably play in Phoenix. Creating the means for domestic consumers to purchase products or services more easily, either through the wholesale/retail channel or directly from the manufacturer, helped greatly expand sales. Expanding domestic distribution represented one of the primary efforts to grow market share during the 1950s, 1960s, and 1970s.

3. *Mass marketing.* The battle cry of the 1950s, 1960s, and 1970s was clear: Market share! Market share! Market share! Over this 30-year period—the greatest mass marketing hammer in history—television helped corporations spread the word far and wide, and established consumption habits for multiple generations of consumers.

The growth frenzy that started in the 1950s was greatly aided by the introduction of many new innovations. Not all product innovations are the same, however. Some provide new consumer benefits to existing products, whereas others create a whole new category of products that never existed before. The latter can bring an unusually powerful growth dynamic to a corporation, an industry, a sector, or an entire economy.

## DISCONTINUOUS INNOVATION

One of the most important elements necessary to drive growth in an economy is the ability on the part of consumers to buy products that never existed before. Intel cofounder and author Geoffrey A. Moore calls such events *discontinuous innovations* in his best-selling book *Inside the Tornado:*

> Discontinuous Innovations begin with the appearance of a new category of product that incorporates breakthrough technology enabling unprecedented benefits. It is immediately proposed as the natural replacement for a whole class of infrastructure.[1]

After consumers begin to adopt a discontinuous innovation, it then becomes the responsibility of the continuous innovators to make it better, faster, and cheaper. That is the mantra of the continuous innovator who spends his or her entire life managing an innovation that already exists. It is the primary skill set of the continuous innovator that has largely been taught at business schools for decades. Entrepreneurship, or the ability to bring an entirely new product or category to market, is a difficult skill to teach. It would be like teaching someone to be curious: Either they are or they are not.

Often, when a discontinuous innovation is successfully introduced, the impact can be significant on alternative products or product categories. For example, when network television became available for the first time in the United States in 1949, it had an immediate and devastating effect on the movie industry. Theater admissions fell like a rock, from a high of 4.1 billion admissions in 1945 to less than 1.0 billion admissions in 1970. Of course, television did not replace film as a source of entertainment, but it greatly altered the movie business forever.

Figure 2-1 identifies some of the most significant discontinuous innovations over the last 150 years. The introduction

---

1.    Geoffrey A. Moore, *Inside the Tornado: Marketing Strategies from Silicon Valley's Cutting Edge*, A HarperBusiness Book, 1999, p. 4.

of discontinuous innovations—especially prior to 1950—usually signaled that a completely new and better solution relative to existing alternatives was available. For example, when the telegraph was introduced around 1851, it literally caused the Pony Express—in business only 18 months at the time—to completely disappear. The reason was simple: The new solution of instantaneously sending messages over a wire rendered the old application completely inadequate.

Most often when a discontinuous innovation is introduced (e.g., overnight delivery) the previous standard just cannot stand up to the benefits of the new form. A new, higher expectation develops relative to the new and improved benefits associated with a new discontinuous innovation. Who could go back to creating documents using an IBM Selectric typewriter after using a personal computer with Microsoft Windows and Microsoft Word?

| New Category | Year | Impacted |
|---|---|---|
| Railroad | 1825 | Stagecoach |
| Postal telegraph | 1851 | Pony Express |
| Telephone | 1876 | Telegraph, U.S. Mail |
| Automobile | 1885 | Railroad, horse & buggy |
| Radio | 1890 | Newspapers |
| Airplane | 1903 | Automobile, train |
| Television | 1946 | Radio, newspapers |
| Personal computer | 1978 | Typewriter |
| E-mail | 1984 | Telephone, U.S. Mail |
| Instant messaging | 1996 | Telephone, e-mail |

FIGURE 2-1  Discontinuous innovations: The introduction of new product categories. Source: Customer Share Group LLC.

When Alexander Graham Bell introduced the telephone nearly 25 years later, its utility greatly impacted the role of the telegraph. Unlike the Pony Express, the telegraph didn't disappear when the telephone was widely introduced, but its role as a means to communicate one-to-one certainly did. When each of the discontinuous innovations listed in Figure 2-1 appeared for the first time, each claimed supremacy over existing alternatives. Most discontinuous innovations, however, are rarely completely replaced by the introduction of a new discontinuous innovation. Although television greatly impacted radio's role as a source of news and entertainment, as well as a means of mass marketing, radio didn't go away. It's role simply changed.

There was a very high incidence of significant discontinuous innovations from around 1870 to 1900. This was a period of intense curiosity and invention all over the world that resulted in the introduction of mega-categories such as the automobile and the airplane that not only created new industries, but also greatly impacted virtually all other existing industries. When the automobile was widely introduced after the turn of the century, it enabled a faster, more precise form of distribution through the birth of the trucking industry. This allowed for more rapid delivery of orders and reorders to the retail channel that is still the primary means of delivery today.

The most powerful of all discontinuous innovations are those that have the ability to greatly impact all existing sectors and industries around it. For example, when the personal computer became widely available in the late 1970s and early 1980s, it significantly impacted consumers as well as businesses. The wholesale adoption of a new category that moves both businesses and consumers to spend additional dollars is the type of powerful characteristic that can generate enough momentum to impact an economy. This is why discontinuous innovations are so important to the future health of any economy.

## CONTINUOUS INNOVATION

*Continuous innovation,* on the other hand, is the process of developing improvements to existing products, such as the introduction of fluoride to toothpaste or airbags to automobiles. Continuous innovation does not necessarily result in an increase in the number of consumers in a category. More often than not, cannibalization results, causing a consumer to trade out one product for another, sometimes even within the very same corporation. For example, if a user of PertPlus shampoo switches to Head & Shoulders shampoo, there is no net gain for Procter & Gamble. This is why the development of discontinuous innovations or new product categories is extremely important to corporations such as Procter & Gamble, and why they invest heavily in the development of new categories.

Figure 2-2 shows how continuous innovation progressively introduces new benefits to existing products. However, just because a new benefit is introduced to a category, it does not necessarily mean that the category universe will grow. For example, when toothpaste with fluoride added the benefit of a whitening compound, it is unlikely that the universe of users grew. It is more likely that the total universe size remained the same with many consumers switching from an original form of toothpaste with fluoride to the new line extension featuring toothpaste with fluoride and whitening capability. In this case the line extension gains a customer, but the original form loses a customer. The result is no net gain for the corporation, unless the consumer switches brands. In any case, the category does not gain a consumer.

| Original Product | Innovation #1 | Innovation #2 |
|---|---|---|
| Coke | Diet Coke | Caffeine-Free Diet Coke |
| Toothpaste | With Fluoride | With Whitener |
| Telephone | Portable | Wireless |
| Television | Color | High definition |
| Automobile | Seatbelts | Airbags |
| Airplane | Jet engine | Concorde |
| LP | Audiotape | CD |
| Mainframe computer | Desktop computer | Laptop computer |

FIGURE 2-2   Continuous innovation: Introduction of new benefits to existing product/categories. Source: Customer Share Group LLC.

Even though the long-playing (LP) record revolutionized the music industry, when audiotape became available, it brought new benefits to the consumer, including the convenience of portability and the ability for the consumer to record. The LP continued to exist as the preferred means of replicating and distributing music albums until compact disc (CD) technology arrived. When the CD was introduced, it virtually put an end to the LP, and also changed the audiotape industry, especially as CD burners became available.

Continuous innovation is an extremely important and necessary element to any economy because it allows for the distribution of labor across many different jobs to preserve the core revenue streams. Without continuous or incremental innovation, unemployment rates would likely skyrocket. For example, as much as the computer has helped increase the productivity at most corporations around the world, too much rapid productivity could result in the wholesale elimination of jobs—especially in an environment that is pressured to deliver consistent earnings growth.

## CREATIVE DESTRUCTION

Austrian economist Joseph P. Schumpeter believed that one of the unique dynamics of capitalism was that it enabled and, in fact, encouraged constant innovation and the development of new products and new product categories. Ironically, this dynamic caused what Schumpeter termed *creative destruction*—the unavoidable triumph of the newest innovation over the last innovation.

Creative destruction results from the introduction of a new innovation that greatly impacts the last innovation, hastening its demise or destruction. Although the advent of the automobile at the turn of the 20th century did not destroy the train and horse and buggy businesses, they were forever altered because of the introduction of a preferred form of transportation. In the extreme, an innovation can completely replace a less desirable alternative. Such was the case when the telegraph rendered the delivery of mail by men on horseback woefully inadequate.

## MARKETING STRATEGIES AND TACTICS

For the first half of the 20th century, marketing had yet to evolve to the level of art and science that it would later in the century. Figure 2-3 identifies the primary mass and direct marketing tools widely used along the marketing continuum from 1900 to 1975. The national marketing tools that existed from 1900 to 1950 consisted mainly of magazines and newspapers at the beginning of the century, then later with network radio, especially during the 1930s, which became known as the golden age of radio.

### THE MARKETING CONTINUUM, 1900–1975

|  | 1900–1949 | 1950–1975 |
|---|---|---|
| MASS MARKETING | Newspapers<br>Magazines<br>Radio<br>Sponsorships<br>Outdoor<br>POS<br>Promotions | Television |
| DIRECT MARKETING | Face-to-face<br>U.S. Mail<br>Telegram<br>Telephone | 800 number<br>Fax |

FIGURE 2-3    Marketing to the masses: Everything changed when network television arrived in 1949.
Source: Customer Share Group LLC.

Direct marketing and direct sales actually played a very important role in the development of revenue over the first 50 years of the 20th century. The fabled door-to-door Fuller Brush Man was introduced during this period, and face-to-face sales at retail were ordinarily conducted between sellers who intimately knew their buyers. The butcher, the baker, and the candlestick maker all knew their customers by name and by product preference.

Other popular direct marketing methods during this time included mail order catalogs from corporations such as jeweler Tiffany & Co. and outdoor supplier L.L. Bean. However, as World War II ended, a new and powerful marketing weapon was about to change the course of marketing as well as the course of world history.

Once broadcast television appeared, the marketing game changed dramatically, and all forms of marketing that existed before were greatly impacted from 1950 to 1975. Broadcast television ruled as the preferred means of building awareness, trial usage, and brand image for many years. However, even broadcast television had an Achilles heel that was to come in the form of cable television and the videocassette recorder (VCR).

## A TALE OF TWO STRATEGIES: SELLING SODA AND CEREAL

In 1960, two of the world's leading consumer-packaged goods corporations were on the verge of exploding. The Kellogg Company and the Pepsi-Cola Company posted identical net revenue lines that year—$157 million a piece. Both had originally started operations at the tail end of the 1800s, and over that period of time had built respectable if not burgeoning businesses. But that was about to change—especially with an unusually large population of new, young consumers learning about the delights of soft drinks and cereal. The mushrooming generation known as the baby boomers was the perfect target audience for both Kellogg's and Pepsi. And from precisely the same top line starting point in 1960, both corporations aggressively pursued growth with radically different strategies.

Kellogg's fancied itself as a creator, manufacturer, and marketer of some of the world's great cereals. A proud Kellogg's, therefore, embraced a growth strategy that primarily relied on coming up with new variations of cereals, expanding the availability of its cereals in North America and marketing the daylights out of its offerings with animated pitchmen such as Tony the Tiger and SNAP, CRACKLE & POP! Kellogg's initiated early expansion to Japan (1963), introduced the popular POP-TARTS in 1964, created a state-of-the-art cereal manufacturing facility in Battle Creek in 1988, and pushed distribution to Latvia, India, and China in the early 1990s.

Pepsi took a slightly different approach to growth. While it also developed its fair share of new products over the post-WWII years, Pepsi very early on also embraced one of the most aggressive growth strategies there is: Mergers & Acquisitions. Frequent and significant M&A activity—well before it became a vogue means of generating growth—became a Pepsi trademark. And because Pepsi initiated its acquisition strategy during the high-growth decades of the 1960s and 1970s, it enjoyed the added benefit of acquiring companies that were also growing rapidly.

Starting with the merger in 1965 with the Frito-Lay Company, marking the formation of PepsiCo, the corporation also determined early on that it was more than just a non-alcoholic beverage concern. After four full decades, PepsiCo had grown into a global titan in its industry with major acquisitions in every decade, including companies such as Pizza Hut (1977), Taco Bell (1978), Kentucky Fried Chicken (1986), Tropicana (1998), and the Quaker Oats Company (1998).

|  | 1960 | 1970 | 1980 | 1990 | 2000 |
|---|---|---|---|---|---|
| Kellogg's | $157 | $614 | $2,150 | $5,181 | $6,955 |
| PepsiCo | $157 | $1,122 | $5,271 | $17,515 | $20,438 |

From a dead-heat starting point in 1960, the two corporations entered a new century at very different places from the perspective of top line revenues with PepsiCo topping $26 billion in net revenue in 2002 and Kellogg's just under $7 billion. After nearly a half-century of product development, domestic and global expansion, and M&A work, which strategy worked best in terms of increasing shareowner value?

## A TALE OF TWO STRATEGIES: SELLING SODA AND CEREAL (CONTINUED)

Based on an investment of $10,000 in both Kellogg's ($39.75 per share) and the Pepsi-Cola Company ($39.375 per share) stock on January 4, 1960, the return on those investments, not including dividends, as of January 3, 2003:

Kellogg's  =  $70,019*

PepsiCo  =  $1,177,664*

\* Based on the following stock splits: Kellogg's (January 28, 1986 = 2:1; December 17, 1991 = 2:1; August 25, 1997 = 2:1) PepsiCo (June 9, 1967 = 2:1; May 5, 1977 = 3:1; May 28, 1986 = 3:1; September 4, 1990 = 3:1; May 28, 1996 = 2:1). ■

## EXPONENTIAL GROWTH

It is unlikely that we will ever witness the level of growth produced around the world in the three decades following World War II. Corporate revenue, as well as advertising budgets and television audiences, consistently grew over a 30-year period from 1950 to 1979. This unique confluence of events created unusually fertile conditions for growth. The number of U.S. consumers that even had access to television consistently increased each year for close to 30 years. As corporations grew through the 1950s and 1960s, they continued to invest ad dollars back into media, helping to grow the very marketing machine that drove sales.

Figure 2-4 shows that the installed base of households with televisions consistently grew through the 1950s, 1960s, and 1970s before effectively reaching saturation in 1980. Quite a remarkable feat considering that only 10 percent of U.S. households had TVs just 30 years before.

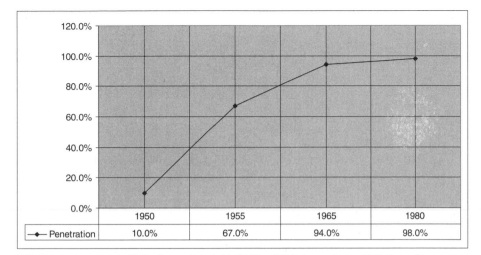

**FIGURE 2-4**    Penetration of U.S. television households, 1950 to 1980. Source: Nielsen Media Research.

Helping corporations mine dynamic growth starting in the 1950s were two fledgling industries whose growth path would literally parallel that of their clients during the post-World World II era. Advertising agencies and media—especially the broadcast television industry—were mere infants in 1950, each struggling to build foundational growth one client at a time.

The explosion of new products and new product categories, coupled with the reach of network television and the voracious appetite of hungry consumers packed a powerful punch that not only helped grow entire industries, but also that of fledgling media companies and advertising agencies that helped them mine the growth. The more consumers bought, the more ad dollars manufacturers plowed back into media. The more ad dollars manufacturers plowed back into media, the more sales they generated.

## FORMULA FOR GROWTH

The formula for building revenues shown in Figure 2-5 was both powerful and enormously successful through the 1970s for all parties: the manufacturer, the ad agency, and the media it used to communicate its commercial messages. It was the extraordinary success of corporations such as Procter & Gamble and the Coca-Cola Company that enabled both ad agency and media companies to flourish.

As the Ford Motor Company and Kraft Foods grew, so grew J. Walter Thompson, as well as broadcast network partners ABC, CBS, and NBC. As the Campbell's Soup Company and Mattel grew, so grew Ogilvy & Mather, as well as the broadcast networks. As Kellogg's and Procter & Gamble, so grew Leo Burnett, as well as the broadcast networks.

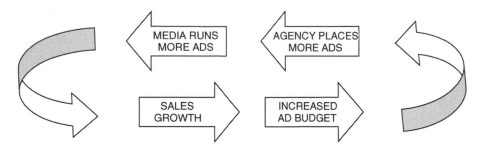

**FIGURE 2-5**    The formula for building revenue growth. It worked through the 1970s; why wouldn't it work forever? Source: Customer Share Group LLC.

In many ways, corporate advertisers helped create one of the greatest mass marketing assets of all time in network television. It was their ever-increasing investment through advertising during the 1950s, 1960s, and 1970s that built the quintessential mass marketing machine. Ironically, although corporate advertisers helped fund the creation and subsequent growth of the machine, they didn't share in the ownership of it. The only way that many advertisers could communicate with their vast, far-flung customer bases was by paying media for the privilege of talking to their own customers. In some ways, corporations that advertised over the airwaves as the primary means of communicating with their customer bases were paying ransom to access the millions of loyal users they had paid millions if not billions to acquire.

## NEW PRODUCT CATEGORIES

Corporations desperately seek to develop new categories all the time (e.g., Swiffer, Spin Brush, Viagra). After 50 years of research and investment dedicated to producing solutions to life's day-to-day problems, it becomes nearly impossible to introduce new categories today. For example, although the automobile was introduced as a new category more than 100 years ago, no new category has come along to replace it. It's unlikely to happen anytime soon, but there will come a day when there is an alternative form of transportation that will begin to replace the automobile just as the automobile replaced the horse and buggy.

As more and more product categories were successfully introduced over the course of the 20th century, it became more difficult for corporations to develop more new categories. Each successive generation, therefore, was introduced to a dwindling number of new categories simply because so many fundamental categories had already been introduced to prior generations. For example, consumers who were part of the World War I generation made many first-time decisions relative to the most basic of categories such as buying their first radio, phonograph, or car.

When the offspring of the World War I generation became adult consumers themselves, it was not a matter of whether they would buy a car, it was simply a matter of when and what model. For many in the World War II generation, the decision to own a car had already been made by their parents. The significance of this is that the longer a product category is on the market, the greater chance it has to reach user saturation levels. For example, it is unlikely that any new consumers will enter the toothpaste category this year.

Figure 2-6 identifies many of the product categories that were adopted by the World War I generation or earlier generations. These are fundamental categories, more consistent with day-to-day survival than personal comforts or leisure-time pleasures.

| GENERATION | FOOD | HOUSEHOLD | PERSONAL | CONSUMER ELECTRONIC |
|---|---|---|---|---|
| World War I | Hot/cold cereal, milk, eggs, bread, ice, sugar, salt, flour, coffee, tea, alcohol, tobacco, fresh produce, meats, poultry | Home indoor plumbing, electricity, laundry flakes, washboard, ice box, car | Bar soap, toothpaste, lye, straight razor | Phonograph, radio, telephone |

**FIGURE 2-6**     First-time product categories, World War I generation, born 1900 to 1924. Source: Customer Share Group LLC.

Now look at what happened a generation later in Figure 2-7. Many new product categories that never existed before became available just as this generation was buying their first homes and starting a family. It was this generation that was faced with the decision about whether to buy so many of the household appliances that were an early version of the staples that are standard equipment in most homes today: electric washing machines, electric dryers, electric stoves, electric refrigerators, and electric vacuums. All of these household basics were available for the first time.

There was also a clear shift in the type of product categories from one generation to the next from a lifestyle standpoint. New product categories for the World War II generation were clearly more geared to making life easier.

For the first time in the 20th century, we witnessed the introduction of many new categories that required a relatively hefty price tag for consumers. Even what we consider today to be basic household appliances were major purchases for most families that were either just getting started or getting back on their feet. The lure of a new car and the open road was a very powerful opiate for the masses, especially with a bombardment

| Generation | Food | Household | Personal | Consumer Electronic |
|---|---|---|---|---|
| World War I | Hot/cold cereal, milk, eggs, bread, ice, sugar, salt, flour, coffee, tea, alcohol, tobacco, fresh produce, meats, poultry | Home indoor plumbing, electricity, laundry flakes, washboard, ice box, car | Bar soap, toothpaste, lye, straight razor | Phonograph, radio, telephone |
| World War II | TV dinners, frozen food | Electric refrigerator, electric washing machine, electric dryer, electric stove, electric dishwasher, toaster, electric vacuum, electric can opener, power lawn mower, Snow-blower | Shaving cream, razor blades, feminine hygiene products | Television, camera, color film, instant photography, home movies, 45s, LPs, hi-fi, transistor radio |

**FIGURE 2-7**  First-time product categories, World War II generation, born 1925 to 1945. Source: Customer Share Group LLC.

of buzz from TV and word of mouth. Although purchasing a new washing machine today might be considered a thankless chore, in 1948 such a purchase was often a major neighborhood event. Consequently, as the World War II generation earned more, they spent more—most often on first-time purchases in categories such as the washing machine. The World War I and World War II generations made more first time buying decisions than any other two generations in history.

This type of consumer pioneering had an impact on generations to come. When the baby boomers arrived as the next generation of adult consumers, their parents had already made most basic household category buying decisions. The boomers, then, were faced with a whole new set of categories that weren't around when their parents started outfitting their homes.

Figure 2-8 adds the baby boomer generation to the mix along with a new set of first-time category decisions. Most of what their parents and grandparents had considered luxuries were necessities for the largest generation in history. This mindset helped guarantee an installed base of basic household appliances for each succeeding generation. Outstanding dynamics to help grow the economy. The new categories continue to suggest that we want things to be faster and more convenient as well as portable.

The boomer generation was the first to embrace the concept of disposable goods. The idea of washing a diaper would not fly with this generation that would begin to change the traditionally defined roles of the average household. Two-income households became more the rule than the exception starting with the boomers. They also helped pioneer the divorce factor that, unfortunately, helped create many more single-parent heads of households; all the more reason for categories of products to help make life easier on the way to and from work. The divorce factor also had an accretive impact on certain industries and the economy in general. In many cases, a divorce required the hiring of at least two attorneys and two real estate agents. The near-term result was at least three real estate transactions: selling one house and buying two others. Over the longer term, where once there was one household to accommodate the family, two households become necessary, creating the appearance of growth.

By the time the youngest boomers turned 21 in 1985, a fully outfitted home with what had become the bare necessities had become an expensive proposition. The estimated cost of outfitting a home with one product from each of the categories listed under the Household and Consumer Electronic columns in Figure 2-8 would today be in excess of $20,000!

| GENERATION | FOOD | HOUSEHOLD | PERSONAL | CONSUMER ELECTRONIC |
|---|---|---|---|---|
| World War I | Hot/cold cereal, milk, eggs, bread, ice, sugar, salt, flour, coffee, tea, alcohol, tobacco, fresh produce, meats, poultry | Home indoor plumbing, electricity, laundry flakes, washboard, ice box, car | Bar soap, toothpaste, lye, straight razor | Phonograph, radio, telephone |
| World War II | TV dinners, frozen food | Electric refrigerator, electric washing machine, electric dryer, electric stove, electric dishwasher, toaster, electric vacuum, electric can opener, power lawn mower, Snow-blower | Shaving cream, razor blades, feminine hygiene products | Television, camera, color film, instant photography, home movies, 45s, LPs, hi-fi, transistor radio |
| Baby boomers | Light beer, Nutrasweet | Microwave, toaster oven | Disposable razors, disposable diapers, birth control pills | VCR, Walkman, answering machine, fax audiotape, videotape, calculator, portable telephone, car phone |

FIGURE 2-8    First-time product categories, baby boomer generation, born 1946 to 1964. Source: Customer Share Group LLC.

## THE INFLATIONARY 1970S

Although many economists point to skyrocketing oil prices brought on by the Organization of Petroleum Exporting Countries (OPEC) in the early 1970s as the primary reason for runaway inflation during the decade, often overlooked is the impact of one of the simplest of all economic theories: demand and supply. Consider the unique demand dynamics that existed in the 1970s:

- Households grew at an increasing rate.
- Baby boomers began to head their own households, boosting growth rates.
- There was an explosion of product categories, products, and line extensions, many of which were considered necessities.

The same boomers that helped generate growth for Procter & Gamble and Kellogg's during the 1950s and 1960s were now coming of age as adults. This unique dynamic alone helped to create an ever-increasing demand during the 1970s. Every year during the decade, another batch of boomers joined the adult ranks as heads of their own households.

In 1970, only about 20 percent of boomers were 21 years of age or older. By the end of the decade, nearly 80 percent or more than 62 million boomer adults over the age of 21 had joined the ranks of U.S. consumers—the single largest increase in U.S. history. Simply put, with each passing year during the 1970s, demand increased consistently with the expanding universe of self-sufficient consumer boomers. Additionally, the offspring of boomers were eating truckloads of Corn Flakes and using mountains of diapers.

## TREND: INCREASING RATE OF GROWTH

It's doubtful that we will ever again witness the unique convergence of events that occurred during the 1950s, 1960s, and 1970s that helped fan the flames of demand. Unusual population dynamics and consumption dynamics also helped fuel the increasing rate of growth for products, corporations, industries, sectors, and indeed, the economy. The particularly robust nature of the dynamics in the 1970s probably hastened the inevitable: A trend of increasing rate of growth would ultimately give way to a trend of decreasing rate of growth.

Every successful business experiences two major revenue trends over the course of its life:

- *Increasing or up trend.* The period of time when the rate of revenue growth is consistently increasing, or trending up.
- *Decreasing or down trend.* The period of time when the rate of revenue growth is consistently decreasing, or trending down.

The chronological progression of a rate of revenue growth that consistently rose from around 1950 to 1979 was a once in a century event that will be difficult to replicate going forward.

## A PHENOMENAL RUN

As the remarkable 1970s drew to a close, there clearly was reason for optimism in corporate America. We had just experienced the greatest decade of inflation-adjusted revenue growth in the history of capitalism. Figure 2-9 illustrates the upward path of growth of the Dow 30 corporations through the 1950s, 1960s, and 1970s. Overall results were incredibly impressive. As a group, the Dow 30:

- Improved its average rate of revenue growth for the third decade in a row (1950s: 6.9%, 1960s: 7.1%, 1970s: 13.6%).
- Reflected the same pattern as most individual corporations around the world.

All sectors were experiencing healthy growth and Wall Street analysts could look across many industries to find numerous pockets of investment opportunity. There wasn't a dog corporation in the Dow 30 in the 1970s. Sectors were consistently growing at double-digit rates and the outlook for the 1980s was one of optimism, even with the ever-present threat of inflation.

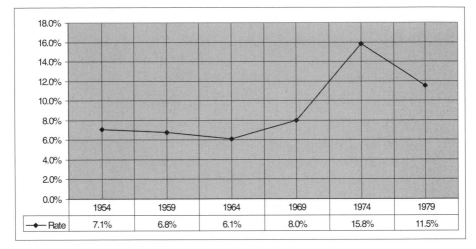

**FIGURE 2-9** Dow Jones component corporations' five-year revenue growth rates, 1950s, 1960s, and 1970s, inflation-adjusted. Source: Moody's (Mergent) Industrial Manuals.

By the end of the 1970s, 26 of the Dow 30 corporations were generating annual net revenues of $5 billion or more. Just a decade before, only seven could make that claim. By almost any measure—dollars, units, price, ratings, share, or market share—corporations had momentum. The future looked bright and the sky truly was the limit, or so it seemed.

## LIVING UP TO NEW EXPECTATIONS

The 1950s, 1960s, and 1970s provided some fairly exciting times for the men and women charged with growing corporations around the world. We had taken advantage of conditions, used a growing media base to communicate the benefits of dozens of new products that would make our lives easier. And it worked.

Virtually every existing industry was galloping forward, growing at historically high levels. The prospects for the future seemed boundless. The outstanding growth from 1950 through 1979 established new and loftier expectations from Wall

Street, the business press, and the boardroom. We had built sales and market share at blinding rates, and there appeared little that would get in our way. We kept clearing the bar and then raising it over and over again. Would we be able to live up to those higher expectations?

Someone once said that, regardless of the endeavor, it is far better to under-promise and over-deliver than over-promise and under-deliver. At the beginning of this chapter, you read about conditions and expectations. By the end of the 1970s, the conditions and expectations had dramatically changed since the end of World War II.

As the 1980s dawned, there was little reason to believe that we would not be able to continue to charge forward, growing corporations to levels beyond our wildest dreams. Would we be able to keep up the pace of corporate revenue growth—double-digit revenue growth—as we moved into a new decade? Would we be able to meet the higher expectations that we ourselves had created?

# 3 CHASING REVENUE AND MARKET SHARE: 1980 TO PRESENT

There's an old tale about a newly elected CEO who has inherited a struggling business. She is finding it very difficult to grow. The determined and optimistic CEO arrives early to work to hit the ground running on her first day in the corner office. After sitting down at her desk for the very first time, in the middle of the desk she spots an envelope with her name scrawled on it. She opens it and reads:

> I wanted to wish you the best of luck on your first day. You have some challenges ahead, but that's why they hired you. The only advice that I have to offer is this: I have left three envelopes in the top drawer of this desk. When you face your first crisis, open envelope number one. Then after the second crisis, open envelope number two. Finally, when you encounter your third major crisis, open envelope number three. There's no more for me to say than that. I wish you all the best.

It was signed by her predecessor.

Three months fly by, and for the first time she finds herself leading the quarterly conference call and Webcast when she is forced to defend some pretty soft sales and earnings figures. After being grilled by analysts and the business press for more than an hour, she retreats to her office to reflect on how she handled her first crisis. She suddenly remembers the advice of her predecessor, and opens the top drawer of her desk, from which she retrieves envelope number one. She opens it and reads:

1. Blame Your Predecessor

After another difficult six months, she finds herself in front of shareowners, reporters, and analysts at the corporation's annual meeting, where she is once again forced to explain the company's soft sales and the ineffectiveness of a much-bally-hooed advertising campaign that drew major criticism from environmental groups. After a tough two-hour meeting, she again retreats to the sanctuary of her own office, closes the door, and opens envelope number two:

2. Blame Your VP of Sales and Your Advertising Agency

Another six months goes by, and after an exhaustive search, she settles on what she thinks is just the right replacement for the vice president of sales, and a much more creative advertising agency to help solve all of her revenue problems. As she makes these painful and disruptive moves, sales and market share continue to slip, new product introductions are quite disappointing, a prized acquisition is snapped up by the competition in the eleventh hour of negotiations, domestic expansion is curtailed, 7,700 employees have been laid off over the last two quarters, 50 percent of the marketing budget for the quarter has been cut to prop up earnings, and morale is in the pits. After a particularly difficult face-to-face meeting with the board, she's back in her office searching for some answers to some extremely difficult questions, when she turns to her desk to retrieve the third envelope. What wisdom would her predecessor share with her this time? She opens the third envelope and reads:

3. Start Preparing Three Envelopes

## HIGH EXPECTATIONS

Anyone who was in the world of business after 1980 should be able to relate to this story, if not personally, then certainly from friends or at least through the pages of the world's business press. Even though we had experienced a couple of recessions and runaway inflation during the 1970s, the corporate world came through the 30 years immediately following World War II remarkably well, and the numbers bear this out.

There is no denying that revenue grew at ever-increasing rates through the 1950s, 1960s, and 1970s—the most consistently robust stretch in history. If you were to pick a time in history to choose a career in sales, it would have been the 30-year stretch from 1950 to 1979. However, those charged with driving revenue since 1980 have had a much more difficult time of it. Certainly, there have been exceptions, such as in the technology, biotechnology, and pharmaceuticals industries, to name a few. However, for most other industries, the task of generating revenue has simply gotten more difficult every year since 1980. Even though technology continues to grow as an overall sector, it is now growing at ever-decreasing rates.

As discussed in detail in Chapter 2, all sectors of the economy experienced steadily increasing rates of revenue growth coming out of World War II, and continued through the 1970s. The conditions were right and expectations were low. The opportunity to make rain had never been better, and most corporations took advantage, building stellar sales track records as well as future expectations for greatness. After putting up robust revenue growth for three straight decades, including double-digit increases for most of the 1970s, why would anyone think that the rate of growth would ever stop increasing? Standing on the threshold of a new decade in 1980, the future certainly looked bright, especially as it related to revenue.

Consistently putting up the numbers—year in and year out—made planning and budgeting considerably easier. Just add 10 percent to the top line and go to lunch. The steadily increasing rate of growth during this period also gave rise to a now-defunct business-planning tool of years gone by: the five-year plan. Today, business planning is more often limited to focusing on one year or less, and some businesses have even adopted a dynamic form of planning that changes from month to month.

Our great success at building sales from 1950 to 1979 helped to create a business world full of optimists, even cheerleaders. The low expectations of the 1950s gave way to the high expectations of the 1980s. A look at some of *Publishers' Weekly's* business bestsellers of the 1980s speaks volumes about the business psyche after three decades of continuous growth:

- You Can Negotiate Anything
- In Search of Excellence: Lessons from America's Best-Run Companies
- The One-Minute Salesperson
- Trump: The Art of the Deal
- Wealth Without Risk

There was definitely a sense of business immortality. How to succeed in business could be learned in seven easy steps. Simply study the success stories from the recent past, apply those strategies and tactics to your own corporation, and you'd be negotiating deals in less than a minute. There was a new business world order: You were expected to succeed, to break last year's record, and to establish long winning streaks across many consecutive quarters. If you didn't, you'd be considered a failure. This was the new standard as the 1980s began.

---

## NEW GROWTH STRATEGIES

Although product development, line extension development, and the subsequent marketing of those products continued to play a major role in the growth of many corporations, growth from expanding international distribution and mergers and acquisitions activity grew in importance after disappointing sales numbers during the 1980s. It was time to shift gears, expand to other continents to acquire new customers, or acquire them wholesale by snapping up a competitor.

1. *International distribution.* Creating the means for international consumers to purchase products or services more easily, either though the wholesale/retail channel or directly from the manufacturer. This enables consumers to act on advertising messages to acquire the product or service to generate trial usage in foreign markets. International distribution represented an effort to grow market share, especially as domestic sales matured. International distribution was especially popular during the 1970s, 1980s, and 1990s.

2. *Mergers and acquisitions.* The wholesale acquisition of sales, customers, and market share, usually through the purchase of businesses that strategically complement the acquiring corporation. Mergers and acquisitions can expeditiously add to the top line by adding revenue, and to the bottom line through consolidation efforts and the elimination of redundant functions. Although sometimes criticized as lacking in its ultimate delivery of the intended operational and marketing synergies, mergers and acquisitions were especially popular during the latter half of the 1980s and 1990s. M&As are still a popular strategy today, although rapid consolidation since 1990 has greatly reduced the number of corporations that are even available to acquire.

Growth strategies over the second half of the 20th century were typically utilized progressively, from product development and marketing, to domestic distribution, to international distribution, to mergers and acquisitions, especially as each strategy matured. Therefore, product development and marketing was the weapon of choice during the 1950s, whereas mergers and acquisitions became the weapon of choice during the 1990s as other forms of development ran out of steam.

Corporations such as Coca-Cola and Procter & Gamble have utilized all four of these strategies over many decades to build vast global enterprises. The Coca-Cola Company, for example, has had operations in China for more than 30 years, first establishing business relationships shortly after U.S. President Richard Nixon's historic visit there in 1971.

## NEW PRODUCT CATEGORIES

In the first half of the 20th century, much of what we would consider necessities today would have been considered luxuries. The number of new product categories slowed to a trickle from 1980 to 2000. There are fewer and fewer day-to-day problems and needs that are not being met by existing products within existing categories. Certainly, improvements to existing products are introduced all the time, bringing new benefits to consumers. However, the overall impact to the category is, more often than not, negligible.

Nonetheless, Generation X did adopt its share of new categories. As shown in Figure 3-1, two patterns began to emerge as the 20th century progressed: There were fewer and fewer new category introductions, and the new categories that were introduced were almost exclusively communications and entertainment related, such as video games and compact discs.

As the 20th century progressed, our list of necessities expanded, leaving little room for growth after the initial adoption of a new product category. Figure 3-1 identifies the new product categories associated with the generation most responsible for the adoption of that category after introduction. Not intended to provide a complete listing of categories, this chart is designed to illustrate how many basic categories exist today and a sense of the universe of consumers across the socioeconomic strata that participate in those categories.

| Generation | Food | Household | Personal | Consumer Electronic |
|---|---|---|---|---|
| World War I | Hot/cold cereal, milk, eggs, bread, ice, sugar, salt, flour, coffee, tea, alcohol, tobacco, fresh produce, meats, poultry | Home indoor plumbing, electricity, laundry flakes, washboard, ice box, car | Bar soap, toothpaste, lye, straight razor | Phonograph, radio, telephone |
| World War II | TV dinners, frozen food | Electric refrigerator, electric washing machine, electric dryer, electric stove, electric dishwasher, toaster, electric vacuum, electric can opener, power lawn mower, snow blower | Shaving cream, razor blades, feminine hygiene products | Television, camera, color film, instant photography, home movies, 45s, LPs, hi-fi, transistor radio |
| Baby Boomers | Light beer, Nutrasweet | Microwave, toaster oven | Disposable razors, disposable diapers, birth control pills | VCR, Walkman, answering machine, fax, audiotape, videotape, calculator, portable telephone, car phone |
| Generation X | Prepared foods | Swiffer | Teeth whitener, Spin Brush | PC, printer, video games, CDs, Internet access, cell phone, e-mail, PDAs |
| Generation Y | — | — | — | Instant messaging, DVD, MP3, wireless |

FIGURE 3-1   First-time product categories, Generation X (1965 to 1980) and Generation Y (1981 to 1995). Source: Customer Share Group LLC.

Following World War II, many of the luxuries of the past became the necessities of the day. Basics such as homes, cars, televisions, and appliances all became part of a standard checklist for most consumers. Time and time again in the second half of the 20th century we witnessed the introduction of a new category of product at a relatively high cost (e.g., the calculator), only to see it drop dramatically in price in short order due to mass production and competition. This dynamic helped to exponentially increase both the list of must-have products as well as the universe of consumers requiring those necessities. No longer were televisions or stereos possessions exclusively for the rich. These, and many other product categories to follow, became affordable for most consumers.

## NINE WAYS TO PLAY A CD

Consumers have not always enjoyed the luxury of being able to play their favorite recorded music in a multitude of ways. Thomas Edison was again at the forefront of a new industry when he invented and patented a wax-coated cylinder in 1886. Cylinder technology was quickly replaced with the first disc recordings just after the turn of the 20th century. The record then became the preferred method of playing recorded music for more than 50 years, until audiotape cassettes started to become available around 1965.

For 20 years, LPs and cassettes coexisted side by side in music stores, until 1982 when CD hardware and software was introduced in Japan. Where households in 1950 usually had only one consumer electronic device with which to play music, the typical household in the 21st century has a plethora of options. Since the advent of the CD, consumer electronics corporations have dramatically increased the number of devices that have the capability of playing a music CD:

1. CD stereo
2. CD Walkman
3. CD car stereo
4. Personal CD player
5. Boom box
6. Desktop computer
7. Laptop computer
8. X-Box
9. DVD player

As core products began to introduce scores of line extensions, some worried that shifting a consumer's loyalty from one product to a slightly different version of the same product would result in cannibalization. Corporations were much more afraid of losing sales to a competitor if they decided not to play the copycat line extension game. As the theory goes, it was far better to lose sales from one product to another within the corporation than to a competitive product outside of the corporation. This competitive dynamic has probably also caused corporations to hang onto too many unprofitable versions of the same core product for fear of losing even a small amount of top-line revenue to the competition.

The fact that so many consumers participate in so many categories has hastened the onset of saturation because the universe of consumers in any given category is not infinite, and will find its own natural size over a number of years. Volume and frequency of consumption habits also become established and then evolve to be hardened or fixed. Once this happens, it is extremely difficult and expensive to alter those behaviors.

## IF IT AIN'T BROKE . . .

As the 1980s dawned, there was no reason to think that all of the growth strategies that worked so well since 1950 wouldn't just lead us to new and larger markets, and larger shares of those markets. The marketing formula that we had established also seemed to be working like clockwork. Why change it? The marching orders coming into the 1980s were clear: Whatever you did over the last 10 years, keep doing it.

The traditional four Ps of marketing (product, promotion, price, and place) were working like a charm, and business schools everywhere preached the formula for mining market share that seemed both logical and achievable. Even if domestic growth started to slow, there would always be market-share growth through international expansion. If demand was fading domestically, there was also the option of dropping price to increase demand. That was Marshall's theory, and it usually worked.

Even in an extremely slow market, demand inelasticity was viewed as only a temporary condition. This is what we were taught, and this is what we expected of the 1980s and beyond. However, the model—if not broken—was surely beginning to show signs of stress. The first crack in the model was a rapidly changing media world, making it more difficult to reach prospective customers.

## THE FRAGMENTATION OF MEDIA

Not only had business performance expectations greatly changed since 1950, so had the business conditions. The growing influence of technology played a major role in both creating a communications medium (television), and in its relative destruction through the introduction of other forms of entertainment (cable TV, VCR, the Internet). This was Schumpeter's theory of creative destruction at work: innovations replacing other older innovations. More often, though, new innovations don't completely replace a product or service that is already in place, or not immediately, anyway. However, new innovations were more likely to change the role of old innovations that were already in place.

This was certainly true for print when radio came along a century ago, for radio when television came along a half-century ago, for television when cable TV and the VCR came along a quarter-century ago, and for all media when the World Wide Web arrived around 1994.

Although we expected all universes to keep growing at the rates they had been throughout the 1970s, some of the most fundamental *booms* were already behind us.

**The Population Boom.** Baby boomers were not procreating at nearly the rate that their parents did, delaying the start of their families for a number of reasons, including a significant increase in the number of women entering the workforce.

While the 78 million baby boomers were birthed during only an 18-year period from 1946 to 1964, boomers themselves spread their babies over more than four decades, thus greatly dissipating the impact of their offspring as consumers.

**The Broadcast TV Boom.** Although continuing to grow, the universe of users for most media was reaching saturation. Figure 3-2 shows that the universe of television households delivered in prime time by the three major broadcast television networks in the United States actually peaked in 1980. Every household that would ever have a television in the United States essentially had one by 1970 or before, even though the overall number of households would continue to grow. Once the preferred means of communicating to the masses, the average number of households watching the three major networks reached 15.2 million households per average minute in prime time in 1980, and that number has been shrinking ever since. By 2003, the three major networks had lost nearly two-thirds of their audience to thousands of other entertainment options.

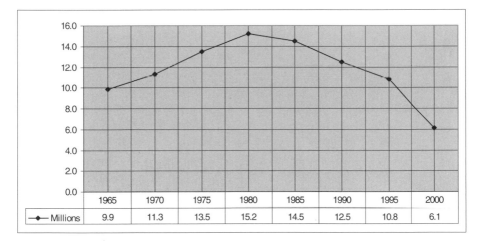

|  | 1965 | 1970 | 1975 | 1980 | 1985 | 1990 | 1995 | 2000 |
|---|---|---|---|---|---|---|---|---|
| Millions | 9.9 | 11.3 | 13.5 | 15.2 | 14.5 | 12.5 | 10.8 | 6.1 |

FIGURE 3-2    Big Three major television networks' number of households per average minute in prime time: Going, going, gone. Source: Based on Nielsen Media Research.

**The Cable TV Boom.** The number of U.S. households with cable grew rapidly, effectively reaching saturation by the year 2000. Figure 3-3 shows that the installed base of U.S. households with cable started to slow after 1985. Even though its growth was slowing, the damage that cable caused for broadcast television in terms of audience defection was done by 2000.

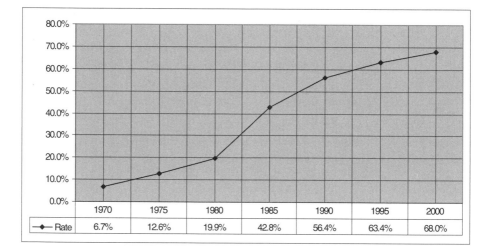

| | 1970 | 1975 | 1980 | 1985 | 1990 | 1995 | 2000 |
|---|---|---|---|---|---|---|---|
| Rate | 6.7% | 12.6% | 19.9% | 42.8% | 56.4% | 63.4% | 68.0% |

FIGURE 3-3    Penetration of U.S. households by cable TV, saturated. Source: Nielsen Media Research.

**The VCR Boom.** Another important technology that caused a shift in consumer behavior during this time period was the introduction of the VCR, the most rapidly adopted consumer electronics category in history. When the VCR became widely available in the early 1980s, the urban myth of consumers rejecting the idea of watching new-release movies on a small screen at home was shattered. Saturday nights would never be the same, even for the movie theaters that carried the brand new first run films that had not yet made it to video. Figure 3-4 indicates that by the year 2000, VCR penetration was very close to the saturation point, right around the time that the DVD started to gain momentum as the new medium of choice for films in the aftermarket.

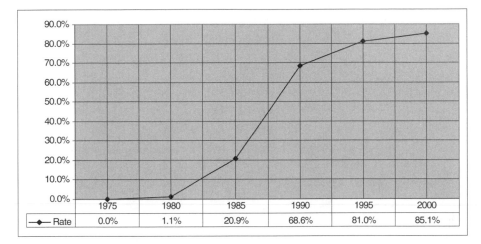

| | 1975 | 1980 | 1985 | 1990 | 1995 | 2000 |
|---|---|---|---|---|---|---|
| Rate | 0.0% | 1.1% | 20.9% | 68.6% | 81.0% | 85.1% |

FIGURE 3-4    Penetration of VCRs in U.S. households, saturated. Source: U.S. Census 2000.

**The Personal Computer Boom.** Enter the personal computer in the late 1970s, and later the ability for consumers on every continent to communicate via the Internet, and a whole new distraction caused consumers to reprioritize their 24-hour days. After the World Wide Web entered the mainstream around 1994, it became clear that no generation would ever spend its time the way it once had. Figure 3-5 shows that the growth of the installed base of computers in the United States picked up speed after 1994. In seven short years between 1993 and 2000, households with computers more than doubled, and the percentage of U.S. households with Internet access grew from virtually none to more than 40 percent.

Some look at the last half of the 20th century as proof positive that we did our jobs, and did them so well that we maximized the growth potential in most existing categories. We had more cars than people to drive them, more telephones than people to talk on them, and more homes than people to live in them. How much more would we be able to push the consumption envelope?

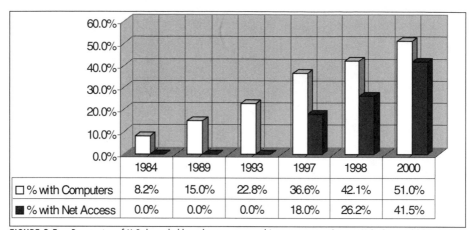

| | 1984 | 1989 | 1993 | 1997 | 1998 | 2000 |
|---|---|---|---|---|---|---|
| ☐ % with Computers | 8.2% | 15.0% | 22.8% | 36.6% | 42.1% | 51.0% |
| ■ % with Net Access | 0.0% | 0.0% | 0.0% | 18.0% | 26.2% | 41.5% |

**FIGURE 3-5** Penetration of U.S. households with computers and Internet access. Source: U.S. Census 2000.

Many whose careers ended around 1979 left a business world that was growing rapidly and probably just past the top of delivering historical rates of growth. Many whose careers started in 1980 have a much different perspective on the business world than their retired predecessors. A business world of rapid top-line growth and infrastructure building in the 1970s soon gave way to a trend toward deconstruction. It was the 1980s that introduced us to *reengineering,* the mother of downsizing, rightsizing, and productivity gains.

## THE TIRED FOUR PS

The traditional tools used to market products and services were showing signs of wear and exhaustion. The elements of marketing had essentially been maximized. Corporations that had so effectively used the marketing skill set to build their franchises were left scratching their heads contemplating what to do next. For the most part, marketers continued to use the same tools in an effort to wrestle market share from the competition. However, this ritual was becoming more and more expensive and was yielding less and less. The traditional four Ps had essentially achieved all that they could:

1. **Product:**
   - There were more line extensions introduced, yet fewer new categories introduced after 1980, resulting in cannibalization of product sales.
   - Without technology, pharmaceuticals, and consumer electronics, the economy would have greatly suffered after 1980. However, even these categories have faded in recent years.
   - Category saturation and lower prices contributed to an oversupply of product, which caused prices to remain depressed.
   - New products that entered mature categories gained market share at the expense of category leaders and more often did not help grow the overall category.

2. **Promotion:**
   - Mass media's ability to deliver an audience consistently eroded after 1980, due in large part to the explosion of entertainment, and two-way communication options:
     - Cable TV
     - The VCR
     - The PC
     - E-mail
     - The Internet
     - Video games
     - Tivo
     - The cell phone
     - Instant messaging
   - It became harder to reach busy consumers who were spending more time with forms of entertainment and communication that carried no advertising at all.

3. **Price:**
   - Lack of sales momentum and volume decreased in some major industries, igniting competitive price wars and leaving most corporations little choice but to lower prices.

- Consumers were conditioned to always expect the lowest price, and learned that they could get it if they waited for predictable seasonal discounting periods.
- Financing became easier to obtain with payments spread over longer and longer periods of time.
- Selling extended warranties at checkout became a popular ploy for retailers to generate additional revenue in the guise of customer service.
- The oversupply of inventory put downward pressure on prices.

4. **Place:**
   - Products became available worldwide.
   - The most dynamic revenue growth of the 1990s was partially driven by aggressive expansion plans from companies such as Wal-Mart and The Home Depot. However, with this type of strategy, as expansion plans slow, so too does the rate of revenue growth.

New marketing channels that were introduced between 1975 and 2000 negatively impacted the major marketing tools that helped build the significant corporate sales foundation from 1950 to 1980. Cable TV and the World Wide Web were added to the marketing continuum between 1975 and 1980 as new tools to help sell more. The introduction of the personal computer in the late 1970s paved the way for e-mail, Web surfing, and instant messaging, all new activities that consumers added to their already busy lives.

## THE MARKETING CONTINUUM

When the *I Love Lucy* show aired on the CBS television network every Tuesday night during the 1950s, a country stopped to engage in a new form of visual entertainment that now resided in the living room. Families often planned their evenings around the show that commanded more than 85 percent of the audience among all the television sets in use at its height. In those days, however, there were only three programming options on television in the United States.

When cable television was introduced in the late 1970s, followed by the advent of the VCR, and finally the World Wide Web in the early 1990s, families that had been entertained by network television for 30 years began to find their own preferred forms of entertainment. What had been a three-option world during prime time suddenly became a 300-option world.

Figure 3-6 shows that the tools that were added between 1975 and 2000 were designed to deliver entertainment to more and more specific groups of people. Segmentation became the marketing buzz word of the time, as buying eyeballs in bulk gave way to cable programming, print, and even the Web as more targeted ways to deliver finite groups of people.

THE MARKETING CONTINUUM, 1900–2000

|  | 1900–1949 | 1950–1974 | 1975–2000 |
|---|---|---|---|
| MASS MARKETING | Newspapers Magazines Radio Sponsorships Outdoor POS Promotions | Television | Cable TV WWW |
| DIRECT MARKETING | Face-to-face U.S. Mail Telegram Telephone | 800 number Fax | DB marketing E-mail WWW CRM CSM |

FIGURE 3-6    A century of mass and direct marketing tools: Trending toward direct marketing. Source: Customer Share Group LLC.

Cable television was introduced around the mid-1970s, and the stronghold that network television had enjoyed over the airwaves began to erode when hundreds of new options started to be delivered through a cable in the wall. When the

VCR followed in the early 1980s, yet another option beyond the three major commercial networks, it further altered network television's historic role. Interestingly, broadcast TV enjoyed a relatively short boom period—about 30 years from 1950 to 1980. After 1980, network television was no longer the only game in town when it came to reaching target audiences.

On the direct marketing front, some powerful new marketing tools were introduced during this period: e-mail and the World Wide Web. Like television before it, the Internet caused people to change the patterns of their daily lives, with e-mail growing in popularity as the preferred means of communication for the X and Y Generations.

With the advent of the personal computer in the mid- to late 1970s, early adopters were ready when e-mail became widely available starting in the 1980s and then online services in the mid- to late 1980s. Ultimately, when the World Wide Web became more commonplace around 1994, the world of communication changed dramatically. E-mail gave the Web an interactive capability that allowed the masses to experience the first new method of live two-way communication since the invention of the telephone.

Ironically, the tool that would largely be credited as the builder of corporate empires also came with a relatively invisible downside: The one-to-one relationship between buyer and seller that was pervasive and effective during the first half of the 20th century took a back seat to the power and effectiveness of television. Consequently, after 50 years of one-way mass marketing to unidentified customers, a gap had formed between buyer and seller. No longer did marketers enjoy true relationships with their customers; more often their customers had relationships with them.

## THE MYTH OF CUSTOMER RELATIONSHIPS

One of the unfortunate consequences of the advent of television was that it helped to distance buyer and seller, resulting in the hibernation of the one-to-one sales and marketing model that was so popular and effective during the first half of the 20th century. Introducing new products to customers was no longer the job of the Fuller Brush Man or the corner grocer. That was TV's job, and it did it extraordinarily well. The love affair with television as an entertainment tool made it an ideal marketing tool, especially during its adoption phase from 1950 to 1980. As a result, corporations have been busy building sales since 1950 and have spent little time and effort building customer relationships. Now as sales continue to slide, customer relationships have suddenly become important.

Fundamentally, all relationships require a dialogue, from one side to the other and back. Business-to-consumer (B2C) companies have largely been engaged in a one-way monologue to unidentified customers, who have responded by buying a product or service. If the product fulfills the promise that the advertising makes, then the customer usually begins a relationship with the brand or company.

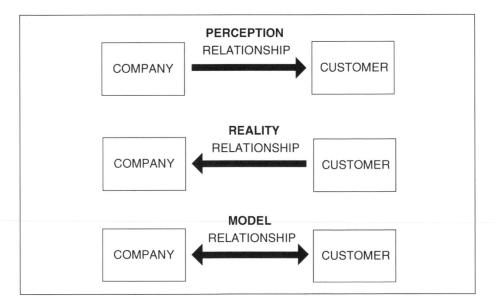

FIGURE 3-7    Perception and reality: Company relationships, not customer relationships. Source: Customer Share Group LLC.

Most companies believe that they do indeed have relationships with their customers, but real relationships require two-way communication, not a one-way sales pitch to the world. The fact is that customer relationships, for many companies, are a myth. More often than not, businesses really don't have a relationship with their customers; their customers have a relationship with them. The difference is not just a matter of semantics.

We have spent the last 50-plus years investing in customer sales, and have more often given only lip service to developing customer relationships. Investments in customer relationship management (CRM) make sense as a tool for data collection, but those investments alone won't build customer relationships. Does installing a new telephone system guarantee great telemarketing results?

Fortunately, more meaningful relationships can be built going forward because customers—long ignored by companies—have developed a relationship with a brand. The challenge now is to leverage the equity in that one-way relationship into a two-way relationship with the loyalists who, in spite of being ignored for 50 years, have an affinity for a corporation and its brands.

## HITTING THE MARKET-SHARE WALL

For most of the 1980s and 1990s, we chased ever-diminishing revenue growth down a slope with the same tools and same skill sets that we had since the end of World War II. For most industries and corporations, the challenge of growing revenue will simply get more difficult with each passing year. Like the former Olympic high jump champion at 55 years old, our personal bests are probably in our past. Our goals for the future, therefore, have to change along with our expectations. As it turns out, the sky does have a limit, and in the pursuit of the sky, some will inevitably fall by the wayside (e.g., Ames, Polaroid, Montgomery Ward) while other corporate titans reorganize under Chapter 11 in an effort to survive.

As it became more and more apparent that domestic markets were tapped, corporations sought market-share gains through global expansion. Although revenue gains from international markets have often provided positive news for earnings releases in recent years, longer term these markets are also limited, and they too are starting to mature. Like domestic market share, international market-share growth also hits a wall after a generation of market presence. Even with the hope of capturing billions of new consumers in China, the market share model is an exhausted source of new growth for corporations that reached peak rates of growth decades ago.

Sometime around the mid-1970s, each of the major pre-technology industries that were represented in the Dow 30 hit a wall. After years of delivering a consistent upward trend, the rate of revenue growth stopped increasing and started decreasing. With market share levels largely established by 1980, the battle was on to wrest fractions of a percent from the competition. Although all industries continued to show actual growth, none were growing at the rate they once did. The erosion in the rate of revenue growth was so subtle over such a long period of time that few even noticed. After all, every industry was still delivering more revenue each year, and the careful management of costs post-1980 made earnings heroes of scores of CEOs. However, the downward trend in the rate of revenue growth kept sliding, even reaching negative growth in some cases.

In the 1960s and 1970s, much of the revenue growth was organic—a natural increase in consumption due to an increase in the number of consumers entering categories for the first time. One of the reasons that the 1980s generated such anemic revenue growth was that corporations expected the organic growth of the 1970s to continue. There was really no clear signal from the marketplace that rising growth rates were over. Instead, revenue growth became more difficult to deliver throughout the 1980s, and few could explain why. Consequently, corporations have literally chased revenue since 1980 with little success in terms of reversing the downward trend.

## PRIDE AND PROFITS

The world of business has always defined success as up and failure as down, except for contrarian investors. Any backward slide in the business has always been viewed as a personal failure, often ending in the resignation of a high-profile executive or the public firing of an advertising agency. In the end, such actions were mostly not necessary.

Few CEOs have opted to publicly educate Wall Street, analysts, media, and shareowners of the limits to growth because it can appear as a sign of weakness. Consequently, a corporation's long-term viability might be compromised for short-term gain, delivering what Wall Street expects and what rewards senior executives.

Another unfortunate consequence of the unrelenting pressures to deliver perpetual earnings growth is unwillingness, on the part of senior executives, to speak frankly about their business to anyone, including boards of directors. Instead, many ignore the realities of aging and boldly push forward, convinced that they are always in the growth phase of a corporation's life. Inflated egos prevent many from admitting that the corporation could be in decline. Therefore, companies end up spending too much time preparing for the quarterly ritual of providing optimistic spin on financial results instead of channeling some of that time and energy into creating innovative new ways to generate revenue beyond acquisitions.

The problem, though, with generating new revenue from the core is that it takes time and patience, neither of which are Wall Street virtues. Cost reductions are often a more immediate earnings driver and consequently have fueled the trend toward Wall Street's love affair with the CEOs who are tough on costs. Where are the CEOs who are tough on revenue, gifted at generating new sources from the core? These are the executives who deserve and earn blue-sky compensation packages.

Delivering consistent earnings growth without consistent revenue growth is a dangerous game that is gaining steam as the strategy of choice for corporations that have run out of revenue juice. Sustainable earnings growth requires more than just midstream cuts in the marketing budget, or wholesale reductions in headcount. Long-term earnings growth requires improvement in both the generation of new top-line growth and the management of costs. Short term, however, many have ignored this premise. Like the sandbagger in golf who cheats to give the impression of achievement, some corporations have kept score with erasers at the end of their pencils.

A popular means of generating legitimate and wholesale revenue growth, especially over the last decade, has been through mergers and acquisitions. Why wait years to develop meaningful top-line growth by incubating new sales from the core when, with one acquisition, billions of dollars in revenue can simply be added to the top line?

## ANABOLIC REVENUE GROWTH

Around 1995, the rate of revenue growth started to climb again, but not for the same reasons it had 25 years before. Significant organic revenue growth was over, especially for many of the pre-technology industries. However, the revenue growth this time was mostly inorganic. A recent study from the DAK Group LTD and Rutgers University's Whitcomb Center for Research and Financial Services found that a corporation's motivation for engaging in mergers and acquisitions has changed in recent years.

Once, mergers and acquisitions were viewed more as a strategic move that allowed corporations to expand their product line or competencies. Now, all pretense of strategy seems to have given way to the corporation's pure, simple need to quickly generate growth. According to the study, close to 90 percent of respondents pointed to growth as the primary reason for acquisitions.

It took a number of unnatural methods to drive revenue rates upward, if only for a brief time. If you look specifically at the Dow 30 from 1995 to 2000, there were four primary reasons why we saw an upward tick in the rate of growth during the 1990s:

- There was an enormous increase in merger and acquisition activity from 1995 to 2000.

- There was aggressive expansion of storefronts in the retail sector.
- There was a new industry on the rise: technology.
- There was an up-tick in population growth rates during the 1990s.

Here's a closer look at each of these elements.

**Mergers and Acquisitions: The House That Jack Built.** After delivering 17 consecutive years of record revenues from 1965 through 1981, General Electric's top line hit a bump in the road, and shrunk as many times as it grew over a 10-year period from 1982 through 1991. Even though GE delivered record earnings in nine of those years, becoming one of Wall Street's darlings, the strain of slowing revenue growth began to wear on its ability to keep its earnings record streak alive in the 1990s.

Figure 3-8 shows that GE's revenue grew by less than $10 billion during the 1980s, beginning the decade with $24 billion in sales while beginning the 1990s with $33 billion in sales.

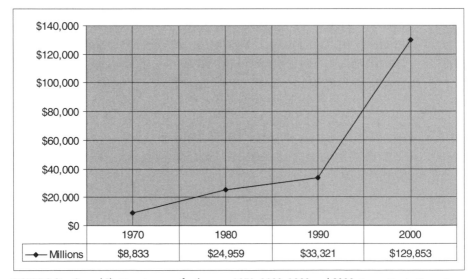

| | 1970 | 1980 | 1990 | 2000 |
|---|---|---|---|---|
| ◆ Millions | $8,833 | $24,959 | $33,321 | $129,853 |

**FIGURE 3-8**   General Electric net revenue for the years 1970, 1980, 1990, and 2000. Source: Moody (Mergent) Industrial Manuals.

There was no way that Jack Welch was going to spend the last decade of his career delivering unacceptable revenue and earnings growth, and it became clear that General Electric had determined that it could not deliver one without the other. What ensued in the 1990s was an unrelenting hunger for growth, when the industrial giant added nearly $100 billion to its revenue line.

Although criticized for "buying growth," General Electric's strategy helped it post record revenues and earnings from 1995 through 2001. During this period, the corporation acquired more than 100 companies a year, according to Chairman Jeff Immelt's letter to shareowners in General Electric's 2001 annual report.

Some skeptics question the long-term wisdom of some acquisition strategies that appear to deliver no long-term benefit to shareowners, and seemingly provide only a means to deliver short-term earnings growth. Even with sizable acquisitions that can bring healthy revenue and earnings improvement, the celebration around such events can often be short-lived. It can take years for corporations to realize the full benefit of an acquisition as cost synergies from consolidation work their way through a combined organization. After acquired revenue has been absorbed into results over four quarters, revenue growth often flattens, and consolidation efforts are normally forced to continue.

The question for General Electric in the future is this: Can it keep up the frenetic acquisition pace that it established during Welch's final years? After all, a $1 billion acquisition barely puts a dent in the top line of a company that is approaching $150 billion in sales.

Welch made an unsuccessful run at Honeywell International just before his retirement. European regulators blocked the deal that would have added roughly $25 billion in revenue to General Electric's top line. Regulators the world over now observe the corporation's aggressive acquisition efforts with increased scrutiny when wholesale chunks of an industry's market share are in its crosshairs. This increased scrutiny will make it even harder for Immelt to keep driving sales north. As the unnatural hockey stick effect of the 1990s begins to fade, one has to ask this question: Although Welch might have served shareholders well during the 1990s, will his unnecessarily aggressive run stack the deck against General Electric shareowners over the next 10 years?

**Aggressive Retail Expansion: Wal-Mart, McDonald's, and The Home Depot.**
Wal-Mart, the world's largest company, more than doubled its number of worldwide stores during the 1990s. Although impressive, particularly given the average size of a Wal-Mart store, Wal-Mart's expansion of more than 2,400 stores pales in comparison to the efforts of McDonald's in the 1990s (see Figure 3-9). McDonald's opened more than 16,000 restaurants during the 1990s, averaging between four and five restaurants per day, seven days a week, for 10 years. However, the most dramatic relative growth in the 1990s might have come from The Home Depot. With only 145 stores in operation to start the 1990s, The Home Depot added nearly 1,000 locations in 10 years—fully a 600 percent increase for the decade.

| RETAILER | 1980 | 1990 | 2000 |
|---|---|---|---|
| Wal-Mart | 276 | 1,525 | 3,989 |
| McDonald's | 6,263 | 11,803 | 28,707 |
| The Home Depot | 4 | 145 | 1,123 |

FIGURE 3-9    The roaring nineties: Record-breaking retail expansion. Number of retail outlets. Source: SEC filings.

In its 2001 annual report, McDonald's predicted that it would have more than 50,000 restaurants as part of its worldwide chain by 2005. However, even the restaurant made famous for its seemingly limitless ability to serve billions and billions has hit the wall, announcing the closing of more than 700 restaurants in the United States in 2003.

**The Rise of a New Sector: Technology.** When the rate of revenue growth in most industries started trending downward beginning in the 1980s, the fledgling technology sector arrived on the scene, causing both consumers and business to open their checkbooks wide. This is a powerful dynamic that can generate enough energy to impact an entire economy. When both the business and consumer worlds are moved to adopt a new innovation, significant sales are often generated for an extended period. Technology was also the last major sector that was introduced. The introduction of a new sector is a very rare occurrence in history, and it provides new reasons for new spending that typically cause a shift in the way people live their lives.

**Up-Tick in Population Growth Rates During the 1990s.** Largely driven by aging boomers who delayed the start of their families until after establishing their professional careers, the incidence of women giving birth over the age of 40 more than doubled in the 1990s. Figure 3-10 shows that the high incidence of births by mothers over the age of 40 was actually a throwback to the 1950s and 1960s when, during the original baby boom, women gave birth to many more babies and often kept having babies well into their 40s.

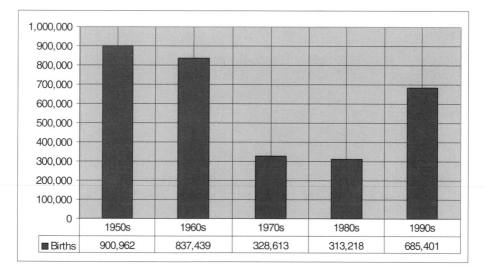

| | 1950s | 1960s | 1970s | 1980s | 1990s |
|---|---|---|---|---|---|
| ■ Births | 900,962 | 837,439 | 328,613 | 313,218 | 685,401 |

FIGURE 3-10    Total U.S. births by decade, mothers 40 years old and over. Source: U.S. Bureau of the Census.

## UPGRADING THE DOW

Creating the illusion of growth during the 1990s, either in revenue or stock performance, took many forms, but the most obvious might have been the revolving door into and out of membership of the Dow 30 component corporations. Even with all the initiatives designed to help boost the performance of corporations during the 1990s, the collective rate of revenue growth for the Dow 30 only marginally responded, improving from 5.2 percent to 8.9 percent between 1995 and 1999. However, the upgrade of the components themselves might have provided the most significant positive ripple effect of all.

In the 1950s, five component corporations were swapped out for five others, where in the 1960s there were no changes at all to the group. In the 1970s, three components were replaced, and five components were swapped out in the 1980s. However, in the 1990s, more than one-third of the Dow components (11) were replaced, the highest number of upgrades during a decade in the history of the Dow.

The Dow 30 trade-outs in the 1990s greatly improved the overall operational performance of the collective group. Figure 3-11 shows that Sears, Chevron, Goodyear, and Dow Chemical were eliminated from the Dow 30 in 1999. The reason was wildly erratic and unpredictable revenue and earnings performance. Replacing the underperforming components were up-and-comers Microsoft, Intel, The Home Depot, and SBC. At the time these corporations were added to the Dow 30, each had been posting impressive and consistent growth—in the case of The Home Depot, 17 consecutive years of record revenue growth.

Similarly, in 1996 and 1991, tired workhorses gave way to more consistent performers, some of which continued to impress well into the 21st century (Wal-Mart, Johnson & Johnson), where others faded (Walt Disney, Caterpillar).

The Dow 30 is designed to give us a quick read on the performance of the stock market on any given day. Virtually every major sector is represented as part of the Dow 30, giving us a fairly good sample of corporations from which we can discern the relative health of stock performance over some period of time. Using the Dow for the purpose of measuring operational

| Year | Components Out | Components In |
|------|----------------|---------------|
| 1999 | Sears<br>Chevron<br>Goodyear<br>Union Carbide | Microsoft<br>Intel<br>The Home Depot<br>SBC |
| 1996 | Texaco<br>FW Woolworth<br>Bethlehem Steel<br>Westinghouse | Wal-Mart<br>Johnson & Johnson<br>Hewlett-Packard<br>Citigroup |
| 1991 | Navistar (IH)<br>Primerica<br>US Steel | Walt Disney<br>JP Morgan Chase<br>Caterpillar |

FIGURE 3-11    The Dow 30 component corporations: Trading up. Source: dowjones.com

performance of corporate America was used here in the very same spirit: using a highly recognized and respected stock performance barometer to measure corporate revenue performance, not just earnings.

In many ways, we have played all of our cards and used up much of the gunpowder. Although merger and acquisition activity will surely continue, voracious M&A activity will simply make acquisitions harder to find and pull off in the future. We are at the end of the retail expansion boom. It is more likely that we will see contraction than expansion in retail outlets over the next decade. The technology boom is over, too. It's possible that we will witness a second technology boom, but that is difficult to predict.

As for upgrading the Dow 30, surely there are robust corporations in growth industries out there that could replace AT&T or Kodak, but because the aging process of corporations has so dramatically quickened, it's doubtful that any moves would generate a significant or long-term positive impact. Just look at the last group of corporations that joined the Dow 30 in 1999: The Home Depot, Microsoft, SBC Communications, and Intel. None of these corporations is as robust as it was in 1999.

The number of strategic options to generate corporate growth has dwindled, and it will be the CEOs who are not close to retirement who will be forced to face and fix this challenge for the balance of their careers.

## INSIDIOUSLY SLOW EROSION

Folklore suggests that if you place a frog in a pan of water on a stove and slowly increase the temperature of the water, the slow warming will make the frog sleepy and content, and it will eventually cook itself to death with no reaction at all. In many ways, the erosion of the rate of revenue growth since 1980 has occurred so slowly that most corporations have focused on the continuous upward movement of total revenue, effectively lulling themselves into a false sense of security. Unfortunately, these changes were so subtle that many corporations never saw them coming while others pushed forward, cutting costs and virtually abandoning investments in R&D.

Figure 3-12 shows a steady upward trend in the rate of revenue growth for the Dow 30 through the 1950s, 1960s, and 1970s until hitting the market-share wall around the mid-1970s. Executives, who had always been a part of an industry that delivered a steady rise in the rate of revenue growth, scratched their heads when the revenue growth rate plummeted during the 1980s. For about 10 years—from 1975 to 1985—the rate of revenue growth dropped dramatically before stabilizing at around 5 percent annual growth for another 10 years.

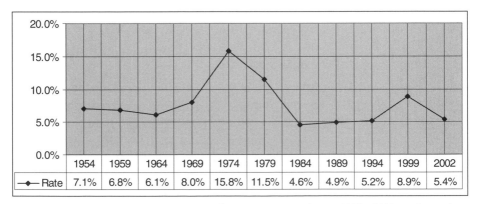

| | 1954 | 1959 | 1964 | 1969 | 1974 | 1979 | 1984 | 1989 | 1994 | 1999 | 2002 |
|---|---|---|---|---|---|---|---|---|---|---|---|
| ◆ Rate | 7.1% | 6.8% | 6.1% | 8.0% | 15.8% | 11.5% | 4.6% | 4.9% | 5.2% | 8.9% | 5.4% |

FIGURE 3-12   Dow Jones component corporations' five-year revenue growth rates, 1950s–2000s, peaking in the mid-1970s. Inflation adjusted. Source: Moody (Mergent) Industrial Manuals.

## ONWARD AND DOWNWARD

Even though we had hit a market-share wall in the mid-1970s, proud and naturally optimistic senior managers, who themselves were part of the revenue boom just a decade before, pushed forward. They spent increasing sums of money on media to communicate to an increasingly fragmented society that, to a large degree, had already selected their brand of soap and had little time or motivation to change.

Now consider that management threw in everything but the kitchen sink to help reverse the downward trend:

- Constant staff changes, seeking the perfect salesperson.
- Constant agency changes, seeking the perfect agency partner.
- Better, more creative advertising that "breaks through the clutter."
- A plethora of product line extensions.
- Expanded domestic and international distribution and sales.
- Thousands of mergers and acquisitions.

Yet, nothing could prevent or reverse the downward trend of the rate of revenue growth. Certainly, corporations continued to grow, but at much slower rates—the slowest in history.

The task of generating revenue growth was getting more difficult for established corporations, and senior management that had delivered the goods in record numbers just 10 years before found themselves under delivering and searching for simple solutions to the problem as well as someone to blame. Scores of vice presidents of sales and advertising agencies were handed their walking papers time and time again during what became one of the most disruptive 20 years for workers in history.

More recently, as corporations continue to invest billions of dollars to generate revenue gains through conventional means, the return on those marketing investments is increasingly coming under close scrutiny by corporations that desperately need a healthy jolt of new revenue.

Take away all revenue from acquisitions and international sales in recent years, and sales growth would be downright depressing. It may explain, in part, why some corporations outside of the U.S. that tend to keep employees at all costs are not faring as well as their U.S. counterparts. Perhaps that also explains why the majority of the products on supermarket shelves are no longer supported in any way by conventional advertising, according to industry sources. Investing millions of marketing dollars to wrest a quarter-of-a-percent market share away from a competitor does seem rather futile.

## THE GAMBLE AT CAMPBELL'S

When Douglas R. Conant arrived in Camden, New Jersey in 2001 to take the helm of the Campbell Soup Company, he was accepting responsibility for one of the most enduring brands in the history of consumer-packaged goods. He was also inheriting a 130-year old company that was losing steam, fighting hard to return to its record revenue and earnings performances in 1996 and 1997.

Campbell's, the undisputed heavyweight champion of condensed soup, rules a category that is way off-trend having peaked decades ago. Chief competitor Progresso has captured a significant share of the growing ready-to-serve soup category, in recent years, causing real problems for Campbell's and their new CEO. However, Conant has the right resume for the job. An alumnus of Kraft Foods, he knows something about mature food brands.

Back in the beginning of the 1990s, Campbell's top line showed steady if not stellar improvement from 1990 to 1996, while earnings showed even greater health through 1996. Consequently, the stock price made steady gains from 1994—almost tripling on the way to a 2:1 stock split on March 18, 1997. However, during the five-year period from 1998 through 2002, both the top and bottom lines retreated in 4 of 5 years, and the company's stock reflected that inconsistency of performance.

But at least part of the earnings slide was planned as Conant sought and received Board approval to cut the dividend to .63 cents in order to help fund a major revitalization of the company.

## THE GAMBLE AT CAMPBELL'S (CONTINUED)

His options greatly narrowed, Conant rolled the dice and set off to retool the process of making Campbell Soup on the way to upgrading product quality. Conant also substantially increased product marketing, product innovation, and sales execution. EPS for 2002 reflected an 18 percent decrease—actually better than the 20 percent predicted by Conant in his 2001 letter to shareowners.

Though Conant is making progress on a number of fronts, most observers agree that he has far to go. Results after his first two years showed some signs of life with back-to-back sales increases in 2002 and 2003 coupled with expected earnings shortfalls. One measure of the difficulty facing Conant's climb: 2003 results of $6.67 billion in net revenue and $626 million in net income match almost identically the company's results of a decade ago when it posted $6.69 billion in net revenue and $630 million in net income in 1994.

Conant's challenge is to stir demand for a product that many fondly remember more as part of their past than their present—an issue today for dozens of consumer brands. Stay tuned. It's not exactly soup yet. ∎

## THE CURSE OF THE CLASS OF 1980

With approximately 25 percent of the workforce retiring every decade, 75 percent of those in the business world who experienced the roaring 1970s brought their optimism and high expectations for delivering sales records with them into the 1980s. However, after the first few years of the 1980s, it was becoming clear that this would not be much of an encore to the 1970s. By the end of the decade, corporations that had hit it out of the park in the 1970s were left scratching their heads. Where did the growth go in the 1980s?

Not deterred by the disappointing numbers in the 1980s, the 50 percent of executives that experienced the double-digit rush of the 1970s pushed on into the 1990s seeking to return to the glory days. Senior executives, disappointed with sales executives in general in the 1980s, sought scapegoats for the shortfall and handed pink slips to executives from entry level to the vice president of sales. These blame-based firings became associated with the decade and particularly the class of college graduates that entered the workforce at the beginning of the decade.

For those entering the workforce immediately following the greatest decades of postwar revenue growth, they had the great misfortune of following a generation that enjoyed the ride up when rates of revenue were increasing. In some circles, this ill-timed entry into the corporate world became known as the *curse of the class of 1980*, especially because most of their bosses were part of the greatest sales period in the postwar era just a decade before.

There was also much bloodletting and blame directed at the advertising agency world, which was being cut by the double-edged sword that it had lived by through the major postwar growth decades. Praised for their great creative work in helping many corporations introduce new products on the way to building corporate empires, the agency world probably took too much credit for the sales successes of their clients during the 1950s, 1960s, and 1970s. However, the agencies similarly took too much of the blame when sales greatly slowed in the 1980s. The agency's creative personnel became the scapegoat and naive corporations were quick to seek new agency partners whose creativity would help move soup sales to yet another level. Such moves resulted in a lot of unnecessary trauma that had absolutely nothing to do with the agency or their creative staffs in most cases.

There is one other unfortunate element to the *curse of the class of 1980*: The majority of people who graduated around 1980 or after still have a significant number of years remaining in their careers, which requires them to have to deal with the issue of whimpering demand until they retire. For the 63-year-old executive on the verge of retirement, the issue of corporate growth is a riddle for the next generation to figure out. Unable to skirt the issue will be the unlucky members of the class of 1980, who will have to deal with the lack of demand head on, most likely for the rest of their careers.

## DESPERATE TIMES CALL FOR DESPERATE MEASURES

As the rate of revenue growth continued to slide in the 21st century, corporations reacted in a variety of ways from delaying the release of bad results to reporting outright fabricated results. Some schemes stretched Generally Accepted Accounting Practices (GAAP) standards where others simply broke the law, keeping SEC and state officials very busy. New media stars such as New York State's Attorney General Eliot Spitzer suddenly found themselves in front of the cameras talking about a whole new breed of felons: corporate crooks.

The times were not only changing, the times were getting desperate. Often desperate times call for desperate measures, especially if it means protecting personal wealth.

# 4 Desperate Times, Desperate Measures

**W**hile cleaning out the junk drawer in her kitchen, a Chicago accountant came upon two plastic gift cards from a popular consumer electronics retailer that she had received two Christmases ago. Neither of them had ever been redeemed. For Mary Berry, it was like finding two $20 bills in an old coat on the way to the cleaners.

In many ways, the same could be said of the retailer, because the unused balance that had been sitting on the electronic strip on those cards for close to two years was slowly dropping to the retailer's bottom line. When Mary finally cashed in her cards, instead of finding a total value of $40 in credit, the value on the cards totaled only $26. The retailer had imposed a $2 per month penalty on each of the cards after they went unused for more than a year.

Mary Berry's situation is by no means unique. In fact, the estimated amount of unused value from gift cards each year is beginning to amount to significantly more than just pocket change. According to industry sources, more than $2 billion is left on such cards each year, and that figure is growing.

Even though the cards might have been purchased with cash many months before, the revenue associated with the increasingly popular gift cards is not recognized as earned revenue until the cards are redeemed. Although cash might flow into the retailer on original purchase of a gift card, that cash typically sits on the corporation's balance sheet as unearned revenue until it is redeemed. Some retailers, however, have devised ways to take the matter into their own hands in turning that balance sheet asset into earned revenue. Instead of waiting for Mary to find and redeem her cards months or even years later, some retailers impose an administrative fee to defray the costs of managing the gift card process.

Consumer groups, retailers, and a number of state attorneys general are organizing efforts to simplify the process of gaining access to the unused cash. In the meantime, it's certain that revenue-hungry retailers will continue to recognize this valuable newfound source of revenue, most of which translates into pure profit.

## DESPERATE TIMES

When it comes to revenue, these days corporations are pulling out all the stops to recognize every penny they can. With organic growth at most corporations slowing to a trickle, the individuals responsible for generating revenue growth are under the gun to do whatever it takes to deliver more. Revenue-boosting strategies have literally run the gamut from deep discounts to the outright fabrication of sales.

With an uncertain geopolitical climate on virtually every continent, lack of consumer confidence only dampens an already lackluster economic picture. Add to this the fact that the corporate revenue bar has been dramatically raised over the last decade, and aging corporations are having increasing difficulty clearing the bar at all.

The more successful a corporation becomes, the harder it is for it to continually outperform itself. Take Wal-Mart, for example. Wal-Mart sales now eclipse a quarter of a trillion dollars a year. That's approaching the size of Mexico's GDP. The Dow 30 collectively is approaching $2 trillion in annual net revenue or about 10 percent of U.S. GDP. The numbers are getting huge, creating an enormous challenge for those charged with growing the corporation down the line. As the revenue line moves into the stratosphere and the rate of revenue growth declines, it becomes more difficult to move the top line—especially in natural ways.

Consequently, the inorganic growth (acquisitions) of corporations over the last decade has far outpaced organic growth. This puts increased pressure on executives such as General Electric's Immelt to continue to push the acquisitions envelope to be able to continue the revenue and earnings pace set by his famous predecessor. To put this in perspective, the Dow 30 collectively increased by $850 billion in revenue from 1990 to 2000. General Electric alone accounted for nearly $100 billion of that improvement.

Much of the rapid consolidation of the 1990s also caused the premature demise of some standalone corporations whose workforces were decimated as part of the consolidation process. The acquire-and-consolidate strategy will increasingly create a dichotomy between the objectives of the corporation and the objectives of the government. Going forward, it will become very difficult to serve both masters by delivering increased earnings for the shareowners without contributing to the growing rate of unemployment.

Dow 30 corporations The Home Depot and Wal-Mart have followed similar growth strategies that came as a result of the breathless expansion of retail locations throughout the 1990s and into the 21st century. But most aggressive growth strategies are served up with a double-edged sword. Delivering growth by aggressively acquiring competitors or aggressively expanding retail locations around the globe can become a doomed growth strategy unless the strategy continues indefinitely. Any slowdown in acquisition or expansion efforts will almost certainly and immediately dampen growth momentum, and rapidly show up in the quarterly results. In fact, it already has. The Home Depot, a corporation that enjoyed stunning growth in the 1990s, largely tied to new store expansion, reported its first quarter of negative revenue growth in its history in Q4 2002—a significant milestone for a company that delivered 24 consecutive years of record revenues.

## IN THE BEGINNING . . .

In the earnings-focused world of business today, it is sometimes difficult to remember that a corporation usually starts out as the dream of a single individual with a single objective: to deliver the best product or service in the world and make money doing it. Somewhere along the road, however, we lost our way. The tables were turned. We went from a corporation that makes the best widgets in the world while delivering increased shareowner value to a corporation that delivers increased shareowner value while manufacturing something or other. Look at Alcoa's mission statement for example: *to be the best company in the world*. At what?

The success of capitalism requires the consistent delivery of profits. However, before there was profit, there was revenue, and without a more lively top line showing in years to come, our ability to deliver increased earnings keeps slipping away as well. It has been the lack of ability to deliver natural revenue growth that, in part, has driven senior management to both the acquisition pool and to the school of cost reduction to deliver one of the few metrics that executives believe they still control: earnings.

When all is said and done, most jobs in a corporation can usually be categorized in one of two ways: Jobs that help to increase revenues or jobs that help to reduce costs. Accomplish either one or both, and you have gone a long way toward increasing shareholder value. Unfortunately, though, it is becoming much easier to reduce costs than it is to increase revenues. There are limits to revenue growth, limits to the amount of costs that can be cut, and therefore ultimately limits to the level of earnings growth that be can delivered. The disproportionate growth of earnings to revenue that is currently more the rule than the exception can only be "managed" for a limited time. Such a strategy often results in a vicious corporate death spiral:

1. Discounted prices
2. Inferior product quality
3. Decreasing unit sales

4. Lack of demand
5. Oversupply

Once on this course, it becomes next to impossible to move off of it because this strategy conditions consumers to expect the lowest price every day. At the same time, you continue to drive costs out of the equation and are ultimately forced to decide whether to compromise the quality of the product itself. Once the quality of the product is compromised—regardless of what consumers said in focus groups—there will be a negative impact on sales volume. Have we lost sight of what we are supposed to be doing when we sit in a meeting to decide whether to cut back on the amount of milk used to manufacture a product?

The ever-decreasing rate of revenue growth for many corporations has created a much greater challenge in fulfilling the promise of all public companies: increasing shareholder value. However, the line between good fiscal policy and unethical behavior in the name of increasing shareholder value has not only been blurred in recent years, but in some cases it has been blatantly compromised.

## THE MOST FUNDAMENTAL OF FUNDAMENTALS

The term *fundamentals* means different things to different people. To many, the term refers almost exclusively to the performance of the corporation's stock. Click through to the investor relations section on any public company's Web site and you should find an area dedicated to its financial fundamentals. Some corporations choose to highlight stock price, volume, and ratio data in favor of the more traditional operational metrics that include highlights from the income statement, cash flows, and the balance sheet.

Often lost in the chorus of enthusiasts who cheer the market, as if it could exist without the corporations that enable it, is a true understanding of the most fundamental of all fundamentals: revenue.

Remember the Wall Street analyst mentioned in Chapter 1 who said that earnings have always grown faster than revenues? Obviously, she never started a company that had no revenue. When revenue fundamentally hits the wall, corporations have no choice but to aggressively reduce costs. In fact, it is their fiduciary responsibility to do so. However, once a corporation reaches the point in its life when the rate of revenue growth is consistently in decline, it signals the need for careful review of the long-term direction of the corporation. Once the rate of organic growth stops increasing, it will never trend up again.

It is particularly important to gain an understanding of the extent of the corporation's maturity. In other words, how many years have elapsed since hitting the market-share wall? How many years or even decades has the rate of revenue growth been in decline? The aging of the revenue stream is an important metric that most corporations have completely ignored. A look at historical rates of revenue growth over five- or 10-year periods will bring a deeper understanding as to why revenue budgets since 1980 have been for many industries more often missed than made. It's time for CEOs to show some guts and eliminate that portion of your job that is forced to deal with the unrealistic desires of those who know the least about your business.

## SPIN DOCTORS: HEALTHY PATIENTS, NO MATTER WHAT

The simple task of reporting results has been elevated to an art form. Falling short of expectations doesn't always mean that it has to be perceived that way. This has to be the credo of investor relations departments the world over. When revenue estimates were missed in the fourth quarter of 2001, it was because of September 11, but earnings targets were often still met. When earnings targets in the second quarter of 2002 were missed, it was because of the devaluation of the dollar in foreign markets, but earnings per share (EPS) targets were made because of aggressive stock buy-back plans.

Reporting results on an EPS basis has become a popular trend in recent years. The reason is simple: The corporation has probably struggled to meet straight-up earnings estimates. The remedy, in many cases, is an aggressive stock buy-back plan to reduce the number of shares outstanding and therefore increase earnings on a per-share basis. Reporting that EPS is up, corporations argue, is better than reporting that earnings are down. A boost in EPS allows the corporation to create an impression of health and vigor. The corporation that focuses on EPS as a measure of health while engaged in a stock buy-back plan is often kidding itself and its shareowners.

No matter how dire the financial news, the spin coming out of the business *intelligencia* makes even the worst of situations seem acceptable. Corporations have progressively found ways to make a silk purse out of a sow's ear. Spin masters during the dot-com era often referred to a corporation's inability to generate any sales as an *extended pre-revenue generation phase*. The stakes have become so high in the perception game that even the most disappointing results can be packaged in such a way as to calm—or at least confuse—most nervous investors.

## REPORT CARD: ALL A'S ON A PRO FORMA BASIS

The emergence of reporting results on a *pro forma* basis has confused many and made many others nervous. Companies such as Amazon.com made pro forma reporting popular in the late 1990s as a way of highlighting the good news while downplaying the bad. One analyst described pro forma reporting this way, when asking his 14-year-old son how he did on his report card:

"So how did you do?"
"This is the first time I ever got two A's!"

"So how did you do?"
"I'm ranked in the top two-thirds of my class!"

"So how did you do?"

"If you eliminate the two Fs, I'm on the honor roll!"

The SEC has been keenly aware of the dangers of pro forma financial reporting and has, on a number of occasions, cautioned both investors and companies about the practice. The SEC has publicly warned that pro forma results "should be analyzed and viewed with appropriate and healthy skepticism." However, public earnings releases that contain positive spin using pro forma reporting techniques are not required to be filed with the SEC. So although the black and white results are filed with the SEC, the public can be served a very different perspective on the current health and welfare of a corporation.

---

## TRICKS OF THE TRADE: INCREASING REVENUES

As the rate of revenue growth slows to a trickle, there seems to be no shortage of creative ploys designed to generate what amounts to revenue beyond sales. At Blockbuster, it is estimated that late fees on video rentals account for up to 16 percent of all revenue, or roughly $800 million annually. That's equal to what the United States pays in dues each year to the United Nations.

Even with the valuable late fees helping their cause, Blockbuster still has not been profitable since 1996. It's frightening to think that Blockbuster's mere existence could be put in jeopardy if consumers started to return their videos on time.

As an increasing number of consumers gain broadband capability, they move closer to being able to access feature-length motion pictures over the Internet. With average revenue growth sliding since hitting the market-share wall in 1998, it's difficult to imagine any survival scenario for Blockbuster without a severe shift in its business model. As soon as first-run movies are widely available over the Web, Blockbuster in its current form becomes rather superfluous.

## EXTENDED WARRANTIES

Anyone who has purchased a consumer electronics product since the early 1990s has received a pitch at the checkout counter for the opportunity to purchase an extended warranty on products ranging from digital cameras to flat screen TVs. Because of razor-thin margins in the consumer electronics industry, retailers are able to dramatically boost both revenue and profits through the sale of what are essentially service contracts on purchased equipment. With extraordinarily low claim rates, a high percentage of the premiums on these contracts drop straight to the retailer's bottom line.

Extended warranties provide a great example of the lengths to which corporations will go to generate new sources of revenue. Most consumer advocacy groups agree that the extended warranty is designed much more to help the retailer than the consumer. It is no coincidence that the energy around extended warranties has increased in direct proportion with the decrease in the rate of revenue for many corporations.

Possibly the most desperate of all desperate moves was made by a large utilities company that recently offered its customers an opportunity to purchase insurance against the possibility of a experiencing a water leak that, as the brochure said, "could quickly drain your wallet." For a mere $68 per year, residents would be able to sleep at night knowing they were protected against the infinitesimal possibility that the water pipe leading from the road to their house might spring a leak and flood the entire neighborhood. The tone of this and other hat-in-hand efforts smacks much more of desperation than it does true concern for the customer. Ironically, such ploys essential negate any upfront discount on the product itself. More often than not, retailers end up netting more than the Manufacturer's Suggested Retail Price (MSRP) when consumers fall into such traps.

## PENALTIES: SKIES BECOMING LESS FRIENDLY

The airline industry—a group already wobbly on its feet—was dealt a severe blow on September 11, 2001. It's quite possible that air travel volume might never return to pre-9/11 levels, and this has forced the airlines to compete for a much smaller pie. Competing for a smaller pie also makes it much more likely that they will compete almost exclusively on price. Competing on the basis of intangibles such as quality of service becomes a hard value proposition to deliver because good customer service is very expensive. Upstart airlines such as Southwest and Jet Blue have so far been able to deliver a quality customer experience while keeping costs in line. The more recognized airlines face the same problem that established U.S. automakers face: slowing top line growth coupled with a bloated and escalating cost structure. Handcuffed, in many cases, by punishing union contracts that they themselves negotiated, corporations are now finding ways to pass the punishment along to the consumer.

There was a time when consumers could change a reservation on almost any ticket at almost any time without being penalized. Then along came change fees as a penalty for changing a reservation on a nonrefundable ticket. However, starting on September 6, 2002, the penalties for changing or canceling a flight were dramatically increased. On some airlines, for example, unless consumers cancel or change their reservations by midnight the day of the flight, the entire value of the ticket is lost.

Identified by some as the *death penalty* for airline tickets, it's too soon to say if the revenue from this newfound source will help or hurt the airlines over the long run.

Paying additional fees for overweight luggage has also become a revenue producer for some airlines. The maximum allowable weight for customers checking luggage was dropped from 70 to 50 pounds in the hopes of increasing the universe of overweight baggage violators who must pay the price.

## THE OBESITY FACTOR

There are basically three ways to increase sales: acquire new customers, up-sell them more of the same product, or cross-sell them into other products. This was the formula for success that was essentially mastered in the 20th century. The strategy for achieving maximum consumption—though effective cross-selling still has a long way to go—has been successful beyond anyone's wildest dreams. In an increasing number of cases, though, over-consumption has become a serious issue across the globe. Obesity has reached epidemic proportions in the United States, affecting more than 60 million American adults, and more than 30 million American children and young adults between the ages of 11 and 19. According to the American Obesity Association, it is estimated that obesity is the cause of an additional 300,000 deaths in the United States each year.

Marketers have been so successful at convincing consumers to eat more that a number of class-action suits have been filed on behalf of consumers who claim that some corporations should be held responsible in some way for their role in creating a national health problem.

Although obesity is undoubtedly a very serious matter, it's difficult to argue that the disease has not helped increase the revenues of many corporations in the food industry. In a discussion on the inability of consumer packaged goods companies to generate volume increases, one Wall Street analyst identified obesity as a waning contributor to consumption levels in saying, "We've about maxed out on obesity as a source of consumption growth."

The fact that obesity was even remotely viewed as a potential source for increased sales is a disturbing thought, underscoring the depth of desperation reached in some industries. Nonetheless, corporations can no longer expect volume gains from the consumers that they have already acquired. If the ability to acquire new customers is negligible, and the willingness to raise prices for fear of losing customers to the competition is virtually nonexistent, corporations have embarked on a course that cannot last forever. This type of competitive environment provides great short-term value for consumers, while creating long-term stress on the corporations vying for their fair share of the pie.

## LENGTHENING THE SALES CYCLE

General Motors has become famous for its zero-zero-zero discount program designed to generate volume. It certainly worked during the fourth quarter of 2002, when the customer-friendly program helped GM set a new all-time sales record for the month of December. Zero-percent financing helped General Motors beat December 2001 sales by more than 36 percent. However, a look at Q4 2002 and Q1 2003 sales suggests that more and more consumers are aligning their buying habits with predictable discounting seasons of revenue-desperate corporations such as GM.

GM posted record unit sales tied largely to its liberal financing terms. In 2002, the company offered some type of enhancement to its sales and marketing programs in almost every month of the calendar year. With year-to-date sales looking bleak, GM announced its zero-zero-zero retail-marketing program on October 10, 2002, just until the end of October. However, with unit sales off by 163,582 for October, the program was extended on November 1 through the fourth quarter, ending on January 2, 2003.

Figure 4-1 shows sobering unit sales results on either side of the record month of December in 2002. Although it is impossible to measure precisely, it is fair to assume that a healthy percentage of consumers pushed the purchase of a new car forward from October or November into December 2002, where others might have even pulled purchases back into December from January or February 2003. In any case, the numbers don't look good, even with liberal financing. What would GM unit sales look like without its zero-zero-zero program?

Affectionately known by some insiders as *General Mortgage* due to the success of its mortgage business, GM's auto business—once the envy of the world and the quintessential example of business perfection by economists such as Harvard's John Kenneth Galbraith—now struggles to leave any money on the table.

| MONTH | 2002 | 2001 | +/− | % |
|---|---|---|---|---|
| October | 391,030 | 554,652 | (163,582) | (32.1)% |
| November | 309,263 | 363,721 | (54,458) | (18.2)% |
| December | 473,663 | 362,169 | 111,494 | 36.0% |
| Q4 Totals | **1,173,996** | **1,280,542** | **(106,546)** | **(8.4)%** |
| MONTH | 2003 | 2002 | +/− | % |
| January | 293,086 | 299,634 | (6,548) | (2.2)% |
| February | 333,572 | 411,111 | (77,539) | (18.9)% |
| March | 391,752 | 419,410 | (27,658) | (6.6)% |
| Q1 Totals | **1,018,410** | **1,130,155** | **(111,745)** | **(9.9)%** |

FIGURE 4-1    General Motors U.S. car and truck unit sales Q4 2002 and Q1 2003. Source: General Motors SEC Filings.

The lure of favorable financing deals, although powerful, can cause consumers to change their buying habits both in the short term and the long term. In the case of GM, not only did it cause a consolidation of sales in the month of December, probably depressing Q1 2003 sales, it also might have unwittingly lengthened its sales cycle. By pushing the longer 60-month financing terms as part of its strategy to drive short-term volume, GM might have changed the long-term buying pattern of some consumers from two- or three-year cycles to four- or five-year cycles. Such strategies, although effective in driving sales today, puts even more pressure on dealers to deliver sales tomorrow. It is altogether possible that the average number of months in the GM sales cycle will increase over the next five to 10 years, creating even greater sales challenges for individual dealers in exchange for a short-term sales fix.

In April 2003, GM announced a new program, Zero to 60, which more blatantly connects a zero-percent financing deal with the longest available financing term—60 months or five years. GM is inching dangerously closer to simply abandoning all pretense of deals that are available for a "limited time only." These moves also condition consumers to expect the best possible deal with the best possible financing all the time. This Wal-Mart approach to volume selling is beginning to catch up with U.S. automakers, whose average profit per vehicle hovers near $800 per sale or less. The drive-volume-now strategy can be a helpful one if the corporation has a very specific retention plan that is designed to keep customers who are lured by a deal that barely contributes to an automaker's bottom line. But no effective and measurable retention programs currently exist.

The slogan "everyday low prices" has become heroin for tens of millions of consumers. Once hooked on the expectation of perpetual deals, it's very difficult for corporations to go back.

## HAVE YOU DRIVEN A FORD LATELY?

Since losing $5.5 billion in 2001, the Ford Motor Company has been on a cost-cutting warpath. There's no doubt that costs are an issue at Ford, especially relative to its chief U.S. rivals. However, so is revenue. The century-old automaker sold fewer cars in the United States in 2002 (3.62 million units) than it did a full decade before in 1993 (3.78 million units). This is significant, considering that Ford is now a bigger company, representing more makes and many more models than it did a decade ago.

The war that Ford faces is one that must be waged on two fronts. Cutting costs will only allow Ford to win one battle. Without a concurrent boost from the sales side in Dearborn, Ford might ultimately lose the war. The implication is that like the airline industry, demand might only return after a serious reduction in supply. For the auto industry, that might mean getting smaller before getting bigger. Expect to see the evolution of the Big Three to the Big Two over the next decade.

## BARGAIN BASEMENT DEALS

Consumers love a good deal, and it seems as though there are more good deals in more product and service categories today than ever before: airline tickets, cars, stereos, cell phones, and on and on. It's difficult to imagine that anyone pays full price for anything anymore.

Discounting has become so commonplace that the marketing tactic is being introduced earlier and earlier into the sales process. It is not uncommon to find items discounted—especially in the area of apparel—almost immediately, with but a handful of full-priced sales going to naive consumers who are simply not paying attention.

There was a time when discounting was a marketing tactic reserved exclusively for slow-moving items. This tactic gave rise to bargain outlets, or off-price stores, such as Filene's Basement. Edward A. Filene founded Filene's Basement in Boston in 1908 as a way to sell off unsold name-brand clothing from his father's ground-level department store. Nearly a century later, customers are still getting incredible deals on name-brand clothing at Filene's Basement, which is now part of Value City Department Stores of Columbus, Ohio.

Providing great deals for consumers, however, often comes at a price: Value City Department Stores has not made money since 2000.

## DEFLATION: WHEN HAVING TOO MANY GOOD DEALS HURTS EVERYBODY

What appears to be a great deal for consumers in the short term might ultimately come back to bite the corporation over the long term. Some corporations will simply be unable to sustain the current level of discount policies and might be forced to close their doors. Over the last decade, there have been many long-established, high profile department stores that either closed their doors (Montgomery Ward) or filed for bankruptcy protection under Chapter 11 (Kmart).

Deflation is a phenomenon that is far more difficult to manage than inflation and has become a real concern for global economic powers, especially Japan and the United States. The downward momentum caused by price-slashing corporations hungry for volume is very difficult to reverse. The pricing death spiral leaves a corporation impotent, simply unable to even think about raising prices. Ultimately, the weakest will go down, causing serious unemployment issues over the short term that must be anticipated now. However, it goes deeper than that, especially when it comes to the large retailers, because when they go down, they can take large chunks of corporate volume with them. Consider the amount of business that companies such as the Altria Group (Philip Morris), Kellogg's, and PepsiCo have tied up in Wal-Mart, for example. These corporations have entire teams of employees dedicated to the Wal-Mart business to manage what have become substantive chunks of overall volume.

Ironically, though, it might very well be deflation that will ultimately lead a flagging economy out of its slump and onto the road to recovery. Price wars will undoubtedly continue, but not forever. In order for supply to decrease, there will be a purging that will help solve one problem and create another. As supply decreases, causing prices to stabilize, demand will ultimately increase toward a long-awaited equilibrium. However, unemployment is also a by-product of consolidation that is likely to become a serious issue on the road to stimulating any new demand.

## Your Business Is Important to Us

It seems ironic that some of the most flagrant violators of telemarketing conduct are some of the largest corporations in the world. The real irony is that the calls largely come from corporations with which customers are already doing business. Financial services companies and long-distance service providers are the worst offenders. Some long-distance service providers rent the names of their customers to competitors, just days after signing them up for service.

Outbound telemarketing not only damages the customer relationship, but in many cases, it can end it. Unfortunately, these corporations are hooked—like a junkie on heroin—to the revenue stream associated with this Stone Age marketing practice. Shame on the Direct Marketing Association for defending the practice as good marketing. Even Philip Morris admits that smoking can be hazardous to your health. There are some things that are just difficult to defend.

Consumer advocacy groups lobbied hard for the creation of a national Do-Not-Call list that will cost taxpayers close to $20 million annually. Unfortunately, this problem won't go away unless and until some of the most widely known corporations in the world simply agree to stop the practice altogether. Giving up short-term revenue in favor of establishing a less antagonistic approach to customers is the long-term solution. However, corporations are unlikely to willingly retire their efforts if that puts any level of revenue at risk.

## CUTTING COSTS

The practice of cutting costs has gone through its own metamorphosis since 1980. First, there was reengineering in the 1980s, followed by politically incorrect downsizing *and* rightsizing in the early 1990s. Today, cost savings are more often characterized as productivity gains, a more politically correct way of describing how a corporation can increase by decreasing.

Once it became clear in the 1980s that the rate of revenue growth was slowing, it simply became necessary to begin to trim what had become bloated operations that anticipated an ever-upward rate of growth. Like most life-altering business decisions, cost cutting was born of economic necessity, triggered especially by diminishing earnings results in the 1980s. In the 1970s, earnings grew at about 125 percent versus the 1960s, but grew only 40 percent from the 1970s to the 1980s.

Not surprisingly, earnings grew at a much faster rate in the 1990s compared to the 1980s. This is an extraordinarily difficult feat, considering that earnings figures had reached well beyond $1 billion a year for every Dow 30 component corporation, and some even as high as $10 billion or even $20 billion a year. It is, of course, impossible to measure the roles that true productivity gains enabled by technology and good old cost cutting played in the earnings comeback in the 1990s. It's safe to say that without true productivity gains, as well as the wholesale reduction of headcount, an increase in earnings growth never would have happened in the 1990s.

## CUTTING QUALITY

Have you ever noticed that the size of some newspapers and magazines has been getting smaller and smaller? There's a simple reason why. Shaving even a fraction of an inch off of a typical 7×10-inch glossy stock magazine can drop hundreds of thousands of dollars to the bottom line. That's a decision an executive has to make, but it might not be without fallout. There's the story of the CEO of a leading national magazine group who held up an issue of his 100-year-old magazine, and made the following announcement to his group publishers: "I've done the analysis. If you need to save $250,000 this year, you can reduce the width of each issue by one-eighth of an inch. If you need $500,000, you can lop off one-quarter of an inch."

Increasing efficiency is absolutely necessary for a corporation to succeed, especially a maturing corporation. However, when a manufacturer decides to cut the quality of a product, it essentially has decided to change the value proposition with the customer, usually without any discussion with customers. The manufacturer might justify the reduction in quality as fiscally necessary for the product to continue to contribute profitably to the corporation. That is a judgment call only the manufacturer can make. However, such actions are not necessarily without negative ramifications, and could result in the disruption of what is a tacit understanding between manufacturer and customer.

If the product that once was made with a cup of milk is now made with less than a cup of milk, there might be consumer fallout, regardless of what focus group research shows. Cutting the quality of a product is almost always a low-priority choice for a manufacturer, but it does happen. Tampering with the quality of the product is the most desperate of moves, but it implies that the corporation has exhausted all other options in producing and delivering the product at the lowest cost.

## FABRICATING THE NUMBERS

Of course, the ultimate form of corporate desperation manifests itself in the form of personal greed. With revenue growth rates steadily decreasing and earnings growth rates steadily increasing, the long-term ability to deliver increased earnings is most certainly at risk. The SEC should have known this was coming, or should have at least received some type of heads-up from the disappointing accounting industry. Corporations with no top-line energy but increasingly healthy bottom lines should have been more closely scrutinized, and should be going forward.

There is no shortage of corporations that are currently approaching saturation. It's easy enough to identify these mature entities with revenue streams that are maxed and initiatives that are much more about contraction than expansion. The point is that the pressure to cheat has not gone away. In fact, it has intensified. Legislation such as the Sarbanes-Oxley Act of 2002 was written into law to protect investors by improving the accuracy and reliability of corporate disclosures. However, Sarbanes-Oxley cannot improve corporate results. It can only improve on the reporting of corporate results. The need for more stringent controls over the financial results of publicly held corporations has never been greater. The temptation to consider cheating will only increase, which is simply another reason for CEOs to begin to educate shareowners in a more straightforward way about what a corporation can and can no longer deliver.

It's amazing that reform is almost never raised as an issue until people get caught. Whether it's an Olympic figure skating scandal, a church rocked by sexual misconduct, or runaway corporate malfeasance, rarely is there an outcry for widespread reform until a hand is blatantly caught in the cookie jar. Only then do we seek reform.

Corporate governance took on a much higher profile only after improprieties were discovered at corporations such as Enron, WorldCom, and Tyco. Now most corporate Web sites prominently display a button linking to a renewed discourse on governance and playing by the rules. This is no doubt a good thing, and should go a long way toward preventing cheating in the future. There are two edges to that sword, however. Although there is a much higher likelihood that financial reporting is on the up and up, that may mean that the numbers won't get any better for a while. Everyone wants the truth, but is everyone prepared to handle the truth?

## RESTATING EARNINGS

The restatement of corporate financial results reached record levels in recent years, fueled by corporate greed that manifested itself in the form of fraudulent behavior in the late 1990s and early 2000s. In fact, restatements have more than doubled since 1998, according to the Huron Consulting Group.

At the hub of the controversy was Arthur Andersen, formerly one of the Big Five accounting firms. Andersen's role in the Enron debacle resulted in the abrupt end of its audit practice, sending more than 1,300 clients scrambling to find new accountants.

On the heels of Andersen's embarrassment was the introduction of new legislation in the form of the Sarbanes-Oxley Act of 2002, which was designed to put all corporations on notice regarding reporting practices with the SEC. Sarbanes-Oxley was signed into law on July 30, 2002, and not surprisingly, restatements for the balance of 2002 skyrocketed. The top reason given for issuing restatements was revenue recognition. Not surprisingly, the overall corporate revenue malaise caused some firms to get creative on issues such as bill and hold transactions, transactions with rights of return, and transactions with the reseller channel in general.

As natural revenue growth slowed in the 1990s, and with so much equity at stake in the form of stock option grants, the temptation was simply too great for the individuals in power not to break the rules. Outside auditors, some with investment banking interests hanging in the balance, simply looked the other way when push came to shove. The penalties for impropriety are now more clear and more severe.

## TIMING IS EVERYTHING

In 1999, a freshly minted class of Harvard graduates left Cambridge, Massachusetts, and headed out to conquer the world. At the time, all the signs indicated that there couldn't be a better time to enter the workforce. The Dow was charging toward 10,000, and countless young entrepreneurs were becoming millionaires, and even billionaires.

The timing seemed perfect on the surface, but lurking just beneath the surface was the chilling cold reality that revenue was getting more difficult to generate. Whether you were a dotcom startup or a blue-chip Dow component, generating new revenue would be tough for the class of '99. Some 50 years before, however, another group of Harvard graduates were similarly eager to chase their fortunes in the marketplace. For the Harvard class of '49, though, the timing wasn't just right, it was perfect.

# 5 SIX HARVARD CLASSES

The wind is a remarkable force of nature. It can play the role of friend or foe. For the golfer, it can help on one hole and hurt on the next. Driving the ball into or against the wind can be as difficult as the salmon's journey upstream to lay her eggs. Driving the ball with the wind can make even the shortest of hitters feel like Tiger Woods, if only for a brief moment.

The winds that swirled in the business world immediately following World War II were not particularly gusty. It took a few years for millions to decide what they would do with the rest of their lives. With little experience and maybe one or two years of college under their belts, many decided to go back to school to finish their degrees before entering the business world.

By the end of the 1940s, the favorable winds in the business world were beginning to gain strength, just in time to usher in a crop of new college graduates. On the doorstep of a new decade, the Class of 1949 took the first step in what would become an unimaginable ride to the top of the business world.

## THE CLASS OF '49

Much has been written about the Harvard class of 1949, which turned out the leaders of some of the world's most widely recognized corporations. This illustrious group of leaders

127

literally helped build corporate empires such as Johnson & Johnson, Xerox, Goldman Sachs, Bloomingdale's, and many more. The names are legend: Warren Buffett, James Burke, Thomas Murphy, Peter McColough, Marvin Traub, and on and on. Truly, this class helped shape the business world of the second half of the 20th century. How could one college class produce so many incredibly successful captains of industry?

Well, for starters, they did go to Harvard. Second, and with all due respect, they entered the workforce with a gale-force wind at their backs, in fact, the most remarkable period of expansion the world has ever seen.

Because our starting point in this chapter was the vaunted Harvard Class of 1949, we will build on that theme by introducing you to six fictitious graduates of six different Harvard classes spaced exactly 10 years apart starting in 1950. We will follow the individual careers of these graduates from the Classes of 1950, 1960, 1970, 1980, 1990, and 2000, all of which land jobs at the very real Procter & Gamble Company of Cincinnati, Ohio.

With this device, you will be able to experience the careers of six different executives from their unique points of view at six different starting points over a 50-year period. The 50-year period from 1950 to 2000 is a nearly complete business cycle by our definition of the term—a period of time during which an industry or corporation experiences both phases of the long-term business cycle, a period of increasing rate of revenue growth, followed by a period of decreasing rate of revenue growth.

You will learn from the perspective of the executive who starts his or her career at the beginning of the business cycle, the executive who starts his or her career in the middle of the business cycle, and the executive who starts his or her career at the end of one cycle and the beginning of the next. The Class of 1950 will start us off at the very beginning of the business cycle.

Although the graduates are fictitious, the numbers are real and reflect the actual financial results that Procter & Gamble reported as a public company over a 50-year period. We use results for the years 1950, 1960, 1970, 1980, 1990, and 2000 as reported by P & G to the SEC, and look at the following metrics for each of those years based on actual results:

- Net revenues at the beginning of the decade
- Net revenues at the end of the decade and percentage gain
- Average gross margin for the decade
- Average rate of revenue growth for the decade
- Average rate of earnings growth for the decade

We also highlight the actual major growth strategies employed by Procter & Gamble to drive revenue and market share during each decade, including:

- New product and line extension development
- Domestic and international expansion
- Mergers and acquisitions

---

## PROCTER & GAMBLE

Founded in 1837 as a small family-run candle and soap-making operation, Procter & Gamble has grown into one of the world's most-respected corporations, now operating in its third century. The corporation is organized into three main areas of consumer product expertise—family care, household care, and personal care—and within these groups it manufactures and markets more than 250 products in more than 20 product categories to more than 5 billion consumers in 130 countries.

We have purposefully steered clear of reporting on details relating to Procter & Gamble's stock performance, stock splits, dividends, stock repurchase plans, cash flows, and balance sheets so that we can focus on the major operational strategies and the results of those strategies related to running one of the world's great consumer packaged goods company across five decades. This way, we are able to view the corporation at very different stages of its life. However, at the end of this chapter, we show the individual return on investment that each graduate would have realized if they had purchased $10,000 of Procter & Gamble stock on their first day of work.

## MEET THE GRADUATES

We study the business careers of the following six fictitious Harvard graduates: Abel from the Class of 1950, Baker from the Class of 1960, Charlie from the Class of 1970, Delta from the Class of 1980, Echo from the Class of 1990, and Fox from the Class of 2000. Figure 5-1 identifies the names of our graduates, the year in which they graduated, the generation to which they belonged, and their personal heroes at the time that they started their careers at Procter & Gamble.

| EXECUTIVE | CLASS | GENERATION | PERSONAL |
|---|---|---|---|
| Abel | Class of 1950 | World War I | Hero: Douglas MacArthur |
| Baker | Class of 1960 | World War II | Hero: John F. Kennedy |
| Charlie | Class of 1970 | Early boomer | Hero: John Lennon |
| Delta | Class of 1980 | Boomer | Hero: Grete Waitz |
| Echo | Class of 1990 | Early Gen X | Hero: Nelson Mandela |
| Fox | Class of 2000 | Gen X | Hero: Maya Angelou |

FIGURE 5-1    Six Harvard graduates, six different careers. Source: Customer Share Group LLC.

Each of our graduates enters the workforce with the same qualifications. At the time they accept an entry-level position at Procter & Gamble, they are all 25 years old and all have MBAs. Although two of our graduates are women, the most significant difference between the graduates is the date on which they enter the business world. The social, political, and, especially for our purposes, the economic climates vary greatly from one decade to the next, and provide a unique perspective from six different individuals who experience six very different careers.

## CLASS OF 1950

It's 1950. Harry Truman is President of the United States, and Senator Joseph McCarthy of Wisconsin is advising him that the State Department is filled with Communists and Communist sympathizers. The population in the United States stands at 152 million and babies are booming. *All About Eve* starring Bette Davis wins the Academy Award. The top song of the decade is "Don't Be Cruel" by Elvis Presley. The Dow Jones Industrial Average hovers near 175 to start the decade, when our first graduate, Abel, makes the trip west by bus from Cambridge, Massachusetts, to Cincinnati, Ohio, to begin work.

**Major Growth Strategies of the 1950s.** In Chapters 2 and 3, major corporate growth strategies were described in detail. Over the course of the 1950s, Procter & Gamble utilized all four of the major growth strategies that were commonly used to progressively grow an overall business:

1. Product development and marketing:
   - A new research facility dedicated to upstream research opens in Cincinnati in 1952. The first toothpaste with fluoride, Crest, is introduced in 1955.
2. Domestic expansion:
   - The corporation organizes into individual operating divisions to vertically manage the growing line of consumer products. Separate line and staff organizations are created in 1955. This marked the beginning of the traditional vertical corporate structure that supported the development and marketing of individual brands to individual market segments.
3. International expansion:
   - Procter & Gamble sets up operations in Europe by leasing a small plant near Marseilles, France, in 1954.
4. Mergers and acquisitions:
   - The corporation enters the consumer paper products business with the acquisition of the Charmin Paper Mills in 1957, and started to expand its portfolio of product and category offerings.

**Results of the 1950s.** Figure 5-2 shows net revenue in 1950 totaling $632 million, more than doubling to nearly $1.4 billion by the end of the decade, a 7.56 percent average rate of revenue growth. Net income of $102 million in 1950 grew by more than 60 percent during the decade to $168 million, an average annual rate of growth of nearly 6 percent. Gross margin for the decade averaged 12.34 percent. The corporation enjoyed a healthy decade of revenue growth and positioned itself for the development of more new products with expanded global distribution capabilities.

| CATEGORY | AMOUNT |
|---|---|
| Net Revenue in 1950 | $632 |
| Net Revenue in 1959 | $1,368 |
| Net Income in 1950 | $102 |
| Net Income in 1959 | $166 |
| Average Rate of Revenue Growth 1950s | 7.56% |
| Average Rate of Earnings Growth 1950s | 5.91% |
| Average Gross Margin in 1950s | 12.34% |

FIGURE 5-2 Procter & Gamble financial results, 1950s (in millions of USD).

**Checking in with the Graduates.** Abel spent his first five years at Procter & Gamble working on the incredibly successful laundry detergent Tide, "the washing miracle." Introduced in 1946, Tide had become the leading laundry detergent in the United States by 1950, and provided an exciting starting point at the company for Abel.

In 1956, Abel moved from Tide over to help introduce Crest toothpaste and spent the rest of the decade working on a revolutionary new product that helped prevent cavities. Based on his personal quote after 10 years with the company, shown in Figure 5-3, Abel seemed ready for more of the same in the 1960s. For his stellar work during the 1950s, Abel was promoted into middle management.

| | IN 1960 | | | |
|---|---|---|---|---|
| | AGE | YEARS WORKING | JOB STATUS | PERSONAL QUOTE |
| Class of 1950: Abel | 35 | 10 | Middle management | It was an exciting first decade. I got to work on the company's top two brands, Tide and Crest. Working on the introduction of Crest in 1955 was the highlight of the 1950s for me. |

**FIGURE 5-3**    Perspectives from the graduates in 1960.

Procter & Gamble completed a successful decade of innovation and growth, and prepared to welcome a new Harvard graduate to its workforce in 1960.

## CLASS OF 1960

It's 1960. John Fitzgerald Kennedy has just been elected President of the United States, population 180 million. *The Apartment* starring Jack Lemmon and Shirley MacLaine wins the Academy Award. The top song at the beginning of the decade is "Why" by Frankie Avalon. The Dow Jones Industrial Average hovers near 675 to start the decade, and by the end of the decade reaches 800. Newly minted Harvard graduate Baker arrives in Cincinnati to begin work at the dawn of a new decade.

**Major Growth Strategies of the 1960s.** Once again, Procter & Gamble utilized all major growth strategies to build its overall business over the course of the 1960s. However, both the volume and pace of business had increased exponentially since the 1950s, and the corporation stepped up its growth and development plan, including:

1. Product development:
   - Crest sales explode when the American Dental Association recognizes it as "the decay-preventative dentifrice."

■ Downy fabric softener is introduced in 1960.

■ Pampers enters the test market in Peoria, Illinois, in 1961.

2. Domestic expansion:

■ Partnerships with all segments of the retail community explode.

3. International expansion:

■ Procter & Gamble opens its first operations in Germany in 1960.

■ The company establishes Middle East operations in Saudi Arabia in 1961.

■ The company opens the European Technical Center in Brussels in 1963.

4. Mergers and acquisitions:

■ Procter & Gamble enters the coffee business with the acquisition of Folgers coffee in 1963.

**Results of the 1960s.** Figure 5-4 shows both revenue and earnings nearly doubling during the decade. Revenues grew at an average annual rate of 7.12 percent, about the same rate as the 1950s, and the rate of earnings growth improved to 8.58 percent, up from 5.91 percent in the 1950s. Similarly, gross margin for the decade increased to an average 13.33 percent, up from 12.34 percent in the 1950s.

| CATEGORY | AMOUNT |
|---|---|
| Net Revenue in 1960 | $1,441 |
| Net Revenue in 1969 | $2,707 |
| Net Income in 1960 | $195 |
| Net Income in 1969 | $369 |
| Average Rate of Revenue Growth 1960s | 7.12% |
| Average Rate of Earnings Growth 1960s | 8.58% |
| Average Gross Margin in 1960s | 13.33% |

FIGURE 5-4    Procter & Gamble financial results, 1960s (in millions of USD).

**Checking in with the Graduates.** Abel spent the entire decade working in middle management on the burgeoning Crest business, and consistently earned merit raises as well as bonuses almost every year of the decade. For his work, Abel was promoted to a senior management position as the decade came to a close. Baker worked on a number of brands during his first decade at the company, including the introduction of Downy fabric softener in the early part of the decade. In the mid-1960s, Baker shifted gears and spent the balance of the decade working on the revolutionary new disposable diaper Pampers. Abel and Baker reflect on their experiences during the 1960s in Figure 5-5.

| | IN 1970 | | | |
|---|---|---|---|---|
| | AGE | YEARS WORKING | JOB STATUS | PERSONAL QUOTE |
| Class of 1960: Baker | 35 | 10 | Middle management | I spent most of the decade working on Pampers, and learned a lot about mothers and their babies, as well as their local supermarket. It was great working on a product that literally took the market by storm. |
| Class of 1950: Abel | 45 | 20 | Senior management I | It was another great decade of growth and excitement for me. There seems to be no limit to our potential and the 1970s should be even better. The last 20 years has just flown by. It's hard for me to believe that my career is already half over. |

FIGURE 5-5   Perspectives from the graduates in 1970.

The turbulent 1960s gave way to a new decade filled with hope for peace and an end to the war in Vietnam. Through all the political and social strife, Procter & Gamble was just hitting its stride as one of the world's leading consumer packaged goods companies, and a new Harvard graduate was about to join his fellow alumni in Cincinnati.

## CLASS OF 1970

It's 1970. Richard Millhouse Nixon is President of the United States, population 205 million. The United States is again at war, this time in Vietnam. *Patton,* starring George C. Scott, wins the Academy Award. "Someday We'll Be Together" by Diana Ross and the Supremes is the top song at the beginning of the decade. The Dow Jones Industrial Average hovers near 800 to start the decade and breaks through the 1000 mark in 1972. By the end of 1979, the Dow retreats to about 850.

A new employee arrives in town after driving his beat-up Chevy Impala from Boston to Ohio to start his first job. Charlie arrives in Cincinnati, grateful for the opportunity to be joining one of the world's fastest growing companies.

**Major Growth Strategies of the 1970s.** Procter & Gamble continued its tradition of innovation in the 1970s, and although there were no significant acquisitions during the 1970s, the hard-charging corporation was generating significant organic growth as it continued to build market share across a number of major categories.

1. Product development:
   - Bounce fabric softener sheets are introduced in 1972, and quickly grow to number two in the category behind Procter & Gamble's own Downy.
2. Domestic expansion:
   - Partnerships with an ever-expanding number of retailers continue through the 1970s. The rise of national retail drugstore chains such as CVS prove to be a boon to the corporation, particularly for its personal care product division.

3.  International expansion:
    ■ Manufacturing and sales of Procter & Gamble products in Japan begins in 1973.

**Results of the 1970s.** The 1970s proved to be a record decade for Procter & Gamble from a number of perspectives. The most significant, though, had to be the growth of its net revenue. Sales more than tripled during the decade from $2.9 billion in 1970 to $9.3 billion in 1979. Although the 1970s were plagued by abnormally high inflation rates, growth during the 1970s was nothing short of remarkable. Revenue grew at an astonishing average rate of 13.33 percent a year during the decade, where the average rate of earnings growth dropped to 6.40 percent after increasing in the 1960s to an average of 8.58 percent per year. Growth proved costly for Procter & Gamble, requiring a larger infrastructure to fulfill the strong demand of the 1970s.

The average annual gross margin also dropped from the prior decade to an annual average of 9.32 percent versus 13.33 percent during the 1960s (see Figure 5-6). It's also important to note that the gross margin for the first five years of the 1970s averaged 12.56 percent, where the last five years of the 1970s averaged less than half that, at 6.09 percent. This significant drop, as well as the decrease in the average rate of earnings growth, can probably be attributed to fact that the company's infrastructure continued to increase in anticipation of a rate of revenue growth that would continue to increase.

| CATEGORY | AMOUNT |
| --- | --- |
| Net Revenue in 1970 | $2,978 |
| Net Revenue in 1979 | $9,329 |
| Net Income in 1970 | $426 |
| Net Income in 1979 | $577 |
| Average Rate of Revenue Growth 1970s | 13.33% |
| Average Rate of Earnings Growth 1970s | 6.40% |
| Average Gross Margin in 1970s | 9.32% |

FIGURE 5-6   Procter & Gamble financial results, 1970s (in millions of USD).

Retrospectively, there are signs that Procter & Gamble's rate of revenue growth might have peaked in 1974 at around 25 percent, and started to trend down thereafter. It would have been impossible for any corporation to judge just when the rate of revenue growth would stop increasing and start decreasing.

**Checking in with the Graduates.** Abel spent a great part of the decade managing the growth of the household care division, which boasted a battery of laundry as well as kitchen and bathroom products. The sales numbers were stellar, but the bottom line experienced some slippage as Abel entered the last decade of his career.

Baker was busy over in the family care division for the entire decade, working on the company's significant line of brands for newborns, infants, and toddlers.

Charlie worked on many brands within the family care health segment. Like many before him, Charlie worked a great deal on Crest learning the ropes of the consumer packaged goods business. Some of their highlights are shown in Figure 5-7.

As the 1970s began to wind down, Procter & Gamble said goodbye to the greatest sales decade in its history with annual rates of revenue growth reaching percentages in the mid-20s in some years. An enthusiastic new Harvard graduate heads west to Cincinnati to begin her career at a company that seems to be just hitting its stride.

## CLASS OF 1980

It's 1980. Ronald Reagan was just elected President of the United States, replacing Jimmy Carter in the Oval Office. The population of the United States is 227 million. *Ordinary People*, starring Mary Tyler Moore, wins the Academy Award. The top song at the beginning of the decade was "Escape (The Pina Colada Song)" by Rupert Holmes. The Dow Jones Industrial Average starts the decade near 850, breaks through 2000 for the first time in 1987, and then ends the decade at 2750. Our 1980 graduate Delta boards a 747 and wings her way to Cincinnati to begin her career at Procter & Gamble.

| | IN 1980 | | | |
|---|---|---|---|---|
| | AGE | YEARS WORKING | JOB STATUS | PERSONAL QUOTE |
| Class of 1970: Charlie | 35 | 10 | Middle management | What a decade! I couldn't have asked for a better introduction to the business world. Working on Crest gave me a broad understanding of the overall business and at the same time an opportunity to be part of a great success story |
| Class of 1960: Baker | 45 | 20 | Senior management I | The Pampers business grew much faster than I could have ever dreamed. Being a part of it was incredibly rewarding both personally and professionally. I'm looking forward to more of the same in the 1980s. |
| Class of 1950: Abel | 55 | 30 | Senior management II | Although sales continued to be extraordinarily strong, our gross margins really suffered during the last half of the decade. It has become a major concern for management and will take more focused efforts in the 1980s to get our hands around it. |

**FIGURE 5-7**  Perspectives from the graduates in 1980.

**Major Growth Strategies of the 1980s.** After a decade of healthy revenue growth in the 1970s, the pressure was on to continue to keep the sales momentum moving onward and upward. Business planning called for harvesting more of the same with many growth strategies similar to those that worked so well during the 1970s, including these:

1. Product development:
   - Always/Whisper—a new feminine protection product—is introduced. The brand would become the world leader in the category by 1985.
   - Liquid Tide is introduced in 1984.
   - Pert Plus/Rejoice is introduced in 1986, enabling consumers to wash and condition their hair with just one product instead of two.
   - Ultra Pampers and Luvs Super Baby Pants are introduced in 1986.
2. International expansion:
   - Procter & Gamble announces a joint venture to begin the manufacture, marketing, and sale of products in China starting in 1988.
3. Mergers and acquisitions:
   - Norwich Eaton Pharmaceuticals is acquired in 1982, increasing the company's presence in the prescription and over-the-counter health care business.
   - Richardson-Vicks is acquired in 1985 and greatly expands its over-the-counter and personal health care lines of business with products such as Vicks respiratory care and Oil of Olay.
   - The acquisition of the Blendax line of products, including Blendax toothpastes, is announced in 1987, greatly increasing the company's presence in the European personal care category.
   - Noxell is acquired in 1989. Cover Girl, Noxzema, and Clarion products help the company enter the cosmetics and fragrance category.

**Results of the 1980s.** Results from the 1980s were somewhat disappointing, as consistent double-digit revenue growth faded for five years between 1981 and 1985. Net revenue doubled during the decade to $21 billion after tripling during the 1970s. Net income, on the other hand, more than tripled during the decade to a record $1.9 billion in 1989. The average rate of earnings growth nearly quadrupled to an average of 24.09 percent, up from an average of just 6.40 percent in the 1970s (see Figure 5-8).

The corporation's average gross margin fell for the second straight decade to 6.48 percent. The results signal that some fundamental dynamics in the business might have changed. The rate of revenue growth was in decline for the first time since World War II. The rate of earnings growth increased dramatically during the decade—growing almost three times faster than revenues. Many pointed to cost-reduction measures as the reason.

| CATEGORY | AMOUNT |
|---|---|
| Net Revenue in 1980 | $10,772 |
| Net Revenue in 1989 | $21,398 |
| Net Income in 1980 | $640 |
| Net Income in 1989 | $1,939 |
| Average Rate of Revenue Growth 1980s | 8.74% |
| Average Rate of Earnings Growth 1980s | 24.09% |
| Average Gross Margin in 1980s | 6.48% |

FIGURE 5-8    Procter & Gamble financial results, 1980s (in millions of USD).

**Checking in with the Graduates.** Abel completed his 40-year career at the corporation in 1990, took his pension and gold watch, and retired. Baker, a 30-year veteran of the corporation, worked primarily on acquisitions during the 1980s, and he was kept quite busy with four major deals culminating during the decade. Charlie worked primarily in the product development area and similarly had his hands full with five new product introductions during the decade. Delta started out working on Crest, but then in 1986 was involved with the introduction of Pert Plus. Their comments are shown in Figure 5-9.

| | Age | Years Working | Job Status | In 1990 Personal Quote |
|---|---|---|---|---|
| Class of 1980: Delta | 35 | 10 | Middle management | Working on some of the world's best known brands such as Crest was great. But there is a growing pressure to reduce costs at the company—especially during the last five years. Marketing budgets greatly tightened up as the 1980s came to a close. |
| Class of 1970: Charlie | 45 | 20 | Senior management I | I've learned that product development is a good place to be. It's new, it's exciting, and, at least for a time, you enjoy the benefits of new sales that keep out-delivering the prior year. I like the development area and definitely don't want to spend the second half of my career looking for nickels and dimes to cut. |
| Class of 1960: Baker | 55 | 30 | Senior management II | Although I missed the day-to-day involvement on the product side, the merger and acquisitions area allowed me to play a more strategic role in laying the groundwork for future growth here. Identifying major potential acquisitions that complement our portfolio of products has been a great place to work. |
| Class of 1950: Abel | 65 | 40 | Retired | I can't say that the last 10 years were as much fun as the first 30. I feel fortunate to have been there during the frontier years. Cost-cutting and layoffs really took a toll on me during the back half of the 1980s. I'm afraid that there will be more of the same in the 1990s. I'm glad that I'll be playing golf in Phoenix! |

FIGURE 5-9  Perspectives from the Graduates in 1990.

The five-year sales slump from 1981 to 1985 might have been much worse without the work of both Baker and Charlie during the decade. Three of the four acquisitions that Baker worked on came after 1985, and therefore contributed to the corporation's top line in a wholesale way, primarily during the last four years of the decade. Similarly, three of the four new product introductions shepherded by Charlie also came during the second half of the decade, helping the corporation to return to double-digit rates of revenue growth starting in 1986 and running into the 1990s.

## CLASS OF 1990

It's 1990. George Herbert Walker Bush is President of the United States, which has a population of 249 million. *Dances With Wolves*, starring Kevin Costner, wins the Academy Award for Best Picture. The top song at the beginning of the 1990s is "Another Day in Paradise" by Phil Collins. The Dow Jones Industrial Average starts the decade at 2750 and then, for the first time ever, proceeds to steamroll through 3000, 4000, 5000, 6000, 7000, 8000, 9000, 10000, and 11000 before settling at 11500 at the end of the decade. Echo arrives in Cincinnati fresh from a rainy Harvard graduation anxious to get her first paycheck and buy a new car.

**Major Growth Strategies of the 1990s.** The corporation stepped up efforts in three major growth strategies during the 1990s. After acquiring a bigger appetite for mergers and acquisitions in the 1980s, the corporation more than doubled its major acquisition efforts in the 1990s. The acquisitions were fairly evenly spread across the decade, serving to impact the corporation financially in a consistent manner. Product development continued to play its role during the 1990s with a number of new product introductions, and international activity also heated up during the decade.

1. Product development:
   - Procter & Gamble's new compact technology enables the reformulation of most of the company's laundry detergents in 1990.

- Pantene Pro-V is introduced in 1992 and becomes the fastest selling shampoo in the world.
- Giorgio Beverly Hills is added to the company's fine fragrance line.
- The company opens a Health Care Research Center in Cincinnati in 1995 to promote innovation in the development of new pharmaceuticals.
- Calorie-free fat replacement Olestra is granted approval in 1996 by the U.S. Food and Drug Administration (FDA) for use in snacks and crackers. In 1998, Olean becomes widely used in snack foods in the United States, including Procter & Gamble's own Pringles chips.
- Procter & Gamble introduces innovative new products Febreze, Dryel, and Swiffer worldwide in 1998.

2. International expansion:
- The company's Japan Headquarters and Technical Center opens on Rokko Island in Kobe City in 1993, consolidating both headquarters and product development in one location.
- The company reestablishes its presence in South Africa in 1994 after U.S. sanctions against the country are lifted.
- After U.S. sanctions against Vietnam are lifted, the company establishes a joint venture to build a manufacturing plant just outside of Ho Chi Minh City in 1995.
- The company forms a global pharmaceutical alliance in 1997 with Hoechst Marion Roussel to market Procter & Gamble's new bone health drug Actonel.

3. Mergers and acquisitions:
- Shulton's Old Spice product line is acquired in 1990, expanding the company's presence in the male personal care market.
- The acquisition of Rakona in Czechoslovakia in 1991 signals the company's first operational foray into Eastern Europe, enabling expansion into Poland, Hungary, and Russia in the same year.

■ Max Factor and Betrix acquisitions in 1991 greatly expand the company's global presence in the cosmetics and fragrances businesses.

■ The acquisition of German-based VP Schickedanz in 1994 helps the company enter the European tissue and towel business.

■ U.S. baby wipes brand Baby Fresh is acquired, bolstering the company's global position in the segment.

■ The acquisition of feminine protection product-maker Tambrands in 1997 helps the company expand its presence in the category worldwide with the help of its lead tampon brand Tampax.

■ The acquisition of Mexico-based Loreto y Pena—a successful maker of tissues—helps the company compete in the Latin American tissue business for the first time.

■ The company enters the pet health and nutrition market worldwide with the acquisition in 1999 of Iams Company, the leader in premium pet foods.

■ Procter & Gamble acquires Recovery Engineering, Inc. in 1999 to bolster its expertise in the development of home water filtration systems brought to market under the PUR brand.

**Results of the 1990s.** Even with all of the growth initiatives during the 1990s, revenue grew at an average annual rate of just 6.03 percent, underscoring two important principles: First, the bigger you get, the harder it is to grow. Second, there can be limits to growth, especially in categories that have been available for at least a generation. Growth in these categories comes almost exclusively out of the competition's hide. This means expensive and backbreaking work with little return.

Net revenue increased by only 58 percent from the beginning of the decade to the end of the decade. Earnings continued to grow during the decade, and 1999 reached record levels of $6.2 billion. However, earnings grew at a much slower rate compared to the 1980s. The average gross margin improved greatly from the 1980s to an annual average of 12.30 percent (see Figure 5-10). International expansion became more and more critical to the corporation during the decade, and, for the first time ever, represented more than 50 percent of sales in 1993—a sign that domestic growth was on the wane and had already seen its best days.

| CATEGORY | AMOUNT |
|---|---|
| Net Revenue in 1990 | $24,081 |
| Net Revenue in 1999 | $38,125 |
| Net Income in 1990 | $2,421 |
| Net Income in 1999 | $6,253 |
| Average Rate of Revenue Growth 1990s | 6.03% |
| Average Rate of Earnings Growth 1990s | 8.06% |
| Average Gross Margin in 1990s | 12.30% |

FIGURE 5-10   Procter & Gamble financial results, 1990s (in millions of USD).

**Checking in with the Graduates.** Abel, our graduate from the Class of 1950, had already been happily retired for 10 years. He enjoyed living in Phoenix, drawing his well-earned pension from his former employer. After his 40-year career with Procter & Gamble from 1960 to 1999, Baker retired. Retrospectively, he remembered his career in two distinct parts: 20 years of sales growth, followed by 20 years of earnings growth. He retired to Florida with a healthy pension from his former employer.

Charlie is now a 30-year veteran of the corporation, and over the last decade continued in his role in the development of new products. He had a very busy decade, helping introduce some new categories of products such as Swiffer in 1998. Delta celebrated her 20-year anniversary with the company in 1999, and at mid-career looked back on the 1990s as a decade when she moved over to work in the extremely busy mergers and acquisitions area. Echo worked on Crest for much of the decade before moving over to work on the introduction of Febreze in 1998. The graduates' perspectives are shown in Figure 5-11.

| | AGE | YEARS WORKING | JOB STATUS | PERSONAL QUOTE |
|---|---|---|---|---|
| | | | | IN 2000 |
| Class of 1990: Echo | 35 | 10 | Middle management | Working on Crest was interesting, but I found that it was hard for a product like Crest to grow. There are lots of ideas to extend the Crest name to other categories related to oral hygiene. That's really the only way that the brand can grow. I'm ready to work on something that has a chance to explode. |
| Class of 1980: Delta | 45 | 20 | Senior management I | I'm glad that I moved over to the mergers and acquisitions area when I did. Many of the company's most recognized brands are maturing. I like the challenge of strategizing growth through acquisition—but frankly, the list of potential acquisitions is getting shorter and shorter as our chief competitors do the same thing. |
| Class of 1970: Charlie | 55 | 30 | Senior management II | Working on new product development and introductions has been challenging for me. It's getting more difficult to develop new products categories in our markets—especially ones that won't cannibalize other products that we already have. I worry what new category introductions like Swiffer do to brands like Mr. Clean, for example. |
| Class of 1960: Baker | 65 | 40 | Retired | I'm looking forward to retirement. The last 20 years since 1980 were rewarding financially but very tough on me personally. I always looked at the cost-reduction efforts of the 1980s as a temporary event, especially because all we did from 1960 to 1980 was add costs as we built revenue. Now I think cost cutting is a forever thing, a necessity to deliver expected results. |
| Class of 1950: Abel | 75 | N/A | Retired | Retirement has been great, but I'd like to see some better results coming out of the corporation to help my retirement portfolio. After a great decade of appreciation, I worry about the future value of my holdings. There was a time when all the stock did was go up, but there aren't any guarantees today. |

FIGURE 5-11   Perspectives from the graduates in 2000.

The continued erosion in the rate of revenue growth required the corporation to be even tougher on costs to continue to deliver the level of shareowner value that the corporation had always delivered. Without a steady flow of new revenue, from whatever sources, it would become more difficult for the corporation to generate increased earnings down the road. If revenue and productivity continued to slow, then it naturally follows that earnings would not be able to grow indefinitely.

## CLASS OF 2000

It's 2000, the dawn of a new millennium. George W. Bush has just been elected President of the United States, with a population of 281 million. *Gladiator*, starring Russell Crowe, wins the Best Picture Academy Award and the number one song at the beginning of the decade is "Smooth" by Santana. The Dow Jones Industrial Average starts the decade at 11500, and within three years has retreated to under 8000. The market bubble had burst as our new Harvard graduate Fox from the Class of 2000 makes her way out to Cincinnati to start her career.

**Major Growth Strategies of the 2000s.** The early part of the new century brought more challenges for the company, as it continued to aggressively seek growth through the development of new products and new product categories, as well as through acquisitions. The acquisition of Clairol from Bristol-Myers Squibb in 2001 is a good example of the type of aggressive moves the corporation continued to pursue to keep revenue moving forward.

1. Product development:
   - The U.S. FDA approves 5 mg Actonel in 2000 for use in the prevention and treatment of postmenopausal osteoporosis.
   - The company introduces a number of innovative new products, including Crest Whitestrips, Pampers Bibsters, Charmin Freshmates, Eukanuba Dental Defense, and Torengos.

2. Mergers and acquisitions:
   - The company acquires global hair color and hair care product leader Clairol from Bristol-Myers Squibb in 2001.
   - The company acquires Wella AG in September 2003.

**Results of the 2000s.** Although it is too soon to draw any conclusions about the first full decade of the new century, it is clear that after three years, the corporation continued to struggle to deliver new revenue growth. The average rate of revenue growth for the first three years of the new century was a meager 1.86 percent (see Figure 5-12). The corporation also delivered negative year-over-year growth in 4 of the first 12 quarters of the new century. After a record-breaking year in 1999, earnings experienced a significant drop in 2000 and 2001 before rebounding in 2002.

| CATEGORY | AMOUNT |
| --- | --- |
| Net Revenue in 2000 | $39,951 |
| Net Revenue in 2003 | $40,238 |
| Net Income in 2000 | $3,542 |
| Net Income in 2003 | $4,352 |
| Average Rate of Revenue Growth 2000s | 1.86% |
| Average Rate of Earnings Growth 2000s | 11.60% |
| Average Gross Margin in 2000s | 9.04% |

FIGURE 5-12 Procter & Gamble financial results, 2000–2003 (in millions of USD).

**Checking in with the Graduates.** The graduates from the Harvard Classes of 1950, 1960, 1970, 1980, 1990, and 2000 certainly all had experienced quite different fictitious careers at one of the world's great companies. Figure 5-13 shows that timing is everything when it comes to shaping the typical 40-year career. Abel's experience of riding the crest of a wave to the top and just beyond does not at all resemble the ride that Fox experiences before her retirement in 2039. Only Abel, Baker, and Charlie can reminisce about the old days when the rate of revenue growth was barreling skyward. After Charlie's Class of 1970, no other class has experienced a decade when the rate of revenue growth was increasing on average.

Delta came to Cincinnati haunted by the "curse of the Class of 1980," the first class of the first post-World War II era when the rate of revenue growth stopped increasing and started decreasing. Echo came to the corporation at an even lower point than Delta, and Fox started her career when revenue growth rates were less than 2 percent. Compare that to Charlie's first decade when the rate of revenue growth topped 13 percent. What can Fox expect over the remaining 30 years of her career? Is there anything that could reverse the ever-decreasing rate of revenue growth at the corporation?

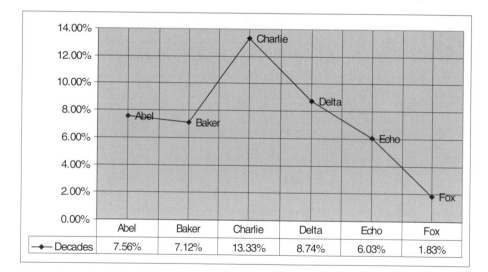

| | Abel | Baker | Charlie | Delta | Echo | Fox |
|---|---|---|---|---|---|---|
| Decades | 7.56% | 7.12% | 13.33% | 8.74% | 6.03% | 1.83% |

FIGURE 5-13     Procter & Gamble rate of revenue growth when our graduates started working. Source: Moody's (Mergent) Industrial Manuals.

Both the conditions and the expectations inside the corporation have changed over time. It is the conditions that lead the change and therefore establish new expectations. When Abel started at the corporation, there was no expectation to deliver double-digit revenue growth. However, after reaching that level of growth consistently through parts of the 1960s and all of the 1970s, expectations changed.

During the 1950s, Procter & Gamble delivered double-digit revenue growth in 3 out of 10 years, and only 1 out of 10 in the 1960s. However, in the 1970s, the corporation experienced double-digit growth 8 out of 10 years, and that performance established an expectation in the minds of many executives that this was the level of performance they could expect going forward. In fact, those expectations were fulfilled half of the time in the 1980s when the corporation delivered double-digit growth in 5 out of 10 years. However, even as the expectation for that level of growth remained, the conditions of the market changed and in many categories began to approach saturation.

From 1980 to 2000, a widening gap formed between expectations and results. Although many in the Classes of 1950, 1960, and 1970 expected growth to continue in the 1980s, that was not at all the perspective or expectation of the Classes of 1980, 1990, or 2000. In some ways because of this perception, it's as if Abel, Baker, and Charlie worked for a different company than Delta, Echo, and Fox.

## INVESTING $10,000 IN PROCTER & GAMBLE

If each of our graduates invested $10,000 in Procter & Gamble on their first day of work, each one of them would have made a wise investment. But without question, Abel would be the happiest of the bunch. His original investment of $10,000 on July 1, 1950 would have multiplied more than 800 times—or nearly $160,000 a year for 53 years! Even though Baker's original investment topped $1.5 million by 2003, it still pales in comparison to Abel, averaging only $36,000 a year for 43 years.

|  | ABEL | BAKER | CHARLIE | DELTA | ECHO | FOX |
|---|---|---|---|---|---|---|
| Original Investment Date | July 1, 1950 $10,000 | July 1, 1960 $10,000 | July 1, 1970 $10,000 | July 1, 1980 $10,000 | July 1, 1990 $10,000 | July 1, 2000 $10,000 |
| Value on June 30, 2003 | $8,442,324 | $1,539,736 | $743,448 | $367,074 | $52,657 | $16,791 |

Source: Procter & Gamble Investor Relations

## THE LAW OF LIMITATIONS

As much as we want to believe that there is no limit to the sky, the realities of the business world suggest otherwise. Although most don't believe that revenue growth will ever permanently flatten, even if it did they are comforted by the fact that gains in productivity will always be able to help a corporation deliver earnings growth that Wall Street expects. Or can it?

With no new sector on the horizon to cause both consumers and businesses to add to their current spending levels, pressure to cut costs and increase productivity is more intense than ever. With such an unrelenting focus on generating benefits from the cost side, it's possible that there might be limits to productivity as well. If there are limits to revenue growth due to saturation, and there are limits to productivity gains due to nearly two decades of incessant pressure to deliver more and more efficiency, then there will ultimately be limits to the ability to deliver earnings growth. The law of limitations suggests that there are limits to everything, and that unless additional means of accretive revenue generation can be developed soon, there is no plausible reason to expect earnings to grow ad infinitum.

# II THE NEW ECONOMIC REALITY

There are signs in every sector of the economy that suggest a fundamental plateau has been reached as the result of a century of selling the maximum number of products to the maximum number of people who consume the maximum amount in the maximum number of countries.

In the best of scenarios, rates of growth have greatly slowed while mounting pressure to deliver increased earnings has intensified. The new economic reality suggests that we have effectively killed demand, and we have been living with that reality for some time now by shifting our strategies away from revenue that we can't grow to costs that we can cut.

How does a mature economy move forward with little demand driving little output growth and at the same time deliver increased earnings results? Business is anything but usual in the *new economic reality*.

# 6 THE LAW OF LIMITATIONS

No matter how much we want to improve, there can be natural forces that prevent us from doing so. At the 1984 Summer Olympics in Los Angeles, Dietmar Mogenburg of West Germany cleared 2.34 meters and won the high jump gold medal. Sixteen years later at the 2000 Summer Olympics in Sydney, Russian high jumper Sergei Kliugin cleared the exact same height of 2.34 meters and took home the gold.

If Kliugin was a vice president of sales at a major corporation, and his sales performance in 2000 equaled that of the vice president of sales in 1984, he would be fired. Just because athletes are not always able to continually outperform their predecessors doesn't mean that they still aren't the best in the world at what they do. One of the major differences between sports and business is that in business we expect to break a world record every year. Fortunately for Kliugin, Olympic officials recognized his performance for what it was—the best that anyone in the world could muster—and was subsequently awarded the highest honor in sport.

## PERFORMANCE LIMITATIONS

There are limits to what we as humans can achieve over the course of a lifetime, and often performance improvements come in smaller and smaller increments as we age. After all, we are only young once. Not even Lance Armstrong can keep winning the Tour de France indefinitely. Businesses are no different. They are living, breathing organisms, and they have performance limitations just like humans.

More often than not, however, our expectation is that a corporation can grow indefinitely, especially revenues. This is why we look at lackluster sales as a corporate failure, and we affix blame to individuals or market conditions that prevented us from meeting our goal. Sometimes meeting our goal is simply not possible. Our expectations often challenge the laws of limitations. We can want a human to high jump 5 meters, but it is unlikely to ever happen in our lifetime.

The fundamental slowdown in GDP as well as corporate revenue growth suggests that such "failures" are far less about the lack of ability, energy, creativity, intelligence, or dedication of the CEO, the vice president of sales, the vice president of marketing, or the advertising agency, and much more about customers reaching a point of consumption saturation. If anything, corporate management of the second half of the 20th century did their jobs so well that we might be approaching volume limits. After all, corporate managers did create the single largest commercial market in the world in the United States in a relatively short period of time.

Now, here we are well into a new century and we must begin to consider that it is not so much that we have reached sales capacity as much as we have reached consumption capacity. For the first time in history, we must consider the possibility that our customers can't drive any more cars, can't live in any more houses, and can't eat any more Big Macs. The evidence undeniably supports this assertion, yet few are willing to acknowledge it. In fact, many are in denial because of the unrealistic expectations, largely set by outsiders who are stuck in the past and look at performance as a matter of talent and hard work. If it were only that simple.

We are able to accept the prospect of limitations when we deal with universes that have a fixed capacity. We understand that there is a limit to the number of people who can watch a baseball game in Yankee Stadium or a concert at Carnegie Hall. We know that once the seating capacity is reached, the venue is sold out. On the other hand, it is much harder for us to accept that there could be limits to the number of people in the world who will drink Coca-Cola Classic simply because the universe of prospects is so vast. A shrinking global village, however, is greatly reducing the number of people in the world who have yet to decide whether or not to drink Coke.

## ONE SIZE, 176 STYLES

Remember the days when one pair of sneakers was all we needed for a trip to the playground for a full day of every activity under the sun?

In 1950, anyone owning a simple pair of rubber and canvas sneakers had the good fortune of enjoying a shoe that did it all. Tennis anyone? Let me get my sneakers. Want to jog, play baseball, basketball, football, soccer, skateboard, or just go to the movies? One shoe fit all occasions back in the day. But not so today. The specialty footwear market has literally exploded in recent years with a shoe for every occasion and an occasion for every shoe.

A quick tour of Nike.com reveals that the mega-shoe manufacturer offers 15 major categories of shoes from running to basketball to just plain old walking. Over 200 styles of men's and women's shoes in all. Figure 6-1 focuses in on just one of those categories—men's and women's running shoes. These categories are further broken down into seven subcategories that are all listed in Figure 6-1.

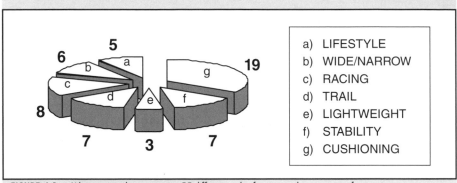

a) LIFESTYLE
b) WIDE/NARROW
c) RACING
d) TRAIL
e) LIGHTWEIGHT
f) STABILITY
g) CUSHIONING

**FIGURE 6-1**   Nike running shoe category: 55 different styles for men and women, just for running.
Source: Nike.com.

If none of the options in the running shoe category suit your fancy, then you can select from one of almost 200 different styles in Nike's Basketball, Jordan, Cross Training, Tennis, Lifestyle, Soccer, Golf, Walking, or Outdoor categories.

The number of categories, subcategories and styles for many consumer products has been segmented and subsegmented to appeal to every conceivable taste since 1950. The days of one-shoe-fits-all-activities are long over—especially considering the explosion of extreme sports in recent years. While continued fragmentation in consumer categories might offer an opportunity for companies such as Vans or Etnies shoes to grab a piece of a growing niche, it's difficult to imagine that consumers will simply add new categories without dropping others. In the case of athletic footwear, the days of owning one pair of high white Converse sneakers are certainly over. But how much more can the expansion envelope be pushed without experiencing a significant trade out effect—where a pair of Vans replaces a pair of Nikes? ■

## EVEN YOUR OWN HYPE SAYS YOU'RE MAXED

Sometimes we are so used to reaching higher and higher that we don't even realize that our own hype is beginning to underscore the fact that we are everywhere, selling everything to everybody on the planet. What surely are efforts intended to highlight strength, some corporations reinforce their omnipotence when they tout incredible stats about their own brands. For example, it sometimes is difficult to figure out who a corporation, such as Procter & Gamble, is trying to impress when it promotes the vast reach of its products:

- *Charmin*—More than 50 million households in North America squeeze the Charmin every day.
- *Tide*—This laundry soap cleans more than 32 million loads of laundry every day.
- *Bounty*—Used by more than 50 million households in North America every day.
- *Pampers*—More than 30 million babies experience the comfort and dryness of Pampers every day.
- *Crest*—This toothpaste brings a beautiful smile to more than 150 million faces every day.
- *Downy*—This fabric softener softens more than 21 million loads of laundry every day.
- *Pringles*—People pop 275 million of them every day.
- *Folgers*—Americans drink 85 million cups a day.

When your press releases and annual reports focus on superlatives that describe your widespread distribution and in some cases world domination of product categories, it certainly reinforces your success as a marketer. However, the sheer size of sales in virtually every commercial country on the planet unwittingly calls attention to the fact that you might be approaching global sales limits.

## FEW CATEGORIES, FEWER CONSUMERS

At the beginning of the 20th century there were far fewer product categories than there are today, as covered in Chapters 2 and 3. There was also an enormous disparity between social classes around 1900. The rich participated as consumers in many more categories than did the working class.

Figure 6-2 lists some of the major product categories circa 1900, and identifies those categories in which the rich participated, but the working class did not. At the turn of the 20th century, only the rich owned cars, homes, telephones, radios, or phonographs. Only the rich enjoyed the luxury of electric light, indoor plumbing, a college education, and butter with every meal. The working class essentially existed to serve the rich, perhaps getting a glimpse of the good life before returning to their tenements or shantytowns.

| CATEGORY | THE RICH | THE WORKING CLASS |
|----------|----------|-------------------|
| Automobile | Yes | No |
| House | Yes | No |
| Telephone | Yes | No |
| Phonograph | Yes | No |
| Radio | Yes | No |
| Butter | Yes | No |
| College Education | Yes | No |
| Electric light | Yes | No |
| Indoor Plumbing | Yes | No |

FIGURE 6-2    The *haves* and the *have nots*. Circa 1900. Source: Customer Share Group LLC.

However, over the course of the 20th century much of that changed. The ability to produce goods in mass quantities at lower costs closed the gap between what was affordable and what was not for a class whose wages were also on the rise. The rich were still rich, but categories that had been exclusive to them for decades increasingly came within reach of the average working-class family's means.

Although the rich might own a $75,000 Mercedes-Benz at the turn of the 21st century, those in the working class that had broadened into a middle class also owned a car of some type. Figure 6-3 identifies the same categories that existed at the beginning of 20th century plus a few more, all of which are within the means of the working class. Most classes now participate in categories of products that were considered luxuries 100 years ago. Homes, telephones, phonographs (stereos), college educations, televisions, VCRs, personal computers, and cell phones. It's difficult to identify a category that is exclusive to the rich today.

| CATEGORY | THE RICH | THE WORKING CLASS |
|---|---|---|
| Automobile | Yes | Yes |
| House | Yes | Yes |
| Telephone | Yes | Yes |
| Phonograph | Yes | Yes |
| Radio | Yes | Yes |
| Butter | Yes | Yes |
| College Education | Yes | Yes |
| Electric Lights | Yes | Yes |
| Indoor Plumbing | Yes | Yes |
| Television | Yes | Yes |
| VCR | Yes | Yes |
| Personal Computer | Yes | Yes |
| Cell Phone | Yes | Yes |

FIGURE 6-3  The haves and the haves, circa 2000. Source: Customer Share Group LLC.

Over the course of the 20th century, more consumers became participants in more categories than at any other time in history. Although new innovations will always be introduced, it is unlikely that the world will ever again witness this level of first-time linkage of new consumers to new categories ever again.

Once a new product category becomes widely available for an extended period of time, it will attract its natural level of consumer participation. Sometimes the level of participation is nearly 100 percent of the population, as with telephones or toothpaste. Other times, forces will dictate that the ultimate size of a universe of consumers will be much smaller. Some of these forces relate to access, some of the forces are financial, and some of the forces that restrict the size of a consumer universe simply can't—and never will—be explained.

## THE LAW OF LIMITATIONS

Why are there 3.2 million subscribers to *Sports Illustrated*? Why are there 138 million movie tickets sold every month in the United States? Why do 150 million consumers use Crest? Why are 16 million cars and trucks sold in the United States every year? Why isn't the figure 20 million or 10 million, for that matter? Why are these relatively unrestricted universes the size that they are?

These are not easy questions to answer. There is no precise formula for why *Sports Illustrated* has a circulation of 3.2 million. Would the folks over at Time Warner prefer it to be 10 million subscriptions? Of course they would. However, over a period of time, *Sports Illustrated* has found its natural universe level. As subscriptions rapidly grew during the 1960s and 1970s, it would have been impossible to guess the ultimate size of the universe.

Certainly, Time Warner officials can discount the cover price and try to unnaturally boost subscriptions to 4 or 5 million. However, the direct marketing scientists at Time, Inc. know what they are doing. If more subscribers were willing to pay full price for the magazine, then the number of subscriptions would naturally go up. The universe of sports fans has spoken and the natural level of the magazine's universe has settled at approximately 3 million and has been there since the early 1990s.

As the saying goes, water finds its own level. Like water, every consumer universe also finds its own level. After some period of time—ordinarily between 20 and 25 years, or about one generation's time—every new consumer category finds its own natural size. This is not to say that the universe won't continue to grow—it probably will—but it will grow at a decreasing rate of growth until it stops growing altogether. The reason is that there are known and unknown forces that dictate the size of a universe. Collectively, these forces are the elements of *the law of limitations:*

### The size of every consumer universe is limited because:

- There are a limited number of people in the world.
- Not all people have access to all products or services.
- Some with access can't afford all products or services.
- Some who have access and can afford the products or services might not have a taste for them.
- Those who have access, can afford, and have a taste for certain products or services establish a limited frequency of consumption.
- Those who have access, can afford, have a taste, and have established a frequency of consumption of certain products or services also establish a limited volume of consumption.

After a particular consumer universe exists over at least a generation's time, then it will arrive at its natural and relative size, and its future natural growth becomes more a function of population growth and less a function of influencing frequency and volume.

At the point when the natural size of a universe is established, three important new dynamics come into play relative to the profitable mining of the universe:

1. *Returns from marketing investments gradually diminish.* With each passing year, the return from marketing investments diminishes and, therefore, requires a corporation to determine an accurate means of measuring ROI going forward.
2. *Demand fades and pricing becomes elastic.* In an effort to help maintain volume levels, prices trend down or even become commoditized.
3. *Cost efficiencies gain in importance.* To preserve profit levels, the ability to continually reduce costs becomes more and more important. However, productivity gains associated with the manufacture and delivery of a product or service are also limited.

In short, there are limits to everything: unit sales, pricing, marketing impact, and cost reductions. This is why it is imperative to fully understand the age of the revenue stream. Understanding that a revenue stream is well past the top, relative to its highest rate of unit or sales growth, can help provide a much clearer roadmap for the management and maintenance of the revenue stream. Such understanding can help corporations avoid unnecessarily high levels of spending and shape proactive plans for more appropriate levels of marketing spending, pricing levels, staffing levels, and cost-reduction initiatives.

## A Case Study in Growth: McDonald's Corporation

Founded by Ray Kroc in 1955, McDonald's is the world's leading food service retailer with more than 31,000 restaurants in 118 countries. McDonald's Golden Arches became an icon the world over, serving billions and billions of customers on virtually every continent. In 1965, the company went public and established a stellar sales track record through the 1960s and 1970s. In 1985, MCD became one of the Dow 30 component corporations.

## GROWING THE CORPORATION:
## THE SIX MARKET FORCES

In earlier chapters, we discussed the four major growth strategies that corporations employ to naturally and unnaturally grow revenues and profits: product development and marketing, domestic expansion, international expansion, and mergers and acquisitions. There are also six major external market forces that are, for the most part, out of the control of the corporation. These forces, however, impose significant influence in dictating the ultimate size of a consumer universe that develops over at least a generation's time.

**Population.** Starting with the population of the world, and then continent, country, state, county, and finally city, Figure 6-4 identifies that even if everyone in the world ate at McDonald's, the number of customers is limited, and would be no more than 6.3 billion. McDonald's started its miraculous story in 1955 with the opening of the first McDonald's in Des Plaines, Illinois. Today, the population of Des Plaines is around 59,000, or about 1 percent of Cook County's population of 5.4 million, which includes the city of Chicago. The universe of potential customers for all 31,000 restaurants today is 6.3 billion. However, for a single McDonald's location, the universe is, obviously, significantly less than that.

**Access.** Now operating in 118 countries with more than 31,000 restaurants, access to McDonald's has never been greater. Aggressive expansion plans right from the beginning helped McDonald's come within reach of an ever-increasing number of prospects around the world.

Figure 6-5 illustrates the dramatic worldwide expansion of restaurants from 1970 to 2000. McDonald's added nearly 5,000 new restaurants during the 1970s, and then added 5,000 more in the 1980s. However, in the 1990s, McDonald's expansion efforts greatly picked up speed, more than tripling the increases in both the 1970s and 1980s by adding nearly 17,000 new locations in just 10 years.

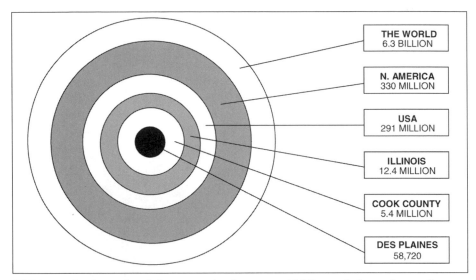

FIGURE 6-4    Population is limited: Maximum number of prospects is 6.3 billion people. Source: Customer Share Group LLC.

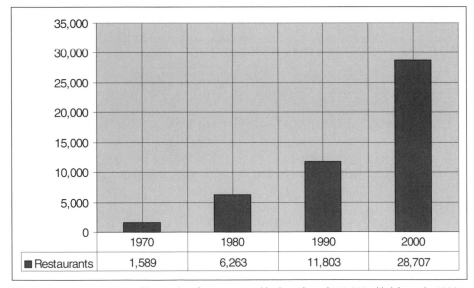

FIGURE 6-5    Access to McDonald's: Number of restaurants worldwide, with nearly 17,000 added during the 1990s. Source: McDonald's Corporation.

The number of new McDonald's locations grew almost 50 percent faster than sales in the 1990s, a common problem for retailers of all types that ultimately leads to serious over-capacity issues. However, even with a record number of restaurants in close to two-thirds of the world's countries, there are still hundreds of millions, if not billions, of people who do not have access to McDonald's because they live in remote parts of the world. A certain percentage of the population does not have access to McDonald's.

**Affordability.** Even though prospective customers might have access to McDonald's, there are billions who cannot afford to pay for food at any price. It is estimated that more than a billion people suffer from hunger and malnutrition in the world today, including an estimated 1 in 10 households in the United States that are either living with hunger or are at risk of hunger, according to the Bread for the World Institute. A certain percentage of the population cannot afford to eat at McDonald's.

**Taste.** Obviously, personal preferences vary greatly, and not all of the 6.3 billion people in the world or 291 million people in the United States or even 59,000 in Des Plaines, Illinois, all have an appetite for burgers and fries. Even though there might be millions who have access and can afford to dine at McDonald's, some people will always prefer a different option. A certain percentage of the population decides not to eat at McDonald's.

**Frequency.** Those who do choose McDonald's as a meal option establish their own pattern of consumption frequency. Some percentage of the population eats at McDonald's at frequencies ranging from once a day to once a year.

Figure 6-6 illustrates the mix of McDonald's customers based on the number of times that they visit the "Golden Arches" over a certain period of time. Some customers might prefer to eat there on a daily basis. These customers represent an intensely loyal yet relatively small group at the very top of the customer segmentation pyramid. Other customers might drift in and out of the customer segmentation pyramid on a monthly basis or even less frequently.

Once frequency habits are established, they become hardened over time, and it becomes very difficult for McDonald's—or any other company in the food service industry—to change those set patterns of behavior. Frequency, then, is one of the dynamics that help drive the business model.

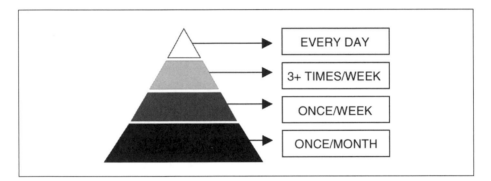

FIGURE 6-6    Customer segmentation pyramid: Universe of McDonald's customers based on frequency.

**Volume.** Volume is the other important dynamic driving the business model for corporations such as McDonald's. This variable is tied to the average number of items—or average order size—that McDonald's customers purchase at each visit (see Figure 6-7). Although the number of items will certainly vary from time to time, volume habits also become established and hardened over time.

Often, volume or cross-sell promotions focus on motivating the customer to purchase another item or two, usually at a very low price. The impact of this strategy is twofold: It usually generates incremental dollars for a temporary period of time, and because the add-on product is usually a low-priced item, this can actually suppress the average order size for a temporary period of time.

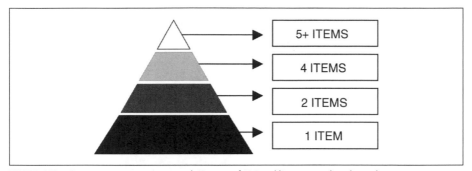

**FIGURE 6-7**    Customer segmentation pyramid: Universe of McDonald's customers based on volume.

Figure 6-8 is designed to illustrate how frequency of visit and volume (number of items) combine to create a variety of different levels of customer contribution. On one end of the scale, there are the infrequent visitors who might come in once a week to purchase one item, resulting in a contribution of $2 for the week. On the other end of the spectrum, there is the five-time-weekly visitor who purchases an average of five items on each visit. The latter contributes $50 a week to the corporation and skews toward the top of the customer segmentation pyramid.

|  | 1 ITEM PER VISIT | 2 ITEMS PER VISIT | 3 ITEMS PER VISIT | 4 ITEMS PER VISIT | 5 ITEMS PER VISIT |
|---|---|---|---|---|---|
| **5 VISITS PER WEEK** | $10.00 | $20.00 | $30.00 | $40.00 | $50.00 |
| **4 VISITS PER WEEK** | $8.00 | $16.00 | $24.00 | $32.00 | $40.00 |
| **3 VISITS PER WEEK** | $6.00 | $12.00 | $18.00 | $24.00 | $30.00 |
| **2 VISITS PER WEEK** | $4.00 | $8.00 | $12.00 | $16.00 | $20.00 |
| **1 VISIT PER WEEK** | $2.00 | $4.00 | $6.00 | $8.00 | $10.00 |

**FIGURE 6-8**    Weekly customer contribution matrix: Example of frequency/volume combinations. Source: Customer Share Group LLC.

McDonald's challenge now is to try to motivate more frequent visits and sell more items per visit, but it won't be easy. Theirs is not so much an issue of marketing as it is an issue of consumption. The frequency and volume variables create a veritable matrix of customer types for McDonald's, but the problem is this:

- McDonald's universe of consumers is relatively established.
- Consumer frequency habits are relatively established.
- Consumer volume habits are relatively established.

After being in business for close to 50 years, McDonald's is a maturing business with maturing business metrics. Its current business model essentially calls for it to generate growth in three basic ways: expanding retail locations, motivating customers to increase the frequency of their visits, and motivating customers to increase the volume or number of items purchased each time they visit. This strategy is becoming harder and harder for McDonald's to pull off. In fact, in 2003 though continuing to build new locations, McDonald's closed more than 700 of its stores, a move that perhaps signals a shift in its growth strategy by eliminating underperforming sites.

## THE LONG-TERM BUSINESS CONSEQUENCES

Even though it might be difficult for us to accept, there are limits to what the human race can consume and, therefore, what businesses can sell. We more often think in terms of the population of the planet—more than 6 billion men, women, and children—as an endless universe of new prospects just waiting to hear about the benefits of our products and services. It is truly hard for us to think that we would ever run out of prospects in a sea of billions of consumers. The *law of limitations* suggests that the world is a finite marketplace, even with the prospect of mining sales from 1.3 billion people in China.

The *law of limitations* challenges the very premise of ad infinitum growth, and suggests that there could be limits to the primary elements that drive any successful public company:

- Revenue growth is limited.
- Productivity growth is limited.
- Earnings growth is limited.

There was a time, not that long ago, when it would have been inconceivable to think that we would reach the limit for new car sales each year in the United States. The fact is that domestic revenue growth for many established public companies is all but over, masked by gains from international sales, retail expansion, and wholesale acquisitions.

The business-to-business (B2B) world, for the most part, has always had to deal with the reality of having limited universes of prospective customers. There are often a finite—and small—number of prospective customers for B2B companies. For example, those B2B companies that sell to the energy industry may only have a handful of major customers. For these companies, the focus is not on the acquisition of new customers at all, but on selling many different products and services to a limited number of prospects.

The business-to-consumer (B2C) world, of course, deals largely with many millions of unidentified customers, marketing to the masses one brand at a time through media that delivers millions of unidentified prospects. However, the overwhelming majority of corporations have largely captured whatever market share they will ever capture. Most corporations have yet to proactively mine enormous sales and profits from the thoughtful cross selling of their portfolio of brands. The reason is simple: They have never had to. Now they do.

## REVENUE LIMITATIONS

From a revenue perspective, we are beginning to experience limits to volume and price for the first time in modern history. Some industries are experiencing demand inelasticity that might not be temporary. Corporations that successfully launch and compete in a free market typically enjoy a number of years when the rate of revenue growth consistently trends up—usually over a generation's time.

Figure 6-9 shows that the rate of revenue growth for McDonald's peaked in the 1970s—roughly around 1975— when growth rates were consistently around 30 percent. However, since the 1970s, the rate of growth has been dwindling— down to an average 12.79 percent in the 1980s, and 8.61 percent in the 1990s. For the first three years in the new century, the rate of revenue growth for McDonald's has slowed to an average of just over 5 percent.

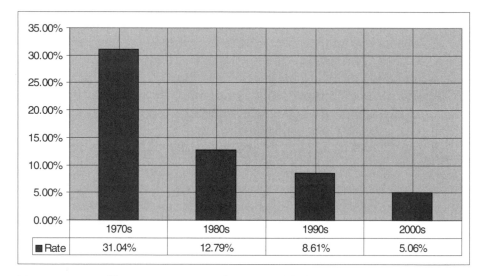

**FIGURE 6-9**   McDonald's Corporation average rate of revenue growth by decade, 1970s–2000s (inflation-adjusted). Source: Moody's (Mergent) Industrial Manuals.

At first blush, a 5 percent annual rate of revenue growth does not look too bad in a sluggish economy. However, at least some of that growth came from aggressive expansion of adding nearly 17,000 new locations during the 1990s. Figure 6-10 provides a different picture of McDonald's performance over the last decade. The corporation's average annual sale per restaurant has consistently eroded since 1993, from a high of $1.67 million in 1993 to a low of $1.33 million in 2002. This declining trend suggests that McDonald's is now staring saturation straight in the face, and the company is at a fork in the road relative to its near-term health. Does McDonald's continue down the "make it up in volume" road by continuing to add to its portfolio as the world's largest food service retailer, or does it take a page from Cott Corporation's Frank Weise and pull back on the reins by shrinking MCD back to a healthier bottom line?

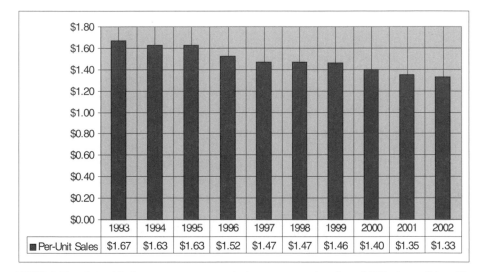

| | 1993 | 1994 | 1995 | 1996 | 1997 | 1998 | 1999 | 2000 | 2001 | 2002 |
|---|---|---|---|---|---|---|---|---|---|---|
| ■ Per-Unit Sales | $1.67 | $1.63 | $1.63 | $1.52 | $1.47 | $1.47 | $1.46 | $1.40 | $1.35 | $1.33 |

**FIGURE 6-10**  McDonald's Corporation average annual sales per restaurant (in millions of USD). Source: McDonald's Corporation 2002 Financial Report.

## PRODUCTIVITY LIMITATIONS

Productivity has always been a fundamental element in raising the standard of living in any culture. Economic optimists point specifically to productivity gains as one of the primary reasons for healthy stock market gains in the 1990s, and fully expect that gains from productivity can and will drive sustainable corporate profit well into the future. However, there is much active debate about exactly how productivity increases have been achieved over the last 20 years, and how much of it can be attributed to new technologies versus wholesale layoffs and the subsequent squeezing of the surviving rank and file.

At least some of the productivity gains that have been realized over the last decade or more are actually being served up by overworked management who absorb those necessary functions that laid-off workers leave behind. Most salaried employees have not seen a 40-hour workweek since the 1980s. Are we really more productive or are we systematically demoralizing and deconstructing a shrinking infrastructure for the sake of earnings?

Because the various sources of productivity are hard to measure, this debate will no doubt continue. However, the undeniable facts suggest that, even though productivity has gained in importance as a driver of earnings growth in recent years, its rate of growth has concurrently dwindled. In fact, contrary to popular belief, the average rate of productivity has actually declined in every decade since World War II. This raises serious questions about the long-term prospects of continued productivity gains as a reliable earnings driver. Even U.S. Federal Reserve Bank Chairman Alan Greenspan cautioned that "the growth of productivity cannot increase indefinitely." In other words, productivity has its limits.

Figure 6-11 shows the decline in productivity growth rates since World War II, and in recent years have been averaging close to 1 percent. The trend over more than a 50-year period is clear: Although productivity might continue to grow—just like revenue—it will continue to grow at ever-decreasing rates of growth.

Of course, no company can reduce its costs to $0, and it will always cost something to produce, distribute, and sell happy meals. With limited revenue and productivity growth on the horizon, it follows that earnings, too, could be in for a tough decade.

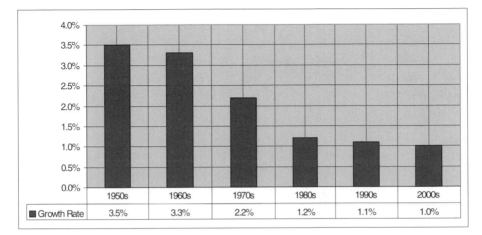

**FIGURE 6-11**    U.S. economy productivity growth rates by decade, 1950s–2000s. Source: U.S. Bureau of Labor Statistics.

## EARNINGS LIMITATIONS

For the first time in history, the concept of a corporation reaching its full potential to generate revenue is now real. Just look at Kraft Foods over the last 10 years. As discussed in Chapter 1, absent the Nabisco acquisition in 2001, Kraft Foods has shown almost no growth since 1995. With the rate of revenue growth at the lowest levels since the 1970s, and productivity rates at the lowest levels in more than 40 years, long-term earnings growth might be at risk at Kraft.

Although it is still too early to tell, some of the mega-aggressive growth strategies of the recent past might ultimately come back to haunt some that are having a difficult time delivering earnings growth as much bigger corporations. In 2002, for example, McDonald's posted net income of $893 million, less than the $959 million in net income in 1992 with 18,000 fewer restaurants.

The frenetic retail expansion and acquisition fest of the 1990s made a lot of people around the periphery wealthy. However, now these super-sized corporations are beginning to show signs of stress and strain. Historically, revenue and earnings grew at rates more consistent with each other. Today, however, earnings are growing much faster than revenues in most cases. For example, after a fairly even split between revenue and earnings growth for each quarter in the year 2000, General Electric earnings grew more than 12 percentage points faster than revenue for each quarter of 2001 and 2002. Can such a gap be sustained indefinitely?

It is not at all uncommon for corporations today to announce earnings growth that significantly outpaces revenue growth. Figure 6-12 illustrates what has to happen for a corporation to consistently deliver earnings growth that outpaces revenue growth by 10 percentage points over a 10-year period. This fictitious corporation starts off in 2004 with $10 billion in net revenue and net income of $1 billion and a net margin of 10.0 percent. To maintain 12 percent earnings growth each year for 10 years, while receiving only a marginal benefit of 2 percent revenue growth, this corporation must more than double its net margin over the 10-year period. Viewed from another perspective, the corporation must essentially hold expenses at the same level for 10 years.

| YEAR | 2004 | 2005 | 2006 | 2007 | 2008 |
|---|---|---|---|---|---|
| Net Revenue | $10,000 | $10,200 | $10,404 | $10,612 | $10,824 |
| Cogs Op-Expenses Taxes | $9,000 | $9,080 | $9,150 | $9,207 | $9,250 |
| Net Income | $1,000 | $1,120 | $1,254 | $1,405 | $1,574 |
| Net Margin | 10.0% | 11.0% | 12.1% | 13.2% | 14.5% |
| YEAR | 2009 | 2010 | 2011 | 2012 | 2013 |
| Net Revenue | $11,041 | $11,262 | $11,487 | $11,717 | $11,951 |
| Cogs Op-Expenses Taxes | $9,279 | $9,288 | $9,276 | $9,241 | $9,178 |
| Net Income | $1,762 | $1,974 | $2,211 | $2,476 | $2,773 |
| Net Margin | 16.0% | 17.9% | 19.2% | 21.1% | 23.2% |

FIGURE 6-12    Earnings growth at 12 percent and revenue growth at 2 percent: Can you more than double your net margin over the next 10 years? Source: Customer Share Group LLC.

Most corporations would simply be unable to transform their business from one that yields a 10 percent net margin to one that yields a 23 percent net margin in 10 years. This scenario is designed to shed light on the difficulties corporations will face if maintaining a significant gap between the rate of earnings growth and the rate of revenue growth. Declining sales rates will only serve to put additional pressure on management to squeeze even more productivity out of the corporation—a necessary but limited proposition. Relying heavily on productivity as the primary earnings driver must be viewed as a short-term fix on the way to creating new revenue growth. Without such growth, earnings of any sort will ultimately be at risk.

The whole purpose of the equity markets is to provide a mechanism to generate investment capital to corporations to help them grow. If the corporation grows its profits, the price of the stock will rise and shareowners will realize a return on their investment. This formula has worked—more or less—for more than a century. However, as long as earnings remain the priority yardstick in measuring corporate health without acknowledging a serious decline in the rate of revenue growth, ultimately the corporation will reach its natural limits, unable to deliver on unrealistic expectations.

## INNOVATION SATURATION

One could argue that McDonald's Corporation has done everything in its power to grow—and it has greatly succeeded in that respect. Along the way, however, it ran into some natural roadblocks that are slowing it down and preventing it from achieving perpetual growth. The *law of limitations* was one of those roadblocks that put limits on revenue growth, productivity gains, and ultimately on earnings.

Another important law of microeconomics that impacts the life of a corporation is the *law of innovation saturation*. This law governs how long a new product, a new business, or a new line extension will experience a trend of increasing rate of revenue growth before reaching its peak. After reaching its maximum rate of revenue growth, the trend starts to decline—a decline that is almost impossible to stop.

# 7 THE LAW OF INNOVATION SATURATION

In 1954, one of the most celebrated products of the 20th century was born when the very first issue of *Sports Illustrated* rolled off the presses and into the hands of more than 450,000 subscribers during its first year. By the end of the 1950s, the popular sports weekly's subscriptions had doubled, and it was well on its way to becoming one of the most successful magazine launches in history.

Over the next 15 years, *Sports Illustrated* subscriptions grew at an astounding rate, doubling again by the end of the 1960s. This breakneck pace began to slow in the 1970s, but still managed to add an additional 400,000, reaching 2,274,819 subscriptions through 1979. The Time, Inc. juggernaut continued to grow in the 1980s, and enjoyed a short burst of accelerated growth during the decade. After briefly approaching the 3.5 million mark, *Sports Illustrated* finally settled at around 3.2 million subscriptions, a level it has maintained since the early 1990s.

During this truly spectacular run, the publication reached two important milestones and probably didn't even know it. First, sometime during the 1960s, the rate at which *Sports Illustrated* subscriptions were growing stopped increasing and started decreasing. To be sure, *Sports Illustrated* continued to add subscriptions to its total, but at an ever-decreasing rate of growth after the 1960s. It reached the second milestone sometime in the 1990s, when the subscription total actually retreated slightly to a more natural level, both from an economic standpoint (the business) and from a demand standpoint (the consumer).

The significance is this: Just as water finds its own level, *Sports Illustrated* found its own natural consumption universe at around 3.2 million subscriptions, pleasing a relatively fixed number of sports fans. The reason is that *Sports Illustrated* reached *innovation saturation,* the point at which the natural size of its consumption universe was established. Consumption universes reach maximum size for a number of social and economic reasons. However, the reason *Sports Illustrated's* customer universe has settled at 3.2 million, or approximately 3 percent of all sports fans in the United States, is unclear.

Corporations are convinced that they should be able to lure some percentage of the overwhelming number of consumers who don't eat their burgers or drink their soft drinks to switch brands. With a total prospect universe of 6.3 billion on the planet, surely even the most established of brands can attract new consumers each year.

On the surface, it makes perfect sense, and the eternal optimists at some of the world's leading corporations will, year after year, agree that it can be done. However, at what point does a corporation check its ego and emotions at the door and begin to manage operations, as well as expectations, more closely connected to reality?

## THE SLOWDOWN: SIGN OF FAILURE OR SUCCESS?

The prospect of approaching a fixed or even shrinking universe of unit sales is not the model that students learn in business school. Conventional wisdom instead suggests that the powers that be at Time Warner can convince an even higher percentage of the population to subscribe to its products. After all, converting another 1 percent of sports fans to subscribe to *Sports Illustrated* would push paid subscriptions up over 4 million. However, it is not likely that *Sports Illustrated* will ever grow to a level of 4 or 5 or 10 million subscriptions. Whose fault is that? Shouldn't heads roll at Time Warner?

The fact is this: It is the fault of every great marketer who worked with all the great editors, photographers, circulation directors, and ad directors at Time, Inc. It's also the fault of scores of talented individuals and agencies in the consumer packaged goods industry, the airline industry, and the auto industry who all contributed to maximizing the potential of the innovations in their respective industries. Unfortunately, too many look at a corporation's inability to generate growth in perpetuity as failure when it should be more clinically viewed as success in maximizing the original opportunity.

The corporate world must take stock and realize that the monumental progress made over the last half-century has both expanded penetration and diminished the ability to expand penetration further. Although it's possible that Ford can sell 5 million cars and trucks in the U.S. again, it is now imminently more difficult to do so, first because the auto industry has lost upward momentum, and second because the auto industry has become so masterful at selling its product that cars far outnumber the population of licensed drivers in the United States.

## THE ETERNAL STAIRWAY

As discussed in previous chapters, the most popularly shared view of revenue or unit growth is the *eternal stairway* perspective shown in Figure 7-1. This view graphically displays the upward calculation of revenue or unit growth over a 50-year period.

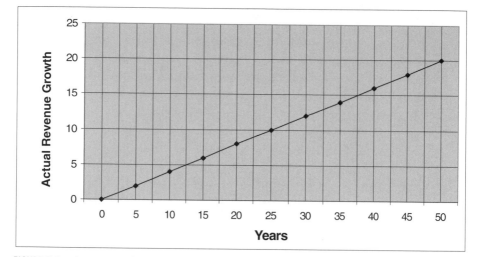

FIGURE 7-1   Revenue growth: Conventional view of a corporation's revenue growth over 50 years. Source: Customer Share Group 2004.

This ever-increasing calculation of revenues or unit sales certainly represents the pattern for most major corporations. This "feel-good" view has lulled some into a false sense of security, leaving the impression that revenue and unit growth can increase forever. Although it's true that revenue and units have increased for most corporations over the last half-century, the eternal stairway perspective often masks an underlying trend that paints an entirely different picture.

## THE INVERTED V

Tracking the rate of revenue growth, on the other hand, can help expose trends and provide a deeper understanding of the relative energy of the revenue source going forward. Figure 7-2 graphically displays the *trend* that revenue and units take when measured on a rate of growth basis. During the early years after the launch of a successful innovation, it enjoys years, even decades, of an up-trending rate of revenue growth.

For many of the successful corporations of the 20th century, this upward trend culminated in the 1960s and 1970s. The point at which the tide turns from an increasing rate of revenue growth to a decreasing rate of revenue growth is known as *innovation saturation*. The pattern when tracking growth rates will form an upside-down or *inverted V*. The rate of growth history of any product, corporation, industry, sector, or even an economy will all track in the shape of an *inverted V*.

As the revenue source of any commercial universe ages, it becomes necessary to take action to supplement or shore up the streams. For example, General Electric took aggressive action in the 1990s by adding tens of billions of dollars in revenue in the form of acquisitions. Fellow Dow Component corporation General Motors instituted increasingly liberal financing terms to boost volume during the early 2000s. As revenue sources continue to age, the overall effectiveness of marketing—particularly the type of marketing that helped drive revenue up the *inverted V*—consistently fades. Like the ocean tide that has turned from flowing *high* to ebbing *low*, it is nearly impossible to stop the forces of this downtrend.

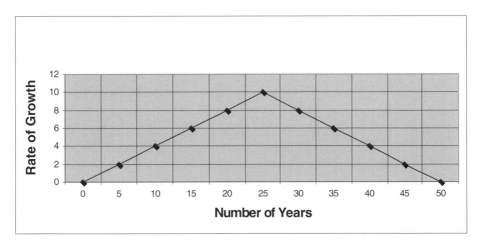

FIGURE 7-2    Rate of revenue growth: Always trends in the shape of *an inverted V*. Source: Customer Share Group 2004.

The *inverted V* can be an effective management tool for the corporation. Many corporations simply cut marketing spending across the board, for example, in difficult economic times. By measuring the age of the revenue stream and its level of maturity since reaching its maximum rate of growth, corporations can develop specific investment formulas based on historical ROI metrics along the downside of the *inverted V*. For example, management might learn that any product that has spent more than 15 years on the down side of this trend benefits little from increased or even sustained marketing investment. Management could then appropriately adjust both human capital and marketing investment from one product to another.

Once *innovation saturation* is reached, the more likely its products and services will compete based on price. Discounting only hastens the decline along the downside of the *inverted V*. The auto industry is a good example of an industry that is competing on the extreme downside of the *inverted V* where price becomes the primary sales and marketing weapon. Pressure to increase volume has created a vicious cycle for the auto industry that results in more and more liberal deals that condition consumers to expect the lowest possible price every time out. What's more, financing deals that are tied to payment terms—such as the popular 60-month term in the auto industry—can actually change consumer-buying patterns by lengthening the sales cycle. Although a marketing tactic might help close a deal today, it often helps make the next sale even harder. With these counterproductive dynamics in play, it's easy to understand why U.S. automakers struggle to generate an average profit of between $400 and $800 per vehicle.

## THE LAW OF INNOVATION SATURATION

*Innovation* is a terribly overused word today. A century ago, an innovation was not just the improvement of a product that already existed. More often, an innovation referred to the invention of something entirely new, such as electric light or the automobile. Historically, corporations have been launched around such innovations. For General Electric, it was the light bulb. For AT&T, it was the telephone. For Ford, it was the automobile. For Microsoft it was a computer's operating system.

However, not every corporation can be the first to introduce a *discontinuous innovation*—a product or product category that is completely new. In fact, Microsoft did not invent the DOS operating system, but it surely made a successful business out of it. Once a *discontinuous innovation* is introduced, a flock of corporations generally follow the leader in hot pursuit of a share of the newly forming market. Once this race is joined, the clock starts ticking and each corporation in the race starts its respective journey up the *inverted V* toward its maximum rate of revenue growth and *innovation saturation*.

*Innovation saturation* is a phenomenon that occurs during the development of all commercial universes. It is an economic reality that impacts every product, category, corporation, industry, and economy. For example, after a product category is introduced, consumers begin to join the universe in increasing numbers over an unspecified period of time that varies from industry to industry. Similarly, competitors begin to join the universe of those responding to the demand created by the new innovation. As consumers consume and competitors compete along the uptrend axis of the *inverted V*, there comes a point in time when the rate of revenue and unit growth for the majority of competitors stops increasing and starts decreasing. *Innovation saturation* is achieved when:

- The natural number of consumers in a category is relatively established.
- The natural consumption levels of consumers in the category are relatively established.
- Competitors fight over that relatively fixed universe of consumers whose consumption habits have been established and hardened habits are extremely difficult to change. Market share levels are established.

Although successful corporations competing in a category will continue to grow both revenue and unit sales for years to come, they will do so at an ever-decreasing rate. Procter &

Gamble averaged double-digit growth during the 1970s, but its rate of growth has consistently declined ever since. This is not an indictment of the corporation's management, its marketing department, or its advertising agencies. In fact, it is because of the success of all of these groups in implementing growth strategies over the last 170 years that Procter & Gamble has effectively reached its full potential—one product at a time. Once *innovation saturation* has been reached, the rate of growth is destined to decline, regardless of the product, category, corporation, or industry.

## THE LAW OF INNOVATION SATURATION

Every successful innovation enjoys two major trends during its life: a period of ever-increasing rate of growth followed by a period of ever-decreasing rate of growth. The point at which an uptrend turns into a downtrend is known as *innovation saturation*. Inventive marketing initiatives and non-organic growth strategies, such as acquisitions or retail expansion, can temporarily slow the declining rate of growth. However, over the long term, once the downtrend starts, it cannot be reversed. ■

The *law of innovation saturation* applies to all products, in all categories, in all corporations, in all industries, in all sectors, in all economies. To drill to a deeper understanding of this law, it is important to break it down into its two most significant assertions.

## EVERY SUCCESSFUL INNOVATION ENJOYS TWO MAJOR TRENDS

Successful innovations are adopted over a period of time. According to Geoffrey A. Moore's *Technology Adoption Life Cycle,* the first to adopt an innovation are the technological enthusiasts and visionaries, followed, in order, by the pragmatists, the conservatives, and finally, the laggards. In some ways, *innovation saturation* is the next natural extension of Moore's thesis relative to the adoption of innovations—especially *discontinuous innovations*.

When an innovation such as the automobile is introduced, it enjoys a robust and ever-increasing rate of growth for some period of time. This period can be years, or even decades. The adoption of the automobile was a very slow process in the United States. Interrupted by two World Wars and a Depression, the major growth of the automobile didn't happen until after World War II. The auto industry rode the uptrend of the *inverted V* for about 65 years before reaching *innovation saturation* in the late 1960s and early 1970s.

*Innovation saturation* is a phenomenon that applies to all corporations and industries, not just those that are considered mature. In the case of the personal computer, for example, its upward trend didn't even begin until after 1978. The upward trend for technology lasted from 15 to 20 years before hitting its peak between 1995 and 1999. Again, this does not mean that the PC industry or corporations such as Dell, Hewlett-Packard, Intel, Microsoft, and others won't continue to grow—of course they will—but at a much slower rate than they did during the 1980s and 1990s.

## THE DECLINING RATE OF GROWTH CAN BE SLOWED, BUT NOT REVERSED

There is no doubt that even in a downtrend, the rate of growth can show marked improvement from one year to the next. Take Procter & Gamble for example. Although Procter & Gamble's rate of growth has been trending down since the mid-1970s, its rate of growth has ranged from a high of +10 percent in 1995 to a low of –1.8 percent in 2001. However, the trend over the same period shows that Procter & Gamble's top line continued to lose steam, averaging 3.63 percent per year since 1995.

Even though a corporation can experience a healthy uptick over a year or even a decade, the increase is short-lived, but can create the impression that the corporation has reversed course. The widely believed idea that a product can "get back on a growth track" is a myth. Ultimately, the downtrend will continue and it cannot be reversed. Moreover, it signals the beginning of what is usually a very long and expensive battle for existing market share, when corporations big and small battle for fractions of a share. *Absolute saturation* occurs when a product or corporation's declining rate of growth turns from positive to negative.

Over the last half-century, the overwhelming percentage of information written, studied, and taught on the topic of business has focused on the upward slope of the *inverted V*. However, little attention has been paid to two significant events in the life of a product, category, or corporation. Figure 7-3 shows the point of *innovation saturation* at the very apex of the *inverted V* at the Number 1. Most people entering the workforce today, for example, will join a corporation that is already well past *innovation saturation* on the downside of the *inverted V*. A growing number of people entering the workforce will be joining corporations that are approaching *absolute saturation* at number 2 in Figure 7-3.

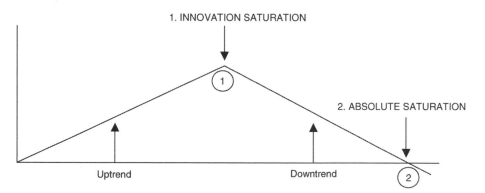

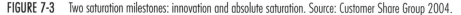

**FIGURE 7-3** Two saturation milestones: innovation and absolute saturation. Source: Customer Share Group 2004.

Corporations approaching *absolute saturation* are typically those in very old industries such as consumer packaged goods (food), retail (clothing), and automotive (transportation).

Margins in these businesses greatly evaporated over the decades. Ironically, the strong market leaders, such as Kraft Foods, have historically had the most to lose because of their overwhelming market share position in many of the categories in which it competes.

## THE LAW APPLIED

The advent of television truly marked a new era in economic development following World War II. Consumers far and wide were exposed to dozens of new products and new product categories, and as a result the major industries that contributed to overall personal consumption in the United States all followed essentially the same growth pattern, experiencing an increasing rate of growth until sometime in the 1970s, followed by a decreasing rate of growth through the end of the 20th century. A look at the consumer packaged goods industry in Figure 7-4 illustrates the classic *inverted V* pattern when measuring the rate of growth as opposed to a calculation of growth.

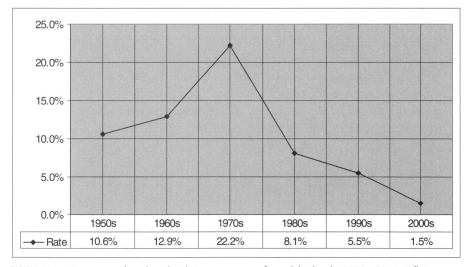

|  | 1950s | 1960s | 1970s | 1980s | 1990s | 2000s |
|---|---|---|---|---|---|---|
| Rate | 10.6% | 12.9% | 22.2% | 8.1% | 5.5% | 1.5% |

**FIGURE 7-4** Consumer packaged goods industry average rate of growth by decade, 1950s–2000s (inflation-adjusted). Source: Moody's (Mergent) Industrial Manuals.

After an enormously successful post-World War II run up, the industry has been in decline since the mid-1970s, and struggles to deliver even a small level of growth today. Although the consumer packaged goods industry might continue to grow, there is no reason to believe that it will grow any faster than the rate of population growth, which today averages around 1 percent or less in the United States, and even less in other countries. These are the long-term growth levels that corporations can expect from markets that are made up of categories that have been part of the global consumption habits of billions of consumers for many decades.

## CAR AND TRUCK SALES

The auto industry has enjoyed an incredible run since it appeared in the United States just after 1900. Interestingly, though, this industry peaked a full decade before the consumer packaged goods industry because of explosive growth immediately following World War II in the 1950s and 1960s. America's love affair with the automobile secured the industry's role as one of the most significant engines of the American economy. Some estimates suggest that the auto industry, and all subindustries directly related to it, accounts for up to 25 percent of real U.S. GDP. In many ways, as the auto industry goes, so goes the U.S. economy. This explains why every recession since 1948 aligns with one or more years of negative unit sales growth in the auto industry. Figure 7-5 shows that the average rate of growth for cars and trucks in the United States actually peaked during the 1960s and has been in decline ever since. Like many other industries, it enjoyed a minor comeback during the 1990s only to begin to slide again after 2000, when cars sales dropped three years in a row for the first time since the recession of the1970s.

When viewed from a linear perspective, the auto industry appears to go through cycles similar to the economy as a whole—the ups followed by the downs followed by the ups again. However, ever since the 1960s, the rebounds have consistently lost steam as the overall rate of growth continues to slide. In fact, car and truck sales have rebounded at lower and lower levels in the year immediately following a recession.

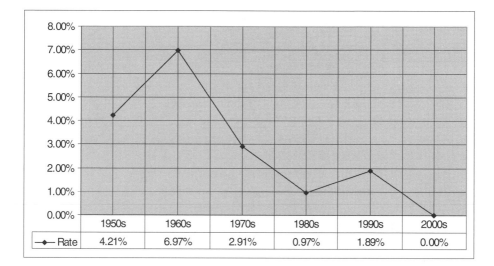

**FIGURE 7-5**    U.S. car and truck sales average rate of growth by decade, 1950s–2000s. Source: ©Copyright 2002, Ward's Communications, Southfield, MI 48075 USA. Redistribution prohibited.

Figure 7-6 shows that cars flew out of the showrooms in 1976, posting nearly a 20 percent improvement over the prior year. Following the recession in the early 1980s, car sales bounced back with close to a 17 percent improvement, but following the recession in 1991, cars sales bounced back at less than 5 percent versus the prior year. Following the recession in early 2001, car sales were flat to down slightly versus the prior year.

The auto industry in the United States is still rebounding from the recession in 2001 with little concrete evidence of a return to increased unit growth anytime soon. In fact, U.S. car and truck sales were down in the first full year following a recession for the first time ever in 2002, reinforcing the fact that overall long-term energy in the consumer marketplace is fading and has been for some time. The impact of deep discounting is also beginning to hit corporations where it hurts most: earnings. Although analysts and the business press have historically focused on the industry's problematic cost structure, that's just half of what is becoming a very bleak story.

| RECESSION YEAR(S) | UNIT SALES INCREASE FIRST YEAR FOLLOWING RECESSION |
|---|---|
| 1975 | 19.72% in 1976 |
| 1980–1982 | 16.77% in 1983 |
| 1991 | 4.61% in 1992 |
| 2001 | –2.00% in 2002 |

FIGURE 7-6    U.S. car and truck unit sales: postrecession increases. Source: © 2002, Ward's Communications, Southfield, MI 48075 USA. Redistribution prohibited.

With almost 31 million more registered cars than licensed drivers in the United States, it's not difficult to understand why it is nearly impossible to increase demand. Only once before has the auto industry posted a four-year losing streak—from 1979 through 1982—when car and truck sales went down versus the prior year in each of those years. That record is now in jeopardy as the century-old industry desperately seeks solutions to its volume sales problems while, at the same time, struggling to keep costs in line.

## THE AIRLINES: SEPTEMBER 11 COMPOUNDS THE PROBLEM

Another industry plagued with high costs and diminishing demand is the airline industry. Many of the woes troubling the airline industry are pinned on the tragic events of September 11, 2001. However, this industry's rate of growth has actually been in slow decline since the 1950s. Although the total number of domestic passenger enplanements has increased most years since the 1950s, the rate of that growth, as shown in Figure 7-7, has consistently declined over half a century, according to the Bureau of Transportation Statistics.

Often obscured by the aftermath of September 11 is the fact that, through August 2001, year-to-date domestic passenger enplanements were tracking virtually even with the first eight months of 2000. It appeared as though 2001 was already on its way to showing little or no improvement over 2000 even without the tragedies. September 11, then, made a weakening

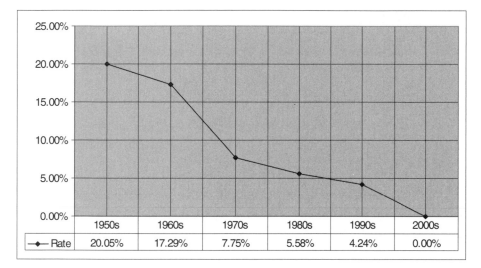

FIGURE 7-7    U.S. airline industry average rate of passenger growth by decade, 1950s–2000s. Source: Bureau of Transportation Statistics.

industry all the more vulnerable. The ripple effect carried over to 2002, as passenger enplanements dropped for the second year in a row for only the second time in history. A $3 billion boost from the federal government in the first half of 2003 helped shore up an embattled industry that was on its way to its first ever three-year losing streak.

A number of underlying issues continue to nag the airline industry, including a lingering unease over safety, as well as corporate cutbacks in travel and technological advances in two-way business conferencing. Similar to the auto industry, the airlines can no longer look at year-over-year unit increases as a given, and must consider the possibility of a no-growth scenario over the near-term given current economic and geo-political conditions.

## GENERAL ELECTRIC: NOT EVEN JACK COULD BREAK THE LAW

There is no corporation or industry that can escape the law of *innovation saturation*. Even those corporations with a voracious appetite for acquisitions, such as General Electric, can only delay the inevitable for so long. Jack Welch certainly made an impact during his tenure at General Electric, but nothing really compares to the last decade before he retired in 2000. After naturally reaching *innovation saturation* in the 1970s as a hugely successful industrial corporation, General Electric created little top-line excitement during the 1980s, averaging a humble 3.5 percent annual rate of growth for the decade. Its chairman was not about to preside over a corporation that delivered mediocre results during the 1990s, his last decade before retirement. Consequently, General Electric went on the most aggressive acquisition spree in corporate history during Welch's final years at the helm.

Figure 7-8 shows a pattern of growth like no other corporation in the world. General Electric transformed itself from a $30 billion giant in 1989 to a $111 billion behemoth before the turn of the century, posting an average annual rate of revenue growth of more than 14 percent for the 1990s. The century-old corporation grew faster than Hewlett-Packard, a company nearly half its age and less than half its size. The final act to Welch's play was complete and he stepped down after using up much of General Electric's gunpowder. Although he made a lot of GE shareholders happy during his last decade as chairman, the challenge that Welch left his successor, Jeffrey Immelt, is a formidable one that will require him to tighten the screws on an already efficient corporation.

The temporary upward move in General Electric's top line during the 1990s will be just one element of Welch's legacy that makes Immelt's job even harder. Welch only temporarily defied the *law of innovation saturation* before retiring. Even then, it took a Herculean effort—about two acquisitions a week during each of his last five years—to leave in a blaze of glory. With the acquisition cupboard greatly stripped, Immelt must look to a stepped up focus on cash management in order to protect the GE dividend. As part of that plan, Immelt's new compensation package will require him to broaden his objectives beyond increasing earnings to a heightened focus on increasing total shareowner return and cash flow.

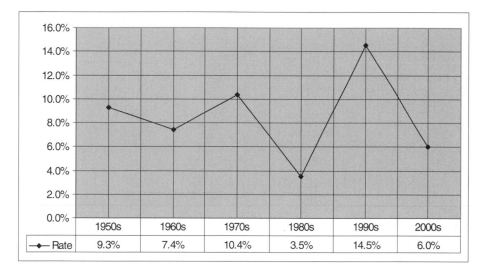

**FIGURE 7-8**   General Electric company rate of revenue growth by decade, 1950s–2000s. Explosive unnatural growth is always a temporary event. Source: Moody's (Mergent) Industrial Manuals.

## EVEN TECHNOLOGY IS ON THE DOWNSIDE

Even the youngest of the major sectors has already seen its best days. Technology, largely driven by the introduction of the personal computer, truly took off in the late 1970s and early 1980s. The growth pattern of technology heavyweight Microsoft provides a good example of how many corporations in this sector progressed toward *innovation saturation*.

Figure 7-9 illustrates that explosive growth over the corporation's first decade helped it reach *innovation saturation* very rapidly in the late 1980s. Although Microsoft continued to grow at healthy rates through the 1990s, its rate of growth was already in decline, starting the decade at 47.3 percent in 1990 and beginning the next decade at almost one-third that rate in 2000. However, since the turn of the 21st century, Microsoft's annual revenue growth rate has begun to resemble mere mortal corporations with growth rates in the 12 percent range, with some quarterly rates in the high single digits.

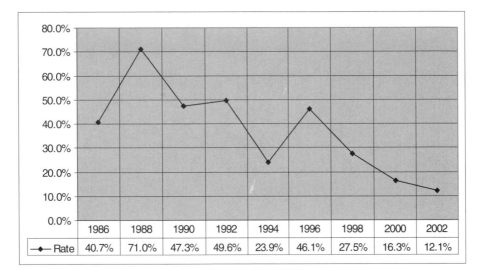

**FIGURE 7-9**   Microsoft Corporation rate of revenue growth, 1986–2002. Source: Moody's (Mergent) Industrial Manuals.

Certainly, double-digit growth rates are few and far between among the world's blue-chip corporations today. Not even technology giant Microsoft can escape the *law of innovation saturation*, for the first time in its history experiencing single-digit revenue growth. One fundamental difference between the technology industry and all other industries that came before it has been a much shorter ride to the top of the *inverted V.* Less than 15 years after its launch, Microsoft, one of the world's most profitable corporations, reached *innovation saturation.* Such a fast ride up begs this question: Will the ride down the *inverted V* be just as quick?

Take a close look at Dell and you will see a corporation that took advantage of a combination of favorable conditions that helped it to ride the wave to the top in less than 15 years as well. After launching in 1984, Dell capitalized on the PC explosion and muscled some healthy market share by using an innovative, on-trend marketing and distribution model by selling direct—first through direct mail and a call center and then later with an e-commerce platform on the World Wide Web.

Experiencing a skyrocket ascent up the *inverted V*, Dell reached *innovation saturation* in 1998 when its annual rate of revenue growth peaked at 58.8 percent. Since 1998, Dell's revenue growth rates have skidded from 47.9 percent in 1999, to 38.4 percent in 2000, to 26.2 percent in 2001, all the way to negative growth in 2002 at –2.3 percent, causing one to wonder about the long-term viability of any corporation that was launched after 1980.

Not surprisingly, many of the successful corporations in the technology sector since 1980 enjoyed steadily increasing rates of growth for about 15 years before beginning to trend down. The significance is this: Because of advances in communication and marketing over the last 50 years, more consumers learned about and adopted new products much faster than consumers did from 1900 to 1950. The implication of technology's swift ride to the top is that it, too, now operates on the downside of the *inverted V*. Although technology continues to grow, its downward slide takes a toll on the economy today because for the first time ever there is no major sector with revenue that is experiencing an increasing rate of growth: not technology, not health care, and not financial. None.

There is certainly some impressive growth at the industry level in biotechnology, for example, but that is a relatively small industry at this point in its life, unable to make even a small dent in a massive world economy.

## FASTEST RIDE IN HISTORY: AMAZON.COM

The phenomenal rise of Amazon.com in the mid-1990s might have propelled it to *innovation saturation* faster than any corporation in history. Launched in 1994, Amazon skyrocketed to the top within its first three years of operation. Amazon experienced wildly successful volume growth in 1996, shooting up a remarkable 2,988.2 percent when it went from a mere $500,000 in revenue to more than $15 million in one year. Although its actual dollars and unit sales continued to increase into the 21st century, it did so at ever-decreasing rates of growth, dramatically dropping for five straight years before stabilizing in 2001 with top-line growth of only 13.1 percent, as shown in Figure 7-10.

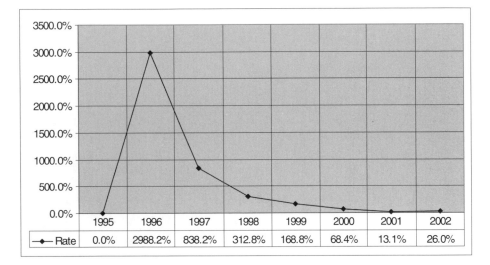

| | 1995 | 1996 | 1997 | 1998 | 1999 | 2000 | 2001 | 2002 |
|---|---|---|---|---|---|---|---|---|
| ◆ Rate | 0.0% | 2988.2% | 838.2% | 312.8% | 168.8% | 68.4% | 13.1% | 26.0% |

FIGURE 7-10   Amazon.com rate of revenue growth, 1995–2002. Source: SEC filings.

Amazon bounced back in 2002 with 26.0 percent growth, fueled by the lure of free shipping on orders of $25 or more. But not unlike the auto industry's zero percent financing tactic that drives short-term growth, free shipping has become a standard expectation at the online bookseller. The unanswered question for both models: Can they generate sustained profit with such liberal sales incentives?

Although the online retailer continues to grow, it now operates on the downside of the *inverted V* and must fight the gravity of a downtrend while devising an infrastructure that delivers on its promises at the lowest possible cost to the corporation. The question for Amazon now is this: Can it continue to deliver healthy, although declining, rates of growth long enough for the cost side to reach an optimum level of efficiency? In other words, will revenue growth rates run out of steam before Amazon can achieve efficiency levels that will allow it to deliver sustained earnings? That is the $64 question.

## CORPORATE PROGERIA

*Progeria* is a rare childhood disease that causes premature aging in the individual. In many ways, some of the most successful new corporations of the last quarter-century suffer from *corporate progeria*, or the accelerated aging of commercial endeavors that move through corporate childhood, adolescence, and young adulthood in the blink of an eye. Where it took AT&T more than 100 years to reach *innovation saturation*, Microsoft reached the same point in its development in only one-sixth the time.

Ironically, technological advances might indeed have created a completely new type of business model that enjoys a limited period of maximum usefulness before it either morphs into something completely different or is absorbed into a much larger organization. Software publisher Lotus introduced the world to electronic spreadsheets in the form of their first and most successful product, Lotus 1-2-3. Lotus avoided certain death as a stand-alone entity when the *one-hit-wonder* was gobbled up by IBM. Now Lotus plays more of a supporting role as part of IBM's strategy to sell more hardware and consulting services.

Such *disposable business models* will make it even more difficult for investors to determine the most appropriate investments and, more importantly, when to get in and when to get out. This is all the more reason why investors need sound advice from professionals who understand these new dynamics. Will the new corporations of the future essentially provide relatively short bursts of growth around an innovation that helps a corporation or industry get from A to B and then disappear into the infrastructure acquired by a larger corporation that will use the innovation to create a short-term competitive advantage? If so, what are the implications for the future of business and the future of investing?

The days of launching a corporation that endures for a century or more might well be gone. Consider the major sectors of the economy shown in Figure 7-11. Each of them occupies a different place along the aging axis, from the toddling technology sector to the 125-year-old communications sector.

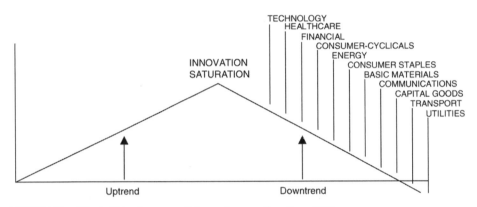

**FIGURE 7-11**   What's driving the economy? Source: Customer Share Group 2004.

Only a few short years ago, some of these sectors were on the uptrend side of the *inverted V*, and 30 years ago all were trending up, still short of reaching *innovation saturation*. Now, some even flirt with *absolute saturation*, the absence of growth altogether.

Over the short term, all of these industries will continue to grow. However, none will be able to naturally reverse the current long-term downtrend, even with continuous product and marketing innovation. Consequently, the economy will move forward more like a tortoise than a hare, especially with no significant new sector on the horizon to cause both business and consumers to add to their spending.

## IMPLICATIONS OF INNOVATION SATURATION

The U.S. economy experienced extraordinary growth during the 1970s, driven by huge gains in personal consumption, despite a deep recession and runaway inflation. As personal consumption growth sputtered during the 1990s, gross private domestic investment grew more than twice as fast as personal consumption and more than six times faster than government spending, according to the Bureau of Economic Analysis. With lackluster growth in personal consumption and a serious pullback in gross private domestic investment since 2000, there is little wonder why the economy struggles to find any momentum at all. It also may explain, in part, the decision to go to war in Iraq, increasing government spending as a percentage of the GDP for the first time since Vietnam. In some ways, war can be viewed as a government's means of fabricating growth, delaying facing the economic facts.

The implications of *innovation saturation* are far reaching, impacting every product in every corporation in every industry in every economy in the world. Once an innovation is introduced, the clock starts ticking as it finds its consumers and grows its universe to its maximum natural size.

From an individual product's perspective, it is very difficult to increase market share once *innovation saturation* is reached. Subtle improvements and endless varieties of a particular product add little to the overall pie. More often than not, consumers will trade out one product for another in a category when a new or improved version is introduced. For example, if a consumer decides to switch from an original formula of bar soap to the unscented version of the same soap, it's unlikely that the consumer will continue to buy the original formula. Therefore, the net gain to the category is often zero, unless the consumer trades up to a premium version.

From a corporation's perspective, if all of the categories in which it competes have reached *innovation saturation*, then obviously the corporation as a whole will steadily lose momentum. Although share of market of the three major U.S. automakers has eroded due to increased competition since the

1970s, the impact of that loss was at least mitigated by the fact that overall U.S. car and truck sales were growing. The Big Three could lose share and gain in sales volume while the overall pie was getting bigger. Now, however, their loss of share is exacerbated by the fact that overall U.S. car and truck sales are shrinking, and the Big Three automakers are now getting a smaller piece of a smaller pie.

From the perspective of an economy, it's difficult to stimulate growth when most major elements of that economy have reached *innovation saturation*. Increasing the money supply in a relatively satiated economy will not necessarily stimulate the level of demand or consumption in categories that have reached *innovation saturation*. When technology arrived in the form of the personal computer, both businesses and consumers added the new category to the long list of categories in which they already participated. That is what is needed to help an economy grow—the introduction of a new category that will attract additional dollars from businesses and consumers. With no major new category on the horizon that would command new consumption, there is little reason to believe that existing consumption levels across the major industries will suddenly and consistently increase.

## THE FADING BUSINESS CYCLE

The developed world has come to a crossroads in the 21st century—a crowded economic and geopolitical intersection that requires a complete rethinking of the concept of progress as we have come to know it. Our expectations are high, but for the first time in more than half a century, those expectations are mostly going unmet. We freely trade livelihoods for the ability to increase earnings and justify it as having the guts to be tough on costs to deliver increased shareholder value. The idea of entertaining the opposite notion—trading earnings growth for livelihoods—would be dismissed as a naive notion that would do nothing but deflate shareowner value and the value of the senior management team's stock options.

Revenue growth drove corporate success in the 1950s, 1960s and 1970s. Cost-reductions drove corporate success starting in the 1980s. Global expansion, acquisitions, and consolidation drove success in the 1990s and into the 2000s. We are witnessing the end of one long-wave business cycle and the beginning of the next. We are riding the tail end of a fading business cycle, and until a new energy arrives to help drive the next cycle, we must adapt and learn how to play the hand we've been dealt.

# 8 THE FADING BUSINESS CYCLE

Economists have studied and debated the phenomena that drive economies for hundreds of years. Central to the discussion has been the general belief in the existence of repetitive patterns of economic activity. This pattern, known as the *business cycle,* refers to the general ups and downs of an economy—the ups representing times of expansion and prosperity, the downs representing contraction and recession.

One of the most remarkable aspects of the business cycle is its resilience—its seemingly endless ability to rebound from adversity—defying Newton's law of gravitational force, when it comes to business: Whatever goes up, must come down, and then must go up again. That's how the business cycle, or short-wave cycle, has always worked. However, although the economy has gone through nine full short-wave cycles since 1948, study of the same data from a different perspective suggests that it is losing steam and rebounding at lower and lower levels.

Think of it this way: Drop a tennis ball from shoulder height and what happens? After each bounce, the ball loses energy and therefore height, each time rebounding to a lower and lower level. First, the ball bounces to a level of about 3 feet, then to a level of about 12 inches, and then to a level of 2 inches, until it ultimately just starts rolling along the flat ground. In many ways, this is how the economy has performed since 1984, and not surprisingly, consistent with the micro-economic view of the Dow 30 components' collective revenue discussed in Chapter 1.

Source: customershare.com

The product categories are losing steam, individual corporations are losing steam, and industries and the major sectors are losing steam. Ultimately, all this lack of steam impacts the entire economy, making it more difficult to grow. Put an age on all existing sectors that make up the economy and you will find that the only one less than 100 years old is technology. Put an age on all existing industries within those sectors and you will find that the largest ones are growing at a decreasing rate and a handful of the smallest ones are growing at an increasing rate—hardly enough to motivate a significantly ample economy to get off its duff and start moving ahead.

## A PATTERN OF SHORT-TERM ECONOMIC DEVELOPMENT

Although there are many events that can impact a country's growth both positively and negatively, the generally accepted belief is that the rolling business cycle in the form of the measurement of a country's GDP provides some measure of the health—if not the welfare—of a nation. A rising GDP is the very engine that drives capitalism and, at least in theory, quantitatively proves that an economy is successful, or at least making progress.

Most economists believe that, while an economy develops along on a continuously upward path, it inevitably is interrupted by events that cause a downturn, and growth slows for a period of time. The downturn can result in a recession, or even a depression, before ultimately moving through to recovery and expansion and the beginning of another cycle.

Historically, economists have pointed to four distinct phases associated with the business cycle: boom, recession, depression, and recovery—or as the more optimistic economists prefer to say: expansion, contraction, recession, and recovery—referring to the extreme top of the cycle as the *peak* and the extreme bottom as the *trough*.

Figure 8-1 illustrates the classic rolling S curve that is normally associated with the business cycle's progressive measurement of results over time. The short-term measurement of results, quarterly or annually, creates a seemingly endless rolling pattern of ups and downs as the GDP naturally expands and contracts.

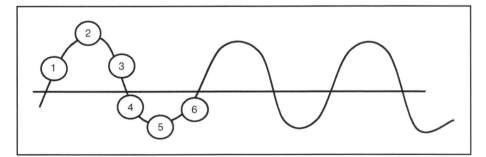

FIGURE 8-1    The rolling business cycle: Ups followed by downs followed again by ups. Source: National Bureau of Economic Research.

The economy moves through this repetitive pattern of phases of varying durations. To illustrate this point, the actual pattern of real GDP growth in the United States from Q1 2000 to Q3-4 2001 is shown in Figure 8-1 and follows this six-point pattern over a two-year period:

1. *Expansion:*
   Q1 2000 Real GDP = +2.6%
   (increasing positive rate of growth)
2. *Peak:*
   Q2 2000 Real GDP = +4.8%
   (increasing positive rate of growth; high point)
3. *Contraction:*
   Q3 2000 Real GDP = +0.6%
   (decreasing rate of growth)
4. *Recession:*
   Q1 2001 Real GDP = −0.6%
   (negative rate of growth)
5. *Trough:*
   Q2 2001 Real GDP = −1.6%
   (negative rate of growth – low point)
6. *Recovery:*
   Q3 2001 Real GDP = −0.3%
   (increasing rate of growth but still negative)

From an historical perspective, this rolling pattern of economic ups and downs has recorded nine complete cycles since 1948, according to the National Bureau of Economic Research (NBER). The economy has experienced nine recessions since 1948. In fact, there has been at least one recession in every decade since the 1930s. However, the economy has always recovered and always expanded after each recession, although at varying rates of speed.

## THE CLIMBING S CURVE

Figure 8-2 provides a graphic representation of how the economy has performed since the end of World War II. This classic upward-climbing S curve is the pattern that is generally accepted by most in the economic community as representative of the business cycle. A series of repetitive and relatively short-term crises temporarily interrupt the ever-upward momentum of the economy.

The blocks across the top of the S curve in Figure 8-2 represent the 10 peaks that have been reached since 1948, whereas the blocks under the S curve represent the troughs of the nine recessions experienced since 1948.

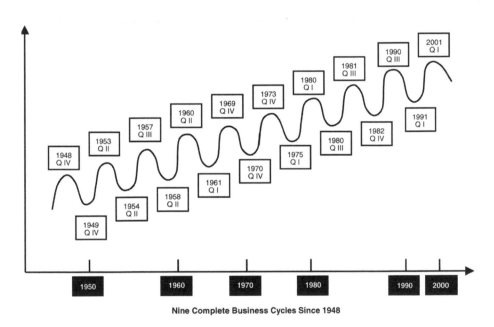

Nine Complete Business Cycles Since 1948

**FIGURE 8-2**    Short-wave cycles: Nine complete business cycles since 1948. Source: National Bureau of Economic Research (NBER).

As the economy moves through the four phases of the business cycle, it almost always reaches new heights each time. Over time, who can say that the economy is not growing? Most years, total GDP increases versus the prior year. The same holds true at the corporate level. Similarly, who can say that Procter & Gamble is not growing?

However, there is an inherent problem when looking at results on such a short-term basis, such as the data in Figure 8-2. Although each phase of the short-wave cycle can be observed, measured, and analyzed, it is extraordinarily difficult to identify trends in the economy over long stretches of time—stretches that can reveal patterns that might be difficult to see over the short term. Just as Procter & Gamble's revenue has continually grown over the years, so too has the economy's. However, applying a rate of growth perspective to the overall economy provides quite a different picture.

Figure 8-3, on the other hand, serves up the same economic data, but from a rate of growth perspective in 10-year increments. The pattern actually shows that, although total GDP continues to grow, it is growing at an ever-decreasing rate. In fact, Figure 8-3 shows that the economy's rate of growth has been in slow decline since the 1960s.

Viewing the business cycle on a quarterly or even annual basis provides only a one-dimensional perspective that often masks trends. Such a perspective emphasizes the short-term crises that are inevitably overcome, perhaps creating an inaccurate impression of the state of the economy.

The perspective provided by viewing the economy over decades shows a rolling, slowly declining trend, not surprisingly consistent with the pattern that most individual corporations have followed since the end of World War II.

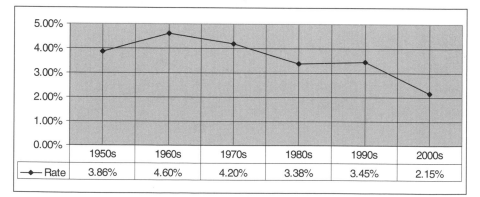

| | 1950s | 1960s | 1970s | 1980s | 1990s | 2000s |
|---|---|---|---|---|---|---|
| Rate | 3.86% | 4.60% | 4.20% | 3.38% | 3.45% | 2.15% |

FIGURE 8-3    U.S. real GDP growth: Long wave rebounding at lower levels. Booms caused by technology: TV in 1950, computer in 1980. Source: U.S. Bureau of Economic Analysis.

This long wave view of the economy in Figure 8-3 shows an upward trend from the 1950s through the 1960s. The economy continued to grow at a healthy rate in the 1970s, but began to show signs of a slide through the 1980s. A minor comeback in the 1990s, driven in part by an uptick in population growth, gave way to further retreat during the early years of the 21st century. Some might say that we can make the economy work by managing a slower rate of growth going forward. Currently, slow growth would be the best case scenario without any new savior sector on the horizon. However, there are few that are even willing to accept and embrace a slow-growth scenario, preferring instead to cheerlead a turnaround that can't possibly be supported.

What are the long-term implications for a corporation, an industry, or indeed the entire economy if such a downward trend continues into the future? Can an economy with foundational elements that continue to age and decline respond positively to historical monetary or fiscal policies that are designed to stimulate demand? So far in the 21st century, it has not.

## RATE OF GROWTH AND THE AGE OF THE REVENUE STREAM

From a corporation's perspective, it is important to understand the rate of growth for every product in the portfolio. Identifying the age of the revenue stream can greatly help a corporation in its planning and strategic development. Simply expecting a product or category to continue to grow has become a naive and arguably irresponsible notion. A corporation is only as strong as its revenue streams. How old are these streams, and more importantly, what are the rates of growth for each of them? This data rolls up into an average natural rate of growth for the corporation, which rolls up to create an average rate of growth for the industry, and ultimately the sector.

An economy, therefore, is only as strong as the individual pieces that comprise it. Too many look at the economy as if it were a never-aging, 24-year-old, world-class athlete in the prime of his athletic career. Once in a while he might twist an ankle or pull a muscle and be down for a few days or even weeks. However, after some ice, a whirlpool, and some rest, he's back performing like an Olympian in his prime. The fact is that the economy is no longer in its prime, but more like a middle-aged man with sore knees, an aching back, and a little too much around the middle. The economy is an aging athlete who moves more slowly, takes longer to climb the stairs, and can sometimes be found taking a nap in the middle of the afternoon. No one expects a former world-class athlete to run at a world-record pace anymore, so why do we expect that of the current economy?

Look at the economy exclusively over the short-wave cycle and you can convince yourself that you see Jesse Owens in his prime and expect prime performance. However, look at the economy over the long-term or long-wave cycle, and you see a different athlete, with different strengths and the ability to move forward, but also with limitations. Seeing and embracing this reality helps to eliminate unnecessary and nonproductive work that is based much more on what was than on what is.

## THE LONG-WAVE CYCLE

The concept of viewing economies over extended periods of time does have some historical precedence, even though the practice is not universally embraced today. Probably the most widely recognized proponent of such an extended view was Nikolai D. Kondratiev, a Ukrainian economist who theorized the existence of 50- to 60-year business cycles around 1925. Kondratiev described a business cycle that was made up of the same four phases as the short-wave cycle (boom, recession, depression, and recovery). However, in Kondratiev's view, these stages occurred over much longer periods of time. Kondratiev identified four long-wave cycles that each coincided with the introduction of a new and significant technological innovation, although it is unclear whether he intended this coincidence. These long-wave cycles later became known as *Kondratiev waves* or *K-waves*.

The first K-wave started with the Industrial Revolution around 1790. The second K-wave coincided with the widespread introduction of the railroad both in the United States and in Western Europe around 1850. The third K-wave coincided with the introduction of electricity and the automobile in both Western Europe and the United States around 1900. The fourth K-wave coincided with the widespread introduction of television around 1950. Some believe that it was Austrian economist Joseph A. Schumpeter who made the connection between K-waves and the introduction of new technology only after Kondratiev's death in 1930. Most compelling about K-waves is that there is logic and reasoning behind their existence. The introduction and widespread adoption of major technological innovations usually stimulate corporate and consumer spending that ignite an upturn in the economy. This was certainly true in the case of the K-waves.

Schumpeter was a firm believer in innovation and technology as important driving agents in an economy. His creative destruction theory suggests that not only does a capitalist economy encourage the development of innovation, but requires it.

The notion that most significant technological innovations—*discontinuous innovations*—ignited periods of robust expansion that drove an economy skyward actually makes perfect sense. Even though that might not have been Kondratiev's intention, the concept of the long-wave cycle, not at all popular among short wave theorists, has attracted new interest in recent years. One reason is that the long-wave cycle can be used to identify overall trends in the short-wave cycle.

In theory, Kondratiev's fourth K-wave is now winding down and, according what he wrote more than 75 years ago, the fifth K-wave is expected to begin around 2010. Maybe it will and maybe it won't. Even though his theory roughly aligns with major *discontinuous innovations*, there was no way that Kondratiev or Schumpeter or any economist could have predicted in the 1920s and 1930s the impact that technology would have on speeding up the very process of introducing new innovations and, along the way, greatly reducing the length of an innovation's life span.

Consistent with the *law of innovation saturation, discontinuous innovations* have historically enjoyed a period of expansion and boom before finding their relative natural size. This was true for the railroad, telephone, radio, automobile, airplane, television, and personal computer. The PC reached *innovation saturation* in less than 20 years, the fastest adoption of a major *discontinuous innovation* ever. The reasons: First, computer use and training was originally funded by business. Second, once the PC became a consumer product, it had the great advantage of having TV, cable, and major print vehicles that were used to both cover the advent of technology as well as to promote it.

## DISCONTINUOUS INNOVATIONS

The introduction of the automobile is a perfect example of a *discontinuous innovation*. It introduced a new category of product (the car) that incorporated breakthrough technology (relatively small gas-powered engine), enabling unprecedented benefits (the ability to transport an individual at anytime to anyplace). Although the introduction of the automobile did not entirely replace the horse and buggy industry, it was never quite the same after the car arrived.

Such major technological shocks or *discontinuous innovations* all had one thing in common: Not only did they create a brand new industry (automobile, television, and computer), they also served as catalysts of growth for most existing industries while spawning a host of new subindustries. These are the innovations that drive an economy—innovations that have a far-reaching impact on the way most corporations and most consumers spend their money.

Figure 8-4 identifies three major *discontinuous innovations* of the 20th century: the automobile around 1900, the television around 1950, and the personal computer around 1975. Certainly, many other *discontinuous innovations* were introduced during the 20th century, such as a number of household appliances and dozens of categories of pharmaceuticals, but no other categories impacted the world like the introduction of the car, TV, and PC.

| AS A RESULT | AUTOMOBILE | TELEVISION | COMPUTER |
|---|---|---|---|
| NEW RELATED SERVICES INTRODUCED | Oil, gas, gas stations, repair, parts, tires, dealerships, seat belts, airbags, driving schools, AAA | Local affiliates, cameras, programming, film, color TV, satellites, videotape, VCR, DVD, movie rental, TiVo | Software, printers, laptop, floppies, paper, IT department, Web design, computer repair, PDAs, wireless, CDs |
| NEW BENEFITS TO ALL OTHER INDUSTRIES | Faster transportation, delivery of products, new construction (roads and infrastructure), more telephones | Consumer product marketing, education, telephone, new construction (roads and infrastructure), more telephones | More telephones, more telephone numbers, productivity (all), e-commerce, new construction (infrastructure) |

**FIGURE 8-4**    These major discontinuous innovations of the 20th century greatly impacted all industries. Source: Customer Share Group © 2004.

In the case of the automobile, dozens of new services in support of the new industry—even other *discontinuous innovations*—appeared as a result of its introduction. Car repair, auto parts, tires, car dealerships, and gas stations are just a few of the many new subcategories that developed as a result of the automobile. The automobile also brought significant new benefits to most other existing industries primarily in its ability to greatly improve the delivery of all kinds of products. The automobile gave rise to the trucking industry, which allowed a faster and wider distribution of products such as food, clothing, and building materials. Suddenly, the world became a much smaller place with access to so much more.

At mid-century, the television started to become widely available, not only as a means of entertainment for consumers, but also as an important marketing tool for corporations. Television was at once a captivating and convenient means of in-home entertainment as well as the mass marketing hammer that helped introduce millions of consumers to dozens of new product categories.

This unprecedented dual nature of TV created an exponential ripple effect that caused new industries to grow, existing industries to grow, and both to develop much larger infrastructures to manage the growth. Because of the corporate expansion it caused, TV helped to create more new construction, more new car sales, and more new jobs simply to meet the exploding demand of a consumption-hungry public.

As the TV audience grew, so grew the new product categories and the ability for corporations to develop even more. Buying advertising time during the 1950s, 1960s, and 1970s often came with the bonus delivery of an audience that grew every week as many families bought televisions for the first time. Growing in parallel with corporations and their media partners was the world of the advertising agency. The ride up the *inverted V* from 1950 to 1980 was a fast and wild one for the media and agency worlds, and the ride down was just as quick, but much more painful.

By the time the personal computer started to become widely available around 1980, broadcast television and the agency world had already seen their best days. Technology sent a shock wave through the consumer and business worlds that caused both to pick up speed. Suddenly, we talked in terms of *Internet time,* where three months equaled a year, and a year equaled four years. Like the car and TV before it, the personal computer not only helped to create a new industry with many new sub-industries to support it, but it also brought significant new benefits to virtually every other industry that already existed.

As these three major *discontinuous innovations* helped boost the economy in their own unique way, a new cyclical pattern was clearly emerging. Not unlike Kondratiev's development theses that appeared to coincide with the advent of the railroad in the mid-1800s and the automobile and electricity in the early 1900s, the introduction of network television around 1950 and the personal computer in the late 1970s ignited new waves that Kondratiev could not have envisioned.

# THE DISCONTINUOUS INNOVATION CYCLE

The coincidence of economic booms in parallel with the introduction of major technological shocks in the 20th century certainly established a cyclical pattern of economic development. The introduction of a *discontinuous innovation* created a consumption explosion that propelled the rate of revenue growth along an ever-increasing path, consistent with the *law of innovation saturation*. The complete cycle from the launch of a *discontinuous innovation* up to *innovation saturation* and down to *absolute saturation* is called the *discontinuous innovation cycle* or *DI-wave*—a long-wave cycle.

There have been seven *DI-waves* since 1800, all initiated by the advent of an innovation of such significant magnitude that few on the planet were not impacted in some way:

## 1. THE FIRST DI-WAVE: THE RAILROAD 1825–1975 (150 YEARS)

The locomotive appeared in the early part of the 1800s as a new and faster means of transporting both people and supplies long distances on land in a faster, safer, and more reliable way. Although the widespread adoption process—first in Europe and later in the United States—was a slow one, by mid-century the railroad had secured its place as the preferred means of long-distance travel on land. This new alternative to existing forms of land transport was significant and forever changed horse-driven transportation, especially over great distances. Like all *discontinuous innovations*, the railroad greatly impacted the lives of both consumers and businesses. Far-away locations became accessible to consumers, and businesses were able to greatly expand the distribution and sale of their goods to many more new prospects in areas that were previously too remote. All *DI-waves* helped make the world a much smaller place. The first *DI-wave* helped make a trip of a thousand miles possible for so many around the world in a fraction of the time.

## 2. THE SECOND DI-WAVE: THE TELEPHONE 1875–2000 (125 YEARS)

One of the most enduring *discontinuous innovations* in history was the invention of the telephone by Alexander Graham Bell in 1876. What the railroad had done for transportation, the telephone made possible for communication. Suddenly, the state, the country, the world became a much smaller place. Like the other early *discontinuous innovations*, the adoption process for the telephone was extremely slow tied to the need to build the technical infrastructure, the distribution of equipment, and the ability on the part of consumers to afford the new technology. In many ways, the telephone was well ahead of its time as a communication wonder enabling the first means of instantaneous two-way communication between two parties in different locations. Ironically, the world would have to wait more than another 100 years before witnessing the introduction of the next means of two-way communication—e-mail. The second *DI-wave* also helped to make the world a much smaller place by making it possible to communicate in real time with people thousands of miles away—greatly improving on the U.S. Mail and even the telegraph by speeding up the delivery of messages.

## 3. THE THIRD DI-WAVE: THE AUTOMOBILE 1900–2000 (100 YEARS)

The third *DI-wave* actually represents the near-concurrent introduction of three *DI*s that in many ways defined what was to come in the 20th century. The introduction of electric light, the radio, and the automobile near the turn of the century dramatically changed the world. But it was the automobile that would prove to be a kind of super *DI*. This wave experienced an extraordinarily long period of expansion—approximately 65 to 70 years until the mid-1970s. Contraction started to slowly impact the automotive industry over a period of about 25 years in the form of a decreasing rate of revenue growth until around 2000. Although trumpeting the greatest car and truck unit growth ever in 2000, the industry started to experience negative year-over-year unit growth, or *absolute saturation*, the very next year.

| | DISCONTINUOUS INNOVATION | EXPANSION BEGINS | EXPANSION ENDS | DURATION |
|---|---|---|---|---|
| FIRST DI-WAVE | Railroad | 1825 | 1975 | 150 Years |
| SECOND DI-WAVE | Telephone | 1875 | 2000 | 125 Years |
| THIRD DI-WAVE | Automobile | 1900 | 2000 | 100 Years |
| FOURTH DI-WAVE | Airplane | 1925 | 2000 | 75 Years |
| FIFTH DI-WAVE | Television | 1950 | 2000 | 50 Years |
| SIXTH DI-WAVE | Computer | 1980 | 2015 | 35 Years |
| SEVENTH DI-WAVE | WWW | 1995 | 2020 | 25 Years |

FIGURE 8-5    Discontinuous innovation cycles: Time to the top getting shorter. Source: Customer Share Group LLC.

## 4. THE FOURTH DI-WAVE: THE AIRPLANE 1925–2000 (75 YEARS)

Although Orville and Wilbur Wright had taken to the air just after the turn of the 20th century, it actually took quite some time after their Kitty Hawk adventure for the widespread adoption of commercial air travel for both consumers and businesses. Commercial adoption was impeded by two world wars and the Great Depression. Consequently, much of the early development of air travel was defense-focused, influenced by the geo-political climate of the day. Throughout World War II, however, the airplane continued to make technological advances, especially by the major warring nations Japan, Germany, and the United States. But it wasn't until

World War II ended that the airplane's major influence on both the consumer and business was felt.

The end of World War II marked the end of a long period of sacrifice for many around the world. The end of the war also marked the debut of a new entertainment and marketing tool that was perfectly designed for the time.

## 5. THE FIFTH DI-WAVE: TELEVISION 1950–2000 (50 YEARS)

Network television debuted in the late 1940s, and with it came the beginning of the fifth *DI-wave*. The most powerful mass-marketing tool of all time became a must-have household appliance in more than 97 percent of U.S. households by 1965. Broadcast television became so successful so fast, both as an entertainment medium and a marketing medium, that it actually hastened its own demise. In many ways, broadcast television was the quintessential example of Schumpeter's theory of *creative destruction*.

TV enjoyed an incredible expansion phase between 1950 and 1979. Then around 1980, the broadcast TV audience began to fragment, largely due to the introduction of cable TV in the mid-1970s and the VCR in the early 1980s. Along for the ride with TV during its expansion phase were the consumer product and advertising agency industries. All three industries were fatefully linked from the very beginning of TV, enjoying the best of times and the worst of times together. Television has undoubtedly been the greatest revenue-generating technology of all time. It helped sell more food, clothes, cars, oil, gas, homes, and appliances than any other innovation in history so far. It helped launch and sell thousands of new products and hundreds of new categories, and it helped corporations do it effectively and efficiently.

It was also during this period that the economy shifted from a so-called goods economy to a service economy. In the 1950s, more than 63 cents of every dollar was spent on durable or nondurable goods such as food, cars, refrigerators, and lawnmowers. The balance of every dollar in the 1950s was spent on services such as hotels, lawyers, accountants, lawn services, and dry cleaning.

Around 1980, the economy crossed over from a goods-based economy to a service-based economy with more than 50 cents of every dollar spent on services as opposed to goods. The shift has continued through the turn of the 21st century with services commanding 59 cents of every dollar and goods only 41 cents of every dollar today.

Meanwhile, just as the automobile, airplane, and television industries begin to decline, the economy received a shot in the arm with the introduction of the PC, and the beginning of the expansion phase of the sixth *DI-wave*. The introduction of the personal computer created a phenomenon of significant new spending, first on the part of businesses, then closely followed by consumers.

## 6. THE SIXTH DI-WAVE: THE PC 1980–2015 (35 YEARS)

Like the automobile and television before it, the introduction of the computer—especially the personal computer—had a profound impact on all existing industries. The computer also spawned its share of sub-industries in support of the mother industry. The very appearance of the computer and its sister industries caused both corporations and individuals to commit new dollars to new products and services that were designed to make life simpler, more convenient, and more efficient.

History will show that during the first 25 years of this cycle from 1975 to 1999, technology not only radically changed the way business was conducted, but how personal lives were conducted as well. Technology proved to be much more of a productivity tool than it did a revenue generator for corporations during its expansion phase. Although the computer was widely adopted by virtually all corporations during the 1990s, it did not provide the revenue-generating boost for non-tech industries that television had during the 1950s, 1960s, and 1970s. Nonetheless, the computer played an important role in the overall management of businesses in the 1980s and 1990s, allowing for the accelerated reduction of costs and improvement in the quality and longevity of products at a time when the rate of revenue growth for most other industries was consistently decreasing. This, in part, explains why earnings grew at a much faster rate than revenues for many corporations during much of the 1980s and 1990s.

Aside from the significant revenue that the technology sector generated for itself through the sale of hardware and software during the first 25 years of this cycle, the computer and information technology industry has yet to greatly enhance the revenue-generating capabilities of corporations outside of the technology sector. This is not to say that technology has not played an important role in enhancing the value chain for many corporations. However, it has played a relatively small role in increasing the sale of automobiles, toothpaste, and clothing, for example. Technology might have made it easier for both corporations and individuals to buy such commodities, but it didn't necessarily cause them to buy more of them. Perhaps the development of technology as a major revenue-generating power—in ways we currently can't imagine—will provide momentum to the boom phase of the next *DI-wave*.

## 7. THE SEVENTH DI-WAVE: THE WWW 1995–2020 (25 YEARS)

The Internet became a more accessible and user-friendly communication tool with the advent of the World Wide Web and the beginning of the seventh *DI-wave*. Electronic mail— the first means of instantaneous two-way communication since the telephone—was slowly embraced beginning in the mid- to late 1980s, when the first online services such as CompuServe and Prodigy gave consumers added justification for their first investment in a personal computer. But once the Web appeared around 1993, suddenly a whole new world of communication and information sharing greatly helped fuel consumer demand for what was becoming the preferred means of privately searching for data and communicating with family and friends.

In combination with e-mail, the Web became one of the most powerful and pervasive innovations in history coming on the heels of the worldwide adoption of the personal computer. Consistent with all other *discontinuous innovations*, the combination of the Web and e-mail greatly altered the consumer and business landscapes in a relatively short period.

The dot-commers of the late 1990s thought that they had found technology's Holy Grail—the secret to technology's revenue-generating power. However, that hope quickly faded when revenues consistently fell short of expenses in thousands of efforts that offered impractical and unprofitable value propositions.

Because technology is already in the waning stages of its productivity phase, and corporate spending on technology has slowed, it is easy to see why the economy struggles for some type of sustained momentum. When television appeared in 1950, it helped drive the economy for 25 years. When technology appeared in the mid-1970s, it helped drive the economy for 25 years. It is frankly unclear exactly what will drive growth in the economy over the next 25 years.

## THE EIGHTH DI-WAVE? STAY TUNED

What new innovation will come along that changes the ways of the consumer and business? The next economic driver could very well be technology's ability to greatly drive new sales. However, technology has not yet enabled the radical transformation of sales models, certainly not like television did. What form that will take is anybody's guess. The economy could certainly use new categories that command incremental spending from businesses and consumers. However, no corporation, industry, or government can mandate the development of *discontinuous innovations*. They more typically are developed in an entrepreneur's garage.

Certainly, there is great hope around the health care sector, especially in the pharmaceutical and biotechnology industries as they search for and deliver new solutions to medical problems through the introduction of new categories of drugs and biotech innovations. However, will that be enough to inspire enough new spending to drive an economy that is near-ing $10 trillion in the United States?

Figure 8-6 graphically illustrates the long-wave *discontinuous innovation cycles* over the last 200 years starting with the Railroad around 1825. Not surprisingly, the length of the *DI-waves* shown here got progressively shorter with the introduction of each *discontinuous innovation*. The reason was that each technological innovation actually hastened the maturation of the last. For example, the introduction of TV (1950) greatly increased the speed at which the automotive and airline industries matured over the second half of the 20th century. Television helped sell millions of automobiles during the 1950s, 1960s, and into the 1970s when the industry reached *innovation saturation* and the rate of growth stopped increasing and started decreasing. Television, along with the PC, e-mail, and the WWW, helped make buying cars easier than ever, and contributed to the auto industry reaching *absolute saturation* around the turn of the 21st century, topping out in 2000 with U.S. car and truck sales of nearly 17.8 million units, and sliding ever since.

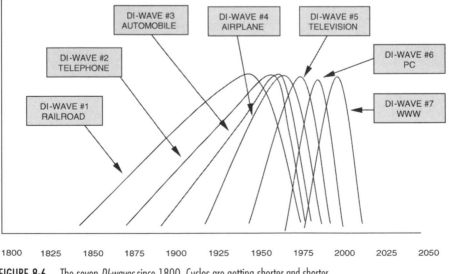

**FIGURE 8-6**   The seven *DI-waves* since 1800. Cycles are getting shorter and shorter.

Another unique characteristic of *DI-waves* is that, unlike many other business cycle theories, *DI-wave* cycles actually overlap as opposed to occurring in an end-to-end contiguous pattern such as the "S-curve." For example, the expansion phase of the first *DI-wave* (railroad) lasted about 150 years before reaching *innovation saturation* and the beginning of its contraction stage. Meanwhile, the second *DI-wave* (telephone) started in 1876, overlapping and in many ways assisting in the railroad's expansion phase, and so forth.

## RECOVERING AT LOWER LEVELS

One of the fundamental issues preventing the world's economy from moving out of its extended slump is the fact that all *DI-waves* have moved through their respective expansion phases—even technology. It therefore becomes extremely difficult to create momentum when:

- The economy is mostly comprised of fading industries that are growing at ever-decreasing rates.

- There is no new sector commanding incremental dollars from both businesses and consumers such as technology did from 1980 to 2000.

Consequently, the economy no longer simply rolls along, creating a consistent short-wave pattern of ups and downs. Like the bouncing ball theory discussed at the beginning of this chapter, the economy begins to show signs that it is losing energy, rebounding from recessions at lower and lower levels.

Figure 8-7 illustrates the bouncing ball theory with actual results from the U.S. economy starting with Q1 1984 when GDP reached a peak at +9.0 percent. Six years later in 1990, the economy slipped into a recession with three straight quarters of negative growth, beginning with Q3 1990 at –0.7 percent, through Q4 1990 at –3.2 percent (trough), to Q1 1991 at –2.0 percent, at which point a recovery had begun.

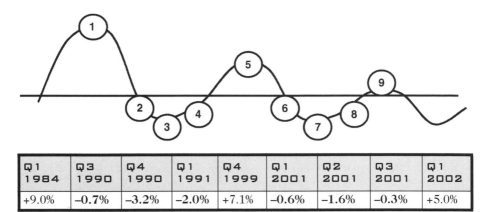

| Q1 1984 | Q3 1990 | Q4 1990 | Q1 1991 | Q4 1999 | Q1 2001 | Q2 2001 | Q3 2001 | Q1 2002 |
|---|---|---|---|---|---|---|---|---|
| +9.0% | −0.7% | −3.2% | −2.0% | +7.1% | −0.6% | −1.6% | −0.3% | +5.0% |

FIGURE 8-7    The fading short wave business cycle: Running out of steam and recovering at lower levels. Source: Bureau of Economic Analysis.

Following the recession in the early 1980s, a new cycle began with a recovery phase after Q4 1982. It took 92 months for the economy to go from trough to the next peak in 1990. Then, after less than 8 months, the economy slid to its next trough in Q1 1991. From there it took a full 10 years or 120 months to reach the next peak in 2001, the longest stretch ever from trough to peak. The recoveries are getting longer as a much larger economy struggles to move back up after bottoming out each time.

Since the recession in 1982, the economy has experienced two other recessions roughly 10 years apart with long stretches of relative stability. However, the economy has rebounded with lower and lower peaks since 1984 (+9.0 percent), reaching +7.1 percent in Q4 1999 and then +5.0 percent in Q1 2002. This is an important trend to watch as major elements of the economy continue to age with no new savior sector on the horizon.

## IMPLICATIONS OF A FADING BUSINESS CYCLE

The vast majority of the population today participates as consumers in the vast majority of existing product categories. Innovators have answered the call over the last 100 years to create unique solutions to unique problems. The development of new product categories ever since the first car rolled out of a garage in Dearborn, Michigan, has been nothing short of spectacular. However, it is precisely this extraordinary response to the challenge that makes it more difficult to develop new categories of products that businesses and consumers will add to their list of consumption necessities.

More often today, the introduction of the garden-variety innovation usually signals the gain of market share for one product and the loss of market share for another. Do consumers continue to buy the original formula toothpaste after switching to the tartar-control formula? The brand might gain, but the category does not, and neither does the economy.

In a microcosm, the challenge facing products, corporations, industries, sectors, and economies is no different from the challenge that the toothpaste brand manager fights each and every day: how to generate new growth from a relatively fixed universe of consumers who have developed relatively fixed consumption habits. This is one of the reasons that the economy drags today, and why it will likely continue to drag for some time.

In the meantime, business as usual becomes more difficult as many industries begin to deal with the reality of flat unit growth and virtually no pricing power. What are the implications for these industries? The question is no longer about selling more cars or airline seats. The call then might be to develop business models that assume a fixed number of sales each year rather than an ever-escalating level of consumption. How can the Ford Motor Company make money selling a fixed number of cars and trucks each year? How can American Airlines make money selling a fixed number of airline seats each year? Say it can't be done? One way or another, it will be achieved. The solution might not be simple to initiate but it is directly connected to resurrecting demand and, along with it, the ability to ultimately raise prices for the first time in a very long time. But it won't be without pain.

## DEALING WITH A NEW ECONOMIC REALITY

Even though we can't see or feel it move, we know that the earth rotates one full revolution every 24 hours. Intellectually, we know that it's rotating, but sometimes such subtleties are lost on us and we end up believing only what we can see, or at least what we are shown. As much as you might not want to believe it, the chances are that you are part of an industry that is in decline. That's the *new economic reality.* Now you have to decide how to deal with that reality.

# 9 THE NEW ECONOMIC REALITY

There is a story about a physician who had a dream that she traded places with the CEO of a large public corporation. Although she had experienced a storied career in the medical profession, she had always wondered what it would be like to be in the position to diagnose the health of a corporation rather than that of a human being. It had to be much less personal and much more clinical, she thought. So, off she went to her first day on the job while her counterpart—the CEO of the corporation—headed off to the hospital to take on his duties as medical chief of staff. After two weeks on the job the two met for lunch to compare notes.

"During my first week," said the physician, "I looked at hundreds of financial reports on each of the divisions, and then provided an assessment to your board of directors."

"What did you tell them?" asked the CEO, nervously.

"I told them that they could expect 1 to 2 percent growth across the board over the near-term, that a few of the product lines were losing money and needed to be either sold, dramatically cut back, or taken off life support altogether. I also suggested a rigorous investment in research and development to help stimulate a flow of new blood."

"What did they say?" asked the CEO.

"They were shocked at such a brutally honest and clinical assessment, and were concerned that my diagnosis might leak to the business press," said the physician. "So tell me about your experience. What happened at the hospital?"

"During my first week, I pored over reports on every department and through histories and physicals, x-rays, MRIs, and lab work for dozens of patients who had complained of one ailment or another," said the CEO. "Then I met with *your* board of directors."

"What did you tell them?" asked the physician.

"I told them that I could see nothing wrong with most of their patients and that since they had been healthy most of their lives, there was no reason to think that would not continue," said the CEO. "For example, the first patient I saw was a 70-year-old man who was complaining of chest pains. He had no prior history of chest pains so I told him that it was probably just some indigestion. Aside from those pains—on a *pro forma* basis—he was in tip-top shape. So I sent him home."

"I think it's time we switched back to our regular jobs," said the physician. "I have some patients to attend to."

"I agree," said the CEO. "And I have some damage control to attend to."

---

## GETTING HIT BY A TWO-BY-FOUR

Cyclist Lance Armstrong was diagnosed with testicular cancer in October 1996. To make matters worse, the disease had also spread into Armstrong's lungs and brain, and forced him off the pro cycling tour and into the hospital. The prognosis was not good. Doctors gave him a 50–50 chance of survival, and suddenly cycling took a back seat to a fight for his life. After three operations and intense chemotherapy, Armstrong started to positively respond to the treatment and after just five months on the sidelines, he was remarkably back on his training schedule.

When Armstrong climbed back on his cycle, he felt as though he had received a special gift after his physical well being had been challenged—something that had never happened before. This incredibly invasive wake-up call had brought about a shift in his priorities and ignited a new resolve in the young athlete. He vowed to do whatever was necessary to not just compete once again at the world-class level, but to win at the world-class level.

Many believe that Armstrong might never have won the Tour de France, much less win it five years in a row, had it not been for his bout with cancer. Sometimes it takes getting hit by a two-by-four to get our attention and force a new perspective, a new resolve. Why is it that necessary changes are often forced on us accompanied by a Chernobyl-like meltdown? Ignoring a health problem can often result in a physical breakdown when the body is simply unable to manage a counter productivity that shuts it down and sends it to the emergency room. It was the threat of mortality that shocked Armstrong into a radically different *modus operandi*. Unfortunately, the same can be said of many businesses. More often than not it takes a serious meltdown for corporations to understand that the game has radically changed.

If physicians were compensated based on the number of patients that they sent back out into the world after diagnosis with a clean bill of health, there would be a lot of sick people walking around under the impression that they were healthy. If CEOs were compensated based on brutal honesty relative to the health and welfare of the corporation's products and divisions, then shareowners, employees, analysts, and the business press would have a much more accurate, much deeper understanding of the short- and long-term health of the corporation.

CEOs seem to take the results of the corporation personally, even though in most cases results have little to do with specific actions they might have taken. On the other hand, the physician takes no personal responsibility for the problems he or she assesses in patients. They simply do their best to fix them. The failure to deliver on expectations that have been built over a very long period of time can be seen as the failure of the individual in our blame-based society. Also, the CEO is often compensated based on the successful delivery of profit or the increase in the share price. This often sets up a dichotomy in a maturing corporation, causing CEOs to initiate action that might not necessarily be in the best interest of the corporation over the long term. In fact, the unrelenting pressure to deliver increased earnings has motivated behavior that has been blatantly unethical, immoral, and, in some cases, illegal.

How can one profession deal so openly and honestly with the day-to-day issues of their profession and the other feel compelled to spin an often baseless story of optimism? Under normal conditions, neither the physician nor the CEO is responsible for the deep-rooted problems in their respective patients.

In the corporate world, prognoses that suggest anything other than good health and perpetual growth are often viewed as a sign of weakness. This is why we often see a hierarchical method of serving up a corporation's results: When there's no revenue growth story, a growth story is often built around earnings. When there's no earnings growth story, a growth story is often built around EPS. When there's no EPS growth story, a story is often built around the fact that the corporation met lowered Wall Street expectations.

There's nothing wrong with putting the best possible spin on results. The problems really start when there's an enormous gap between perception and reality. At a time when confidence in the corporation is at an all-time low, now is the time for Wall Street, the business press, analysts, and boards of directors to demand clinically honest assessments. Why? Because the gap between what can naturally be delivered and what is actually reported is widening. All the boundaries have been stretched, including all generally accepted accounting practices. Without a move away from optimism that is based on hope and toward an optimism that is based on reality, corporations—as well as its employees and shareowners—may unnecessarily suffer. Just observe Detroit over the next five years.

In many ways the job ahead for CEOs will be the toughest in history: managing change while delivering on historical expectations in a marketplace of diminishing demand. "Congratulations! I have good news and bad news. The good news? You've just been named CEO! The bad news? You've just been named CEO!" CEOs who entered the workplace circa 1980 and after will shoulder the burden of managing expectations through the transitional period to an economy that simply grows at a slower rate. CEOs who have 15 or more years left in their careers will be forced to face this reality. CEOs with guts and integrity will embrace the challenge of educating shareowners and Wall Street of this *new economic reality*—because that is the realistic condition of the patient.

## GREAT EXPECTATIONS

The world's spirit was truly challenged from 1915 to 1945. At least two generations were forced to deal with a world in disarray, from World War I, to an influenza outbreak that killed millions, to a stock market crash, a depression, Nazism and Fascism, and a four-year World War that cost the lives of tens of millions worldwide. For more than 30 years, sacrifice was more often the prevailing theme of life in the first half of the 20th century. When World War II finally ended, long sacrifice was transformed into hope for the future of millions whose pent-up dreams had been on hold.

Expectations were fairly low around 1950, as much of the world sought to improve their lives, and especially the lives of the booming new generation that filled maternity wards throughout the 1950s. After healthy expansion in the 1950s and 1960s, and phenomenal growth in the 1970s, many of those from the "greatest generation" lived to see their hopes and dreams fulfilled.

Not only were consumers "outfitting" themselves with the trappings of success, but they were also assuring a better way of life for their children and their children's children. Almost more than anything else, this what the World War II generation

wanted—a better life for their children. This deep desire motivated a generation to continue to work more, earn more, spend
more, and in the process, built new expectations.

Corporations and consumers were the beneficiaries of a
symbiotic formula for success: The more corporations produced, the more consumers bought; the more consumers
bought, the more new products corporations introduced. This
ever-increasing cycle helped drive financial performance skyward along with expectations for more of the same. However,
the high expectations that had been built from 1950 through
the 1970s were not always delivered starting in the 1980s.
What followed was great disappointment in failing to continue
to grow revenue at pre-1980 rates. It was during the mid-
1980s, then, that corporations started to shift their growth
focus from top line to bottom line by engaging for the first time
in projects that were designed to dismantle the infrastructure
that had been built since 1950.

By the early 1990s, expectations had completely changed,
and so had much of the motivation driving key senior executives at public corporations around the world. The formula for
corporate success was a simple and logical one prior to 1980.
Figure 9-1 indicates that the top priority in the corporation
was to drive revenue growth. The reason was because they
could. Driving revenue growth, acquiring market share naturally helped drive earnings growth, which naturally helped
drive the stock price, which attracted new investment dollars
that were invested in growing the operation so that it could
drive even more revenue growth.

After 1980, the formula for corporate growth started to shift
to one that favored the delivery of earnings growth over revenue growth. The reason was because revenue growth was dying.
Figure 9-2 indicates that earnings growth is the top priority in
driving post-1980 corporate strategy. The delivery of earnings
increases drove the stock price, which stimulated investment
dollars, which helped fund corporate acquisition of new revenue growth as well as the opportunity to consolidate operations
and drive down costs to drive increased earnings growth.

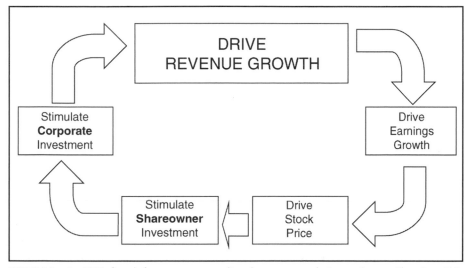

FIGURE 9-1    Pre-1980s formula for corporate success driven by revenue growth. Source: Customer Share Group LLC.

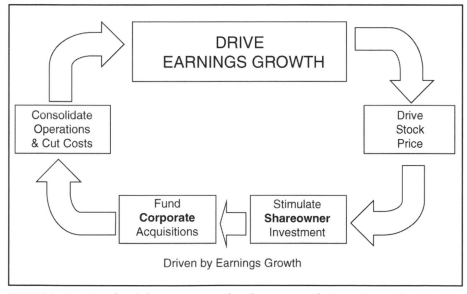

FIGURE 9-2    Post-1980s formula for corporate success driven by earnings growth. Source: Customer Share Group LLC.

As it turns out, though, the formula in Figure 9-2 does not anticipate that there might be limits to the number of corporations in the acquisition pool or limits to the extent of gains from productivity over the long run. If sales at McDonald's slow, then increased pressure is applied to the cost side of the equation. That increased pressure expedites productivity's role in delivering earnings because there are limits to the amount of costs that can be cut. The slowdown in revenue growth sets in motion a chain of events that will ultimately drain all benefits from natural productivity.

The revenue slowdown leads to workforce reductions and cutbacks in research and development, which leads to a reduction in innovation investment, which suppresses the development of new revenue streams, which puts downward pressure on earnings, which drives the stock price lower, that suppresses investment, which puts even more pressure on cost reductions. This counterproductive cycle starts with the slowdown in natural revenue growth and forces corporations to rethink expectations all the way down the line.

Performance limitations are a reality that all parties must accept as simply part of the natural course of a corporation's life. Simple statements such as, "It's only a matter of time before we get back on the growth track," are naive and irresponsibly imply that growth is unlimited. Try to convince the brand managers of Tide, Crest, or Philadelphia Cream Cheese that we will we will soon be getting back on a growth track. Getting back on a growth track for mature brands and corporations is not part of their reality.

It is critically important for corporations to proactively redefine financial success in terms of the *new economic reality*. For example, the maturing corporation that has a strong portfolio of world-class brands, along with an enormous and loyal customer base, but limited opportunity to push vertical consumption beyond current levels, needs to identify product maximization along with plans to generate new growth. Such corporations are mature yet viable entities that can continue to produce slow and steady growth through two types of innovation: product innovation and marketing innovation with smart investment.

## UNREALISTIC EXPECTATIONS

Most business models are based on the assumption that growth will continue in perpetuity. That expectation is simply unrealistic. Just look at the historical rate of growth metrics. The trends do not at all support the thesis of perpetual growth. A number of industries are learning the painful truth that perpetual growth might not be a God-given right.

One of the hottest growth corporations of the 1990s, The Home Depot, hit the wall in 2003. This might have been a sign to management that a fundamental limit had been achieved, especially as inventory levels show that supply is beginning to outstrip demand. Many of the retail models have simply flooded the market with overcapacity for everything from hamburgers to hammers. How many locations within a 10-mile radius of your home sell hammers or hamburgers? Consumers have unprecedented access to everything, yet the expectation and assumption is that The Home Depot, McDonald's, and General Motors will sell more and more every year. Why? Because it has always happened? This is why it is important to analyze results over long periods of time: so that trends can be identified and acted on sooner rather than later.

Undue pressure from Wall Street to live up to an inflexible standard such as perpetual growth can cause corporations to make short-term decisions that deliver short-term shareowner value but might literally put the corporation at long-term risk. This is one of the reasons that the SEC has seen record growth in the restatement of corporate results, the overwhelming majority of which are revenue-related adjustments.

A century ago, four significant innovations caused the world to greatly pick up speed. The invention of radio, electric light, steel, and the automobile—all around the beginning of the 20th century—helped to set in motion an ever-increasing momentum around production and consumption. After 100 years of expansion—of adding to revenue and adding to profits—the rate of that mind-numbing 100-year growth is grinding to a stop. The response to the slowdown has resulted in two decades of improving productivity, cutting costs, and cutting jobs, all to maintain or increase profits.

The sadness is that no one is looking out for the long-term health of the corporation insuring jobs for even the next generation. How many CEOs can you name, in recent years, who have successfully served current shareowners as well as near-term future shareowners? Under present conditions, it will become harder for CEOs to serve shareowners over the next decade as well as they have over the last decade.

## LIVING THE NEW ECONOMIC REALITY

The time has come for CEOs to begin the process of better managing the corporation's expectations. Although a unified effort on the part of CEOs to bring expectations into line is unlikely, it's important to single out the CEOs such as Wells Fargo's Dick Kovacevich, who have a history of throwing out the rulebook when historical practices no longer apply.

Defying conventional wisdom, Kovacevich informed his board in the fourth quarter of 2001 that he would not be preparing a budget for the following year. Preferring to spend the time on more immediate issues, Kovacevich opted out of the hugely time-consuming and questionably productive process of predicting the near-term future, especially when those predictions could be wildly off due to changing market conditions.

There is no doubt that the days of the five-year business plan are long gone and with it the expectation that every year will be an "up" year. However, the euphoria of days gone by still lingers, especially among board members who might have spent the last years of their careers building up the corporations that their successors are now being forced to tear down.

Calling the lack of growth today a failure on the part of existing management does an injustice to the millions of executives who went before, using all in their power to sell as many products and services to as many consumers as possible. To a great degree, the mission of creating the largest possible universe of consumers for the maximum number of products and product categories is complete. The challenge now becomes a matter of intelligently managing a growing number of ever-maturing sectors, while pursuing new innovations that deliver new growth. Expecting an endless inflow of new customers in old sectors is foolhardy and, in fact, counterproductive to the real mission at hand.

## TURNING FOUR BUSINESS BASICS INSIDE OUT

With a $13,000 profit in his pocket from Alaska's Klondike Gold Rush in the late 1890s, Swedish immigrant John Nordstrom and his partner Carl Wallin opened a simple shoe store in downtown Seattle in 1901. From the start, Nordstrom's business philosophy was clear: Provide an unprecedented customer experience. By the time Nordstrom retired in 1928, he had built a retail phenomenon that ultimately grew into an international icon of customer service.

Remarkably, Nordstrom's vision has endured for more than a century, a testimony to the original purpose of a shop owner who understood that the experience of buying shoes could be ordinary or extraordinary. By choosing the latter, Nordstrom sealed the fate of his company and its purpose as a world-class retailer that delivers shareowner value, not just a deliverer of shareowner value that happens to be in the retail business.

The time is now for CEOs to stop running so hard for one day and step back with other senior managers to reconsider four underlying basics that truly shape the day-to-day actions of employees, suppliers, consumers, and shareowners. Remember what happened to Lance Armstrong? He fought for his life and overcame testicular cancer before he won his first Tour de France. He emerged from surgery and chemotherapy, cleared his life of extraneous blather, and turned his life inside out.

### 1. Turning Purpose Inside Out

What are you really doing? This is not about rewriting the mission statement, but about determining priorities in the 21st century. In the face of maturing revenue streams, what is possible and what has become impossible? What lines will the corporation draw in the sand, if any, relative to trading short-term profit for long-term investment in innovation, product quality, and even increased full-time employee levels? The longer a corporation relies on productivity and cost reduction as the primary earnings drivers, the further it gets away from its original purpose.

Some time after 1980, Wall Street took on a life of its own, almost as if it could exist independent of the corporations it serves. Somewhere along the way, the tables were turned when it was Wall Street that was served by public corporations run by executives who were willing to be told how high to jump on the way to becoming wealthy beyond their wildest dreams.

The definition of what is right for a corporation has wide interpretation. Delivering short-term earnings for the purpose of increasing stock price today certainly is an option that makes some percentage of the people happy. However, that focus can be disconnected from strengthening a foundation on the way to becoming the best airline, the best car company, or the best consumer packaged goods company in the world.

Was it John Nordstrom's perspective to build earnings to drive stock price or to build the best consumer shopping experience in the world? It is a slippery slope that most CEOs scale each day in an effort to please so many publics. Prioritizing those publics into hierarchical importance has changed the way many corporations do business, and that is a legitimate decision a CEO has to make.

However, it is difficult to serve more than one master. Which master makes the most sense? Wall Street? Shareholders? Employees? Suppliers? Distribution partners? Customers? Rank them. There can also be long-term consequences to short-term actions. The actions that deliver results today might, in fact, be counterproductive to delivering those same results two, three, or five years from now, making the job of the chief executive in balancing the delivery of profits today and corporate longevity tomorrow an extremely difficult one.

## 2.  Turning the Business Model Inside Out

Rethink the model of *more*. The output and consumption model that requires growth in perpetuity has been embraced for centuries. Although there might be interruptions to this upward climb, ultimately it will get back on its upward course. In the face of maturing revenue streams, what is the corporation's plan for both revenue and earnings growth for the next 10 years? What percentage of revenue growth will come naturally from the existing core, will be acquired through mergers and acquisitions, or will be developed as part of planned research and development? What percentage of earnings growth will be the result of natural growth from the core, mergers and acquisitions work, research and development, productivity, reduction in headcount, or reduction in product quality?

The auto industry has always expected to sell more cars every year. Why? Headed for its fourth consecutive year of unit sales erosion, it is time for a major overhaul of the business model that drives Detroit. No longer can Ford start its budget process by asking how many cars and trucks it needs to sell this year to make money. The question now must be this: How can we make money by selling 7 million cars and trucks this year and perhaps even next year?

There are business models that successfully operate with relatively fixed unit sales, especially in the service sector. With high sunk costs in the durable goods area, it will be difficult for a single manufacturer to change the business model alone. Therefore, it is more likely that some type of forced consolidation will alter many maturing business models before the end of the decade.

### 3. Turning Success Metrics Inside Out

Measuring the success or failure of a corporation based on one number is like proclaiming that a patient is in good health because his or her temperature reads 98.6 degrees. Earnings alone provide an incomplete picture of the patient. Additional metrics are required to paint a more complete understanding of all elements that ultimately boil down to one figure. As with a patient in the hospital, a complete history is critically important to understanding health status today. How can shareholders, analysts, business media, and even the board of directors better understand the health of the earnings that corporations deliver? What is the relative quality of the earnings?

On the surface, increased earnings might appear to be a sign of health, but there are a number of ways to increase earnings in the short term that might not be in the best interest of the corporation over the long term. Under what circumstances were the earnings generated? What is the ratio of the rate of revenue growth to the rate of earnings or profit growth? Is the bottom line growing much faster than the top line? If so, can this disproportionate growth be sustained? For how long?

Figure 9-3 identifies the rate of revenue and earnings growth for four corporations in four different industries over the last 10 years, five years, and three years. In each case, the rate of revenue growth has consistently eroded since 1990 and in some cases before. In most cases, the rate of earnings growth has also dipped over time. However, in all cases the rate of earnings growth has consistently outpaced the rate of revenue growth since 1990. This is a significant change from the 1950s, 1960s, and 1970s when revenue growth consistently outpaced earnings growth at most public corporations.

When revenue growth began to slow for many corporations in the 1980s, earnings growth began to pick up speed, especially as corporations increasingly focused on cost reductions as an important corporate survival strategy. The three columns on the right side of Figure 9-3 identify the relationship of the rate of revenue growth to the rate of earnings growth. This *R:E ratio* provides a single metric that helps measure the relative rate of growth of the top line to the bottom line.

The closer the R:E ratio is to 1.00, the more balanced the performance of the corporation, suggesting an equal contribution on the part of revenue and cost control in delivering earnings. An R:E ratio of less than 1.00 suggests an imbalance in the R:E equilibrium and, more specifically, the overdelivery of earnings and/or the underdelivery of revenue. It also suggests that cost reductions or productivity have played a larger role in producing results during this period. This new metric, like most metrics, should be viewed as just one additional data set in analyzing the health of a corporation and especially of its earnings. Any deviation from R:E equilibrium of 1.00 should cause a red flag to go up and trigger a whole set of questions.

| CORPORATION | RATE OF REVENUE GROWTH | | | RATE OF EARNINGS GROWTH | | | R:E RATIO | | |
|---|---|---|---|---|---|---|---|---|---|
| | LAST 10 YEARS | LAST 5 YEARS | LAST 3 YEARS | LAST 10 YEARS | LAST 5 YEARS | LAST 3 YEARS | LAST 10 YEARS | LAST 5 YEARS | LAST 3 YEARS |
| Procter & Gamble | 3.0% | 2.4% | 1.8% | 7.0% | 4.0% | 2.2% | 0.43 | 0.60 | 0.82 |
| General Electric | 8.7% | 7.7% | 5.7% | 11.8% | 11.0% | 6.4% | 0.74 | 0.70 | 0.89 |
| Johnson & Johnson | 10.2% | 9.9% | 9.7% | 15.6% | 16.1% | 16.4% | 0.65 | 0.61 | 0.59 |
| Microsoft | 26.2% | 20.1% | 12.8% | 28.2% | 18.3% | 6.3% | 0.93 | 1.10 | 2.03 |

FIGURE 9-3    The R:E ratio: The relationship of the rate of revenue growth to the rate of earnings growth. Source: Moody's (Mergent) Industrial Manuals.

Earnings can only grow twice as fast as revenue for a limited period of time. For example, even though Procter & Gamble's R:E ratio of 0.43 over the last 10 years, shown in Figure 9-3, suggests an overdelivery of earnings and an underdelivery of revenue, it has improved its R:E ratio in recent years by increasing revenue, reducing earnings, or both. In the case of Johnson & Johnson, a corporation with a stellar history of performance, both its top and bottom lines continue to grow in a healthy manner. However, the R:E ratio suggests a disproportion of earnings growth to revenue growth especially over the last three years. This is not necessarily a bad thing, but begs deeper understanding, especially for a research and development-focused innovator such as Johnson & Johnson that requires a consistent investment in new product development—even if such investments temporarily suppressing earnings.

Of the corporations shown in Figure 9-3, only Microsoft has consistently delivered close to R:E equilibrium over the last decade. In some ways, this ties directly to both the age of the corporation and particularly the age of its various revenue streams, having reached *innovation saturation* in the mid-1990s. Microsoft's 2.03 R:E ratio over the last three years suggests an underdelivery of earnings that might have been the result of investment spending.

For those products that historically have required healthy marketing budgets, the R:E ratio metric can serve as a valuable planning tool in predicting both future revenue and profits for an entire portfolio of products and services. Such a tool can also help corporations develop a more scientific approach to determining their marketing investment on a product-by-product basis going forward, a sometimes frightening and difficult task when dealing with maturing products and escalating marketing costs.

Figure 9-4 identifies four different hypothetical products that are part of one division of a large public corporation. All products show a declining revenue growth rate over time. Products A and B continue to enjoy revenue growth, as well as fairly healthy R:E ratios. However, Product C might be in trouble, not only showing signs of revenue exhaustion but, more importantly, profit exhaustion with a dangerously low R:E ratio of 0.20.

| PRODUCT | RATE OF REVENUE GROWTH | | | RATE OF PROFIT GROWTH | | | R:E RATIO | | |
|---|---|---|---|---|---|---|---|---|---|
| | 1980s | 1990s | 2000s | 1980s | 1990s | 2000s | 1980s | 1990s | 2000s |
| Product A | 3.1% | 2.5% | 0.9% | 3.0% | 2.6% | 1.1% | 1.03 | 0.96 | 0.67 |
| Product B | 5.2% | 3.5% | 2.1% | 4.0% | 3.6% | 2.6% | 1.30 | 0.97 | 0.81 |
| Product C | 2.9% | 2.4% | 0.1% | 2.7% | 2.6% | 0.5% | 1.07 | 0.92 | 0.20 |
| Product D | N/A | 5.1% | 0.9% | N/A | 3.2% | 1.6 | N/A | 1.59 | 0.56 |

FIGURE 9-4    The age of the revenue stream relative strength of contribution: Product portfolio history and physical. Source: Customer Share Group LLC.

Notice also that Product D, introduced in the 1990s, had a rapid rise and equally rapid decline over its short life, and might not have the legs necessary to survive nearly as long as Products A, B, and C, with an R:E ratio of 0.56 in less than a decade.

A complete history and physical of the profit centers of the corporation using R:E metrics can help statistically support decisions relative to investment in a particular product or product category, not just in terms of marketing dollars, but also in terms of human capital and capital investment. Such a tool can surely help a corporation identify areas of potential cost savings, as well as areas that might benefit from a shift in investment; for example, reducing a product's mass marketing spending in favor of an increase in its direct marketing (database and e-mail) spending.

## 4. Turning Compensation Inside Out

If revenue is the lifeblood of any corporation, then the CEO needs to be motivated to make new revenue happen, especially when it comes to the long term. If the stream dries up, then the clock starts ticking. Incentives that drive CEOs to innovate the revenue side of the equation are needed now more than ever and compensation packages should reflect a reprioritization of objectives in order to prolong health.

A number of corporations are beginning to address the realities of the marketplace by adjusting expectations around results, even in midstream. When it becomes clear four to six months into the year that budgeted levels of revenue and earnings will not be reached, some corporations have called a time out, regrouped, and started over.

After determining the new priorities of the corporation of the 21st century, it is important to construct attainable incentives down though the organization to motivate the desired push. Too many times over the last decade CEOs have negotiated failsafe compensation packages that left dozens of middle managers without bonuses and stock rewards for not coming close to delivering unattainable targets. Now is the time to adjust compensation to motivate new action that will serve the corporation and its shareowners not just over the short term, but for the long term as well.

It's easy to serve all masters in goods times when revenue and profits are freely flowing. But how do the priorities of the corporation change as times turn bad? What is the relative importance of the following groups in good times and bad?

- Shareowners
- Suppliers
- Customers
- Employees

Should shareowners always be served first in a capitalist system? What would cause a shift in priorities?

## MANAGING EXPECTATIONS

It is vitally important to rethink historical expectations of corporations today or run the risk of sitting on the sidelines waiting for the long-expected turnaround. With aging revenue streams, corporations can no longer expect growth as a given. These same pundits need to stop talking about productivity as if it were some magical bottomless wellspring of benefits. American workers who have escaped the unemployment lines have provided more than their fair share to productivity gains since the early 1990s.

Corporations need to better manage expectations. For example, the U.S. car and truck industry sold 17.8 million new cars in 2000. A remarkable feat. But selling 16.8 million cars a year is viewed as a failure. This is Detroit's fault for failing to manage expectations. Selling 16.8 million of anything in one year is still a Herculean task. Now Detroit must figure out how to make money selling fewer cars—but still a lot of cars. If it can't, it is likely that the competitive landscape will change, and Detroit might be spelled with a small "d." The same holds true for the airline industry. It's not the responsibility of consumers to fill the seats of all existing airlines. The numbers are the numbers; more often than not, unit sales are flattening, requiring corporations to completely rethink all elements of the profit equation.

Cheerleading observers, including analysts and the business press, need to decide what their true roles will be over the next decade. Will it be to selfishly predict the onset of growing markets because growing markets better serve their own interests, or will it be to accurately assess what is happening in the world of business? Will they play the role of the clinically honest physician or the shamelessly transparent public relations practitioner? Optimism is important, especially in bad times. However, now is the time for reality-based optimism, not hope or hype-based optimism.

Now is the time for some guts, as well as the leadership to manage through long and steady yet smaller levels of growth.

At the same time, the future revenue stream requires some new, outside-of-the-box thinking, well beyond traditional line extensions and minor product improvements.

## A TIME OF RENEWAL

The 20th century certainly saw the birth of countless new innovations, as well as the death of many old ones. Some of those deaths were long and hard, kept alive by believers. Sometimes, it's best just to say "Goodbye. You've enjoyed a wonderful life," and make way for the models of a new century.

Over the next 50 years, the world will witness marvels that can't even be imagined right now. The next major sector, whatever it might be, will suddenly appear just as the personal computer and the World Wide Web did. To make room for it, something else might have to step aside. Within a decade, we will witness shrinkage in the number of corporations that fly us from city to city, sell us cars, and do our taxes. We will also see a great reduction in the number of product options—fewer versions of salad dressing, toothpaste, and shampoo. With this purging there will be good news and bad news: The good news will be that corporate pricing power will ultimately return. The bad news is that we will need new jobs for the people who will lose theirs along the way.

There is an opportunity now, especially for those who have a number of years left in their careers, to embrace and in fact lead a movement of corporate and, in some cases, self-renewal. Product innovation will always be embraced, but it just might be marketing innovation that will allow corporations to get from here to the beginning of the next *DI-wave*.

# 10 A TIME OF RENEWAL

Ever since it opened its doors as a small Quebec-based soft drink importer back in 1952, Cott Corporation followed the same formula for success that most 20th-century corporations followed: Grow by gaining market share through geographic expansion and product expansion. After Cott's years of chasing industry leaders Coke and Pepsi by expanding distribution to the United States and Europe, and adding dozens of new flavor options, consumer packaged goods veteran Frank E. Weise joined the company as CEO and changed that strategy.

Weise knew he had his hands full when he accepted the job, so one of his first moves was to simplify things by eliminating unprofitable retail accounts as well as scores of soft drink flavors that could only marginally differentiate themselves. After all, competing on the same basis with soft drink titans Coke and Pepsi nearly killed the 50-year-old company that commands a mere 4 percent of the U.S. carbonated soft drink market, compared to Coke's estimated 43 percent share and Pepsi's 31 percent.

By the end of 2002, Weise had restored an ailing corporation on the brink of bankruptcy back to profitability and posted back-to-back years of double-digit sales increases in 2001 and 2002. The corporation is now well positioned in an extremely crowded segment as the world's leading supplier of store-brand carbonated soft drinks.

Weise proved that bigger is not always better. Sometimes a company has to get smaller for it to grow again, and Weise didn't hesitate to take the proactive steps that resulted in foregoing some revenue over the short term in favor of long-term health and profitability. What Weise did took a lot of guts. Few CEOs are willing to sacrifice any revenue for fear of how it will be perceived on Wall Street. But Weise had a job to do, and like an emergency room surgeon faced with a life-or-death situation, he did what he had to do to save the patient.

Every mature corporation hanging on to unprofitable lines of business and dozens of slightly different variations of the same core product should take a cue from Cott's Weise. Sometimes a controlled contraction strategy is far better than a strategy that calls for the costly pursuit of marginal growth with expensive weapons of mass marketing.

The road to breathing life back into demand and the economy starts with reduction for many.

## Too Many Options, Too Much Capacity

The world is over-flavored, over-optioned, and over-supplied, and no amount of price reduction will cause most people to rush out to buy more deodorant or toothpaste. There are simply too many airline seats to sell, too many cars to sell, too many rooms to rent, too many houses to sell—too much of everything. The most fundamental of all economic theories suggests that the remedy for oversupply and a lack of demand is to simply drop prices, and that theory has almost always worked. However, when rates have dropped to historically low levels and deflation becomes a real possibility, inelasticity of demand is no longer a temporary condition.

The world is in a fundamentally different place than it was when Alfred Marshall first theorized on the issue of demand and supply. It must have been inconceivable for Marshall to consider that some day there would be more cars than people to drive them, more houses than people to live in them. When he wrote his opus magnum *Principles of Economics* in 1890, it must have been impossible for him to imagine that so many people would now have such easy access to such a degree of the time; that, rich or poor, most people in the developed world would be able to eat as much as they want, and often do; that the rich own homes, and so do the working class. The rich own cars, and so do the working class. The rich own cell phones, and so do the working class. Hardship in many developed countries today means that you might have to get back in your car and drive three blocks in order to get the "light" version of your favorite salad dressing.

The demand tide has been ebbing now for more than two decades, as billions across the globe approach satiety with respect to the products and services that they consume every day. Marshall must have viewed demand and supply as an endless rolling journey with no destination. Saturation is a destination. In many ways, the relentless quest for more has expedited the journey to a destination that few ever thought possible: saturation. In retrospect, wasn't it inevitable that our drive for progress would get us here?

## WHY THE ECONOMY LACKS ENERGY

Anyone born after the Great Depression has lived during a time when at least one—if not most—major sectors of the economy was experiencing increasing rates of growth. The majority of the sectors slowly gathered steam after the depression and some greatly benefited from the war effort in the 1940s. Then after World War II, all sectors that existed at the time—based on whatever definition you chose—consistently grew at increasing rates for about 30 years. Then, as discussed in prior chapters, all of these sectors hit a wall and started to grow at ever decreasing rates sometime in the mid to late 1970s. Then along came an entirely new sector—technology— and while all other sectors grew at decreasing rates, technology started its rapid accent growing at ever increasing rates in the 1980s until the mid to late 1990s.

To graphically illustrate the point, Figure 10-1 splits the economy into two pieces: pre-technology sectors and the technology sector. The pre-technology sectors are shown here on the rise coming out of World War II, peaking sometime during the 1970s when the rate of revenue growth reached *innovation saturation*. As the pre-technology sectors started to decline after the robust 1970s, the technology sector took off, experiencing a meteoric rise to the top from 1980 to around 2000, as both businesses and consumers bought into technology. The sectors passed each other (pre-technology on the way down and technology on the way up as shown in Figure 10-1) some time in the early 1980s.

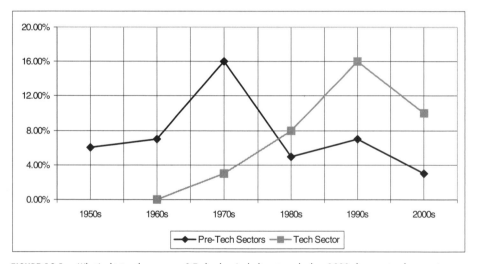

**FIGURE 10-1**    What's driving the economy? Technology's decline since the late 1990s has restricted any major upward movement in the world's economy. Source: Customer Share Group LLC.

The crisscrossing of technology with all pre-technology sectors was a fortunate coincidence for the economy both from a GDP and an employment perspective. At least some of the lack of growth in the pre-technology sectors was mollified by the rapid growth of technology. Without the introduction of the PC in the late 1970s, the economy would have suffered greatly, and more than likely would have spiraled into a serious depression. Fortunately, that did not happen.

However, as the 1990s came to a close, several important new economic realities became apparent:

- The technology sector had already seen its best days.
- There was no new sector on the horizon, no heir apparent to the technology sector as there had been to all other sectors in the early 1980s.
- The days of witnessing a sector or industry that would stand the test of time for a century or more were probably over.

The world was simply running at a much faster pace. Ironically, the introduction of technology actually hastened the aging process of all sectors, putting additional pressure on businesses of all types to do whatever they needed to do to survive.

In the meantime, with the technology sector in decline, it too adopted the cost-reduction strategies—including laying off thousands of employees—that other, more mature sectors had adopted 20 years before. Technology was no longer an adolescent and could no longer, in its current form, be expected to deliver at the rates it once did. A victim of corporate progeria, the technology sector reached middle age while it was still a teenager in calendar years. With all major sectors in decline, there are few CEOs out there who are not dealing with the challenge of growing the corporation with little help from the top line. This is the hand they have been dealt. CEOs have been operating in an environment since the 1980s that requires them to perform a balancing act in determining how to serve multiple masters. There was a time when all major groups that contribute to make a business work all continuously gained from the experience—when *upside* for each of the following groups was more the rule than the exception:

1. Employees
2. Suppliers
3. Customers
4. Distribution Partners

5. Shareowners
6. Government

Ever since corporate revenue hit the wall in the 1970s—when the rate of growth stopped increasing and started decreasing—these groups have not always been treated to an upside. In fact, some have been brutally beaten by the corporation since around 1985. The biggest losers in the equation: employees and suppliers. The biggest winners: shareowners of the day. Managing these publics over the next 10 years will be more difficult than ever as more employees lose their jobs, more suppliers go out of business because of relentless price cutting in their bid to keep business, more customers will become dissatisfied because they are not—no matter what the corporation says—the number one priority at a public corporation.

The relationships with distribution partners and shareowners will be threatened over the next decade including a power struggle with distributors, and the risk of disappointing shareowners. The relationship with the government has also been damaged, and new controls are in place that address improved governance. But will it be possible for corporations to keep shareowners happy without deepening the unemployment problem for the government? The successful CEO of the 21st century has to work all of these groups making the difficult decisions around reward and punishment. It won't be easy, and it will require CEOs who are willing to risk their own livelihoods.

---

# Help Wanted: CEO for the New Economic Reality

With images of former CEOs testifying in front of Senate subcommittees on the actions that cost millions of workers their jobs and life savings etched in the minds of those who trusted, the world has taken a step backward, significantly more skeptical about the individuals charged with running public corporations. Concurrently, and appropriately, new legislation has been written into law that will deal much more severely with senior managers who decide to skirt the law.

Meanwhile, millions of corporations get back to work in an effort to grow severely sagging revenue streams that provided the motive for criminally negligent and morally bankrupt executives seeking to add to their already bulging personal fortunes.

So what are the lessons learned over the last 5 years, 10 years, 25 years, and even 50 years that can be taken back to the board room and the corner office to help shape the future direction of the world's best corporations? What are the new qualities necessary for a 21st-century CEO who is much more likely to be presiding over a corporation that struggles to deliver organic revenue growth and, like an abandoned mountain climber, is forced to cannibalize the workforce to survive just to deliver earnings increases that many have come to expect?

## SEVEN QUALITIES OF THE NEW ECONOMIC REALITY CEO

### 1. Honesty: The Absence of Deceit, Denial, and Spin

Be honest and be straightforward. Everyone respects and looks up to the CEO who tells it like it is. Certainly, the Sarbanes-Oxley Act now requires a much higher level of accountability on the part of CEOs and CFOs of public corporations, but no law can mandate better performance, just better and more accurate accounting of performance. At the end of the day, no one is served by corporate dishonesty. The revenue fabricators of the late 1990s learned this lesson the hard way, along with millions around the world who listened to Wall Street cheerleaders as their personal fortunes evaporated.

In some ways, this recent cleansing is not a bad thing. It sets the stage for honest CEOs to distance themselves even from the gray area of white lies that spin around corporations every 90 days. The lack of momentum at many corporations has been a growing reality for a long time. Deal with it now or deal with it later. Similarly, boards of directors, many of which lived through the grand old days of robust top-line growth, must give latitude to CEOs who must now educate and inform as to what is and what is no longer possible. Don't misconstrue such honesty as a sign of weakness or defeat. It is far easier for a CEO to continue to tell the board that new growth is only a matter of time. It is far more difficult to openly deal with issues such as stagnant or shrinking product lines and the absence of a real, logical corporate growth story.

## 2. Selflessness: Eliminate Selfishness, and Don't Just Run Out the Clock

How much money is enough? Senior managers are well compensated by any measure, and in recent years, one could argue that compensation relative to performance has been way out of whack. When Babe Ruth became the first baseball player to make more than $100,000, he was asked if he thought it was appropriate for him to make more than the President of the United States. "I had a better year than he did," was Ruth's response. Few can argue with Disney-esque compensation packages when they are earned.

There are also far too many CEOs who are willing to run out the clock either until retirement or until they have squirreled away enough of a nest egg so that it just doesn't matter. What would have happened if Edison ran out the clock after inventing the distribution of electricity for the light bulb, if Henry Ford decided to keep his safe and secure job as a machinist, or if Steve Jobs and Stephen Wozniak decided to stay in college?

## 3. Product Innovator: Development of New Categories

There is an inherent problem that most corporations share relative to investing in the next great innovation: The last great innovation is paying their salaries, their bonuses, their stock options, their children's college tuitions, their hefty mortgages, and their country club dues. To preserve the status quo and ensure that those big-ticket items get covered, the focus is not on *discontinuous innovation* but rather continuous innovation, making whatever already exists faster and cheaper.

A dichotomy exists in the conscience of every CEO: How can I serve as a continuous innovator, stewarding the source of today's revenue, profits, and livelihoods, and at the same time serve as a *discontinuous innovator*, championing the development of innovations that will inherently destroy what pays our salaries today?

This thought prevents CEOs and senior managers from pursuing what effectively replaces the current source of their wealth. They opt instead, today, for letting the Class of 2000 worry about tomorrow. It's why the newspaper industry resisted the online world from the beginning, and why the music and movie industries resisted the online distribution model from the beginning. It's why real innovation usually does not come out of the big corporation: The laptop did not come out of IBM, the automobile did not come out of Union Pacific, and Amazon.com was not the brainchild of someone at Random House.

Championing a *discontinuous innovation* from within a corporate structure is tantamount to admitting that whatever pays today's salaries is dying. No one wants to admit that. It requires too much energy, too much disruption, and too much change. On the issue of change, Machiavelli said it best nearly 500 years ago in *The Prince* when he wrote:

> It must be remembered that there is nothing more difficult to plan, more doubtful of success, nor more dangerous to manage than the creation of a new system. For the initiator has the enmity of all who would profit by the preservation of the old institutions, and merely lukewarm defenders in those who would gain by the new ones.

In 21st century terms, it takes a gutsy CEO—one who is secure and selfless—to do what is right for shareowner value both today and tomorrow. Often, these two are at odds with each other, and usually the result is no significant initiatives to create new demand. In many ways, the sales and marketing machine of the second half of the 20th century unwittingly squelched demand by delivering on the ultimate sales and marketing credo: selling the maximum number of products to the maximum number of customers the maximum number of times in the maximum number of locations.

Consumers are now beginning to push themselves away from the dinner table and loosen the top button of their trousers. Convincing them to consume more of what they already consume is not the answer. However, developing new products with new benefits that cause consumers to add to their consumption is one of only two ways that corporations can organically grow in the future. The other is to develop new ways to more effectively market the products that already exist to consumers who already participate in a category. Both are innovations. Both need investment and energy now.

With lackluster top-line performance and continued pressure to deliver on the bottom line, the heat gets turned up to find even more efficient ways to run public corporations. Meanwhile, investment in the future from both a public scorned by the deceit and selfishness of the late 1990s and gun-shy corporations that are held to impossible earnings standards has all but dried up.

## SEARCHING FOR MR. EDISON

Edison, Ford, Farnsworth, Jobs, and Wozniak. They all had several things in common. Each was a restless child who was quickly bored with school and rejected the status quo. None of them graduated from college. And each invented at least one major *discontinuous innovation* that changed the course of the 20th century.

Thomas Edison spent only three months of his life in school, and more often could be found tinkering in an old railroad freight car, his own makeshift laboratory. Henry Ford became a machinist's apprentice at the age of 16 on the way to inventing automobile mass production. Philo T. Farnsworth attended Brigham Young University for a year at the age of 15, then dropped out on his way to developing the television. College dropouts Steve Jobs and Stephen Wozniak spent their early 20s inventing the personal computer.

Most great *discontinuous innovations* have come out of the minds of curious individuals tinkering in their garages. On the other hand, most of the continuous innovation that we see around us every day comes out of existing corporations with diligent workforces that strive to improve what already exists. Both initiatives are necessary if a society is to keep a high percentage of its population employed. Where would the economy be today if the technology sector didn't come along and create new jobs for the legions of workers that were dismissed by the more mature sectors starting in the mid-1980s?

Even though the Segway—the motorless human transporter introduced by inventor and physicist Dean Kamen—might never be as popular as the automobile, it provides an excellent example of the type of thinking required to introduce a *discontinuous innovation*. Kamen, whose successes include the invention of a portable dialysis machine, was not necessarily trying to introduce an improvement to the bicycle, roller blades, or even walking. He was attempting to introduce a wholly new form of transporting people from A to B, just as the train did in the mid-1800s, the automobile did at the beginning of the 20th century, and the airplane did starting in the 1930s.

This type of thinking and perspective is rare. However, encouraging such thinking is imperative to find new ways to be nourished, to be healed, to be educated, and simply to get from point A to point B. ∎

### 4. Marketing Innovator: Development of a New Marketing Perspective

More often than not, the word *innovation* conjures up images of high technology, bells and whistles, and newfangled products. However, there is such a thing as *marketing innovation* that requires looking at existing customer universes in completely new ways. The overwhelming perspective of marketing for more than a half-century has been one-dimensional. The focus on growing sales through market share gains is really most germane to products during the first 10 to 20 years after launch, and perhaps an even shorter period today. After decades of looking at the world from a market share perspective, it becomes necessary for corporations to begin to embrace opportunities from a customer share perspective.

Customer share marketing (CSM) is a discipline that focuses almost exclusively on existing customers, the people who have already purchased products or services from you. CSM is a planned and funded series of customer retention and cross-selling campaigns that are designed to deepen loyalty and sell more to customers who have already said "Yes!"

*More* can mean many things. In the case of CSM, more means motivating existing customers to consolidate more of their business with you. For corporations that sell just one product or service such as hotel rooms, CSM motivates customers to consolidate their business with one source and rewards customer loyalty on a quid pro quo basis. For corporations that sell a portfolio of products or services such as personal care products, CSM also motivates customers to consolidate their business with one source, but across a number of product categories.

The traditional market share view of the world focuses on customer acquisition and up-sell. CSM is the first marketing discipline dedicated to retention and cross-selling. Figure 10-2 graphically illustrates how a corporation has historically viewed a customer from a marketing perspective: as a consumer of one brand at a time.

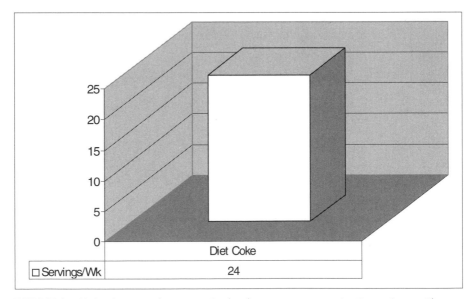

**FIGURE 10-2**   Market share view of a customer: One brand, one customer perspective. Source: Customer Share Group LLC.

The market share view of a customer becomes limiting and costly over time as consumer habits become established and harden. Battling the competition using mass marketing to communicate with unidentified prospects is becoming less and less effective. CSM, on the other hand, is a direct marketing science that manages the development of the customer relationship—something that mass marketing and CRM alone cannot do.

Figure 10-3 illustrates the customer share view of a customer: a consumer who participates in multiple beverage categories, sometimes with multiple brand loyalties. The consumer in Figure 10-3 participates in five categories of nonalcoholic beverages: water, orange drink, sports drink, soda, and orange juice. Such information can be captured using CRM tools in building a customer share profile of category and brand consumption preferences, habits, and affinities.

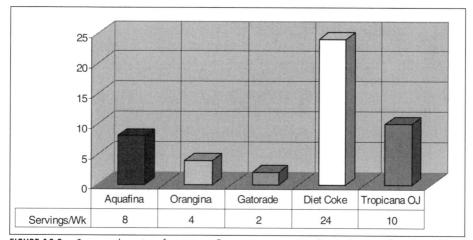

| | Aquafina | Orangina | Gatorade | Diet Coke | Tropicana OJ |
|---|---|---|---|---|---|
| Servings/Wk | 8 | 4 | 2 | 24 | 10 |

**FIGURE 10-3** Customer share view of a customer: Five-category perspective. Source: Customer Share Group LLC.

The customer share profile is central to the development of effective CSM programs. Identifying a customer along with his or her specific product preferences and consumption levels would allow the Coca-Cola Company, for example, to be able to directly influence a consumer who is already in the orange juice category (Tropicana in Figure 10-3) to switch to Coca-Cola's Minute Maid brand of orange juice.

The customer share profile identifies the full category potential for a particular customer. In this case, PepsiCo commands 60 percent of this customer's nonalcoholic beverage requirement, whereas the Coca-Cola Company owns 40 percent of the customer's share. Armed with this data, either corporation is able to more precisely influence brand switching, especially when marketing is done one-to-one.

Unfortunately, most corporations define growth opportunities as the conquest of new customers, as opposed to the nurturing of existing loyal customers. Most define a *prospect* as a consumer who has yet to buy, as opposed to a customer who is loyal to Diet Coke, but who also drinks the competition's water (PepsiCo's Aquafina), sports drink (PepsiCo's Gatorade), and orange juice (PepsiCo's Tropicana).

CSM requires a major shift in the historically vertical nature of the large multiple-product corporation that has been organized and staffed to sell one brand at a time. Marketing innovators such as Indonesia's Indofood Company are already actively engaged in the CSM strategy that helps mine all potential volume across all categories for all current customers.

CSM is a discipline that works for all industries, yet requires a new perspective that looks at each consumer from a multiple-category perspective and targets those categories in which the consumer already participates, but with a competitor's brand. For corporations in the packaged goods industry, the objective is to capture a larger share of refrigerator, share of pantry, share of bathroom, or share of household. For corporations in the automotive industry, it's a larger share of garage; financial services a larger share of wallet.

A CSM perspective can help mature corporations that hit the market share wall decades ago mine new growth from old customers with virtually no cost of acquisition.

## THE AUTO INDUSTRY: FROM CONQUEST AND ACQUISITION TO RETENTION AND CUSTOMER LOYALTY

One industry that has a love–hate relationship with its customers is the auto industry. It has mastered the art of customer conquest and acquisition, and at the same time has notoriously neglected customers the moment they drive off the lot. According to industry experts, nearly 8 out of every 10 customers that buy a car from one dealership end up buying their next car from another dealership. By any standard, this is an embarrassing track record for an industry that is more than 100 years old and in dire need of every sale it can get.

Credited with inventing the automobile, Karl Benz would be proud that a dealership that bears his name has adopted a retention marketing strategy that helps to keep more of the customers who have already been sold. Chicagoland's Autohaus on Edens initiated a unique and specific retention, loyalty, and reward program. The brainchild of marketing visionary Michael Rosengarden, the program has greatly increased retention rates while creating a buzz in the auto industry about Rosengarden's customer share marketing strategies.

The program is driven by a proprietary software program called HENRY© that generates a list of current customers who are nearing the end of their lease or financing deal or who are approaching factory warranty mileage levels. A list of high-probability customers is pulled six months prior to expiration. These customers become part of a highly customized, one-to-one retention marketing program that culminates with a personal test drive in the model of their choice.

HENRY© also organizes customers into a segmentation pyramid that allows an automaker to create a hierarchical view of the active customer base from most loyal at the top of the pyramid to first-time customers at the bottom. Organization of the database in this way allows the automaker to specifically focus on the most elusive of all groups to retain, first-time customers. A minor improvement in retention rate can mean tens of millions of dollars to a dealership over a relatively short period of time, especially considering the profitable service element that is usually captured with every sale. Such a program can help an automaker scientifically improve retention—a major Achilles heel for the auto industry.

This is an example of the type of marketing innovation that mature lines of business must employ to maximize sales efforts that show little life after decades of mass marketing spending in an increasingly noisy media environment. ∎

### 5. Business Model Innovator: Creating New Business Models

The music industry is currently trapped in the classic dilemma of *creative destruction*. Embracing the electronic distribution of music surely would disrupt the existing and significant retail channel of selling physical CDs either at brick-and-mortar outlets or online. Certainly, much needs to be sorted out relative to the protection of the artist's copyrights in the electronic distribution of intellectual property, but the upside is so vast for both the music and movie industries that a model will undoubtedly emerge that will serve all parties.

Though it is unclear precisely what model will prevail—pay-per-play, subscription, or something else entirely, it's a safe bet that the solution will probably not come from the major record labels. Just as Amazon.com was the brainchild of individuals from outside of the traditional book publishing industry, look for this problem to be ultimately solved by innovators from outside of the industry who will figure out how to protect the artists while providing easy and affordable access to virtually everything that has ever been recorded.

For the owners of intellectual property, the Internet truly represents an opportunity to radically change the traditional business model because of two unique attributes: the ability to offer both new marketing and new distribution options. Over the next decade, the Internet will continue to bring a sea of change to the music industry. However, look for another unique Internet attribute—low cost of entry—to throw yet another wrench in the works for the major labels. The ability to start up and market a music label is now well within reach of most junior high school garage bands who dream of stardom. This simply means more original music will be made available over the Web, greatly simplifying what has always been the riskiest, most complex, and most costly part of the music business: marketing and distribution.

## HOORAY FOR HOLLYWOOD

Hollywood has already seen its best days in terms of achieving record numbers of admissions at the traditional box office. That record was established more than a half-century ago when more than 4.5 billion tickets were sold during the final year of World War II in 1945. Given the U.S. population at the time, this would mean that every man, woman, and child in the United States went to the movies more than 30 times that year!

Of course, these figures predate the widespread availability of television. Nonetheless, the overwhelming explosion of entertainment options introduced since 1950 makes it doubtful that Hollywood will ever approach historically high ticket sales under the current distribution model.

Without question, the movie industry does a miraculous job of promoting its films today. It is not at all unusual for the awareness level of a major theatrical release to approach 100 percent of the U.S. adult population, especially when clever studios engage the marketing muscle of partners such as Coca-Cola to build anticipation of a first-run release. However, that high awareness does not always translate into theater admissions.

Figure 10-4 shows the relation of admissions, or movie tickets sold, to the number of indoor screens during the 1990s. Growth in the number of indoor theater screens annually grew much faster than admissions during the decade, with screens growing at 60 percent, and admissions at only 24 percent. This is The Home Depot, McDonald's, Wal-Mart model.

The Internet will make it possible for the movie industry to ultimately market and distribute first-run movies as broadband technology becomes more widely available. Even though there are still major hurdles to clear on the way to creating these new sales and consumption models, including copyright and capacity issues, expect to see first-run films shift to the Web on a pay-per-view basis within the next decade, enabling the movie industry to reach significantly new sales levels as admissions shift from the theater to the home. Hollywood will triumphantly return to the days of selling more than 4 billion tickets in short order once the technology is in place to support the model shift. ∎

| Year | Admissions (Millions) | +/− | Indoor Screens (Thousands) | +/− | Admissions-to-Screens Ratio (Per Week) |
|------|------------------------|------|-----------------------------|------|------------------------------------------|
| 1999 | 1,470.0 | −0.7% | 36.4 | +9.0% | 776 to 1 |
| 1998 | 1,480.0 | +6.4% | 33.4 | +7.7% | 852 to 1 |
| 1997 | 1,390.0 | +3.7% | 31.0 | +7.2% | 862 to 1 |
| 1996 | 1,340.0 | +6.3% | 28.9 | +7.4% | 891 to 1 |
| 1995 | 1,260.0 | −2.4% | 26.9 | +4.2% | 900 to 1 |
| 1994 | 1,290.0 | +4.0% | 25.8 | +4.5% | 961 to 1 |
| 1993 | 1,240.0 | +5.9% | 24.7 | +1.6% | 965 to 1 |
| 1992 | 1,170.0 | +2.6% | 24.3 | +2.5% | 925 to 1 |
| 1991 | 1,140.0 | −4.3% | 23.7 | +3.5% | 925 to 1 |
| 1990 | 1,190.0 | — | 22.9 | — | 1,000 to 1 |

FIGURE 10-4    Screens versus admissions: Screens grew more than twice as fast as admissions in the 1990s. Source: National Association of Theatre Owners.

## 6.  Steward of the Corporation: Invest $1 for Every $2 Cut

Every CEO of every corporation impacts the course of the business in some way. However, few CEOs are irreplaceable, especially if they think that they are. CEOs hold their positions only temporarily until someone else comes along in the long line of successors replacing predecessors. With this view in mind, it becomes critical for every CEO to be viewed as the steward of the corporation, the individual responsible for both today's health and tomorrow's longevity.

It would be naive to suggest that reducing costs will not be a significant corporate initiative over the next decade. However, there are ways to ensure that there is some give with the take, so to speak.

In the mid-1980s, when reengineering was all the rage, the management consulting side of what was then Coopers & Lybrand helped hundreds of corporations significantly cut costs, most of them for the first time ever. However, Coopers & Lybrand's strategy for its clients took a responsible long-term view of the health of the corporation, looking well beyond the short-term need for earnings help. It had an eye on investing in the future as well.

The idea was to work with client management to identify 40 percent of total costs as a target for elimination. Although cuts at that level might have seemed extraordinarily deep at the time, half of the cost savings would be redirected into new revenue-producing innovations. The remaining 20 percent of total costs would drop to the bottom line. This reinvestment strategy not only went a long way to help plant the seeds of new revenue streams, but also helped to mend the scars and build future hope for surviving management and staffers.

Without a consistent inflow of new revenue, corporations cannot just cut costs indefinitely. The global economy is at a crossroads now that requires much more than simple adjustments in interest rates. Stimulating long-term demand must be one of the absolute priorities for the CEO of the new economic reality, and making it part of seemingly endless cost-reduction programs will help bring more of a balance to the give and take.

## 7. Business Evolutionist: A Darwinian Approach to Business

At the very beginning of Chapter 1, there is a quote from economist Alfred Marshall's 1890 economic epic *Principles of Economics*. Marshall made a stunning observation that economic forces can be likened to the stages of a man's life: "growing in strength until he reaches his prime; after which he gradually becomes stiff and inactive, till at last he sinks to make room for other and more vigorous life."

Remarkably, even before the beginning of the 20th century, Marshall was able to correctly observe that nothing lasts forever. Apparently, the Australian government agrees. After experiencing the significant pains associated with bailing out corporations in distress, the Aussies are now taking a different tack. *Voluntary administration* is Australia's version of the popular U.S. practice of reorganizing under bankruptcy protection, more commonly known as filing Chapter 11.

However, *voluntary administration* is far tougher and far more expeditious than U.S. bankruptcy proceedings, with the corporation's creditors quickly determining the fate of the corporation within the span of 28 days. The *voluntary administration* of a corporation starts with the appointment of a single individual to act as the administrator. Once the administrator is appointed, the corporation has one day to notify authorities of the appointment, three days to advertise the appointment in daily newspapers, and five days to convene a meeting of the creditors of the corporation.

Within 28 days, the creditors will meet again to determine one of three options available for swift execution:

1. Liquidate the corporation.
2. Return the corporation to the director of its board of directors.
3. Enter into a *deed of arrangement*.

It is the last option that most closely resembles the more lenient form of U.S. bankruptcy law. However, creditors have been favoring liquidation in recent years, for several reasons:

- Fear that a protected corporation under a *deed of arrangement* might dramatically drop its prices in the competitive marketplace, forcing the balance of the industry to do the same, essentially allowing a weak corporation to negatively impact the healthy ones.
- Fear that protracted proceedings will result in a significant waste of time and money, with lawyers—not creditors, employees, or shareholders—as the primary beneficiaries.
- Fear that the near-term subsidization of what has perhaps been a poorly run corporation will not serve anyone over the long term.

It is quite possible that the only way to resuscitate demand will be to allow some entities that are in decay to continue to follow the natural path of life to the very end. Such a scenario would result in a tightened supply of a particular product, for example, fewer model options and a reduced overall supply of automobiles. A limited supply of available options will ultimately lead to an inventory shortage when the quantity demanded exceeds the quantity supplied and prices can begin to stabilize or perhaps even rise.

The downside to such a Darwinian approach to business, where the strong survive and the weak do not, is that inevitably unemployment can become a serious problem. This is why a constant and concurrent investment in innovation is critical to ensure the creation of new jobs as others are eliminated. Not surprisingly, the highest unemployment rate for any five-year period in the United States since 1970 was a period from 1980 through 1984, averaging 8.3 percent. These could be considered the transition years when maturing sectors began to trim workforces, as a new sector (technology) was adding them.

With the technology sector's rate of growth now in decline, the relatively fledgling sector is already beginning to lay off significant numbers of workers. In some ways, the employment picture in the United States looks very similar to the early 1980s, with unemployment inching higher and higher. However, this time, it is unclear if there is any new sector on the horizon to provide enough new jobs to compensate for those being eliminated.

## A TIME OF RENEWAL

The late John W. Gardner was a remarkable man, a renaissance man, really. He was formally trained as a psychologist at Stanford and then at the University of California at Berkeley. He spent time in the private sector working on the challenges confronting a country that was faced with educating the biggest generation of all time, the baby boomers. His stellar accomplishments with the Carnegie Corporation and Foundation caught the eye of President Lyndon Baines Johnson, who appointed him as Secretary of Health, Education & Welfare, where he played a critical role in the development of Medicare, the enforcement of the Civil Rights Act of 1964, and the landmark Elementary and Secondary School Act of 1965.

Gardner was fascinated by the topic of renewal, especially self-renewal. In fact, he wrote a book on the subject that explored the constant decay and renewal of societies, organizations, and individuals. In a speech to a gathering of McKinsey & Company executives in Phoenix in November 1990, Gardner spoke on one of his favorite topics, and shared a story about an article that he had just read about barnacles:

> The barnacle is confronted with an existential decision about where it's going to live. Once it decides ... it spends the rest of its life with its head cemented to a rock. For a good many of us, it comes down to that.

Gardner was lamenting the wasted life of men and women leading lives of quiet desperation, as Henry David Thoreau wrote. The corporate world is now at a crossroads, a new intersection where, like the drivers at a four-way stop sign, people freeze when it comes to deciding whether to stay or to go.

Everyone in business today is presented with those two options. Most will opt to stay, and there's nothing wrong with that. However, it will be those who decide to go who will pioneer the path to the next new category, the next new industry, or the next new sector in this *new economic reality.*

It will require change for all of us, and can provide a renewal for many of us if we decide to go. Historically, those who decided to go were ultimately responsible for creating new jobs. Edison, Ford, Farnsworth, Jobs, Wozniak—they all created demand. They all created jobs. They all decided to go. What about you? Will you stay or will you go?

# INDEX

Ford Motor Company, 10, 28–
  30, 58, 118, 181, 185,
  227, 241
FPL, 22
Frito-Lay Company, 55
Fuller Brush Man, 53, 87

## G

Galbraith, John Kenneth, 117
Gap, The, 22
Gardner, John W., 269–70
Gatorade, 261–62
Genentech, 22
General Electric, 16, 22, 37, 92–
  94, 107, 176, 183, 185,
  193–95, 243
General Foods, 22
Generally Accepted Accounting
  Practices (GAAP), 35,
  103, 232
General Mills, 22
General Mortgage, 116
General Motors, 22, 28, 30–31,
  44, 115–18, 183, 237
General Motors Acceptance Cor-
  poration (GMAC), 116
Generation X, 74–75, 86, 130
  early, 130
Generation Y, 75, 86
Genzyme, 22
Germany, 10, 134, 219
GI Bill of Rights, 44
gift cards, 105
Gillette, 22
Giorgio Beverly Hills, 144
Goldman Sachs, 128
Goodyear, 96–97

Google, 39
Greenspan, Alan, 19, 174
Gross Domestic Product (GDP),
  201, 207, 225, 252
  United States, 10–11, 26, 106,
  190, 208–10
growth strategies, 131, 140, 143,
  147, 165

## H

Halliburton, 22
Harvard University, 125, 127–28,
  130, 133, 136, 138, 143,
  148–49
Head & Shoulders, 51
healthcare sector, 25, 197, 200,
  223
Health Management Corp., 22,
  26
HENRY©, 263
Hewlett-Packard, 26, 97, 187,
  194
Hilton Hotels, 22
Holmes, Rupert, 138
Home Depot, The, 17, 22, 24, 84,
  94, 96–97, 107, 237, 265
Honeywell, 22, 93
Hoover, Herbert, 29
Hungary, 144
Huron Consulting Group, 124

## I

IAMS, 145
IBM, 22, 26, 199, 257
  Selectric, 49

# 8 reasons why you should read the Financial Times for 4 weeks RISK-FREE!

To help you stay current with significant
developments in the world economy ...
and to assist you to make informed business
decisions — the Financial Times brings you:

**❶** Fast, meaningful overviews of international affairs ... plus daily
briefings on major world news.

**❷** Perceptive coverage of economic, business, financial and political
developments with special focus on emerging markets.

**❸** More international business news than any other publication.

**❹** Sophisticated financial analysis and commentary on world market
activity plus stock quotes from over 30 countries.

**❺** Reports on international companies and a section on global investing.

**❻** Specialized pages on management, marketing, advertising and
technological innovations from all parts of the world.

**❼** Highly valued single-topic special reports (over 200 annually)
on countries, industries, investment opportunities, technology and more.

**❽** The Saturday Weekend FT section — a globetrotter's guide to
leisure-time activities around the world: the arts, fine dining, travel,
sports and more.

**FT** FINANCIAL TIMES
World business newspaper

# The *Financial Times* delivers a world of business news.

## Use the Risk-Free Trial Voucher below!

To stay ahead in today's business world you need to be well-informed on a daily basis. And not just on the national level. You need a news source that closely monitors the entire world of business, and then delivers it in a concise, quick-read format.

With the *Financial Times* you get the major stories from every region of the world. Reports found nowhere else. You get business, management, politics, economics, technology and more.

Now you can try the *Financial Times* for 4 weeks, absolutely risk free. And better yet, if you wish to continue receiving the *Financial Times* you'll get great savings off the regular subscription rate. Just use the voucher below.